MEXICO AND THE SPANISH CORTES
1810–1822

Latin American Monographs, No. 5
Institute of Latin American Studies
The University of Texas

MEXICO AND THE SPANISH
CORTES, 1810–1822: Eight Essays

Edited with an Introduction by Nettie Lee Benson

Published for the INSTITUTE OF LATIN AMERICAN STUDIES
by the UNIVERSITY OF TEXAS PRESS, Austin & London

Contents

MEXICO AND THE SPANISH CORTES
1810–1822

Introduction   *Nettie Lee Benson*

When in 1808 Napoleon attempted to make Spain an appendage of
France with his brother Joseph sitting on the Spanish throne, events
of a political nature were set in motion that were to have far-reaching
effect not only in Spain but in all Spanish overseas dominions and
especially in the area then known as the Viceroyalty of New Spain.
One of the most significant events evolving from the Napoleonic effort
in Spain was convocation of the Spanish Cortes of 1810–1813. True
this was not a new institution to the Spanish world, but the character
it assumed during the period 1810–1814, 1820–1822 was quite foreign
to its previous history.

The Spanish Cortes as developed in the second quarter of the
eleventh century was in its earliest stages a tool of the king to be used
to pit one or two groups against a third that was contending with him
for power. Each kingdom of Spain had its separate Cortes, which was
usually divided into three separate estates, representing the nobility,
the church, and the municipalities. At times the king called for all the
estates to meet at the same time; at times he called only one of them
or two of them for consultation. The several estates met in separate
bodies even when called to meet at the same time. While they were
primarily the tools of the king, the estates, recognizing their useful-
ness to him, managed to use his dependence upon their support to
extract from him concessions in their favor. The towns were especially
effective in exploiting this situation in the early period when the king
was fighting for control of the nobility. Before the middle of the
seventeenth century, however, the kings had won their struggle for
control of the nobility and the church and were no longer dependent
upon the Cortes, which were therefore seldom called and which
even when in session served only as a rubber stamp for the king's
actions.

The Cortes of 1810–1814 and of 1820–1822 were of a totally different character. In the first place, when they met in September,
1810, they met as a single body, composed of deputies elected to

represent, in Spain, (1) the towns, (2) the provincial juntas which had sprung up to direct the struggle against the French invader, and (3) the population on a basis of one deputy for each fifty thousand inhabitants in a province; and to represent, in America, the provinces. As originally conceived by the Junta Central and later the Regency, this first meeting of representatives of all the dominions of Spain was to be simply a means of unifying the efforts of all Spaniards in the fight for national existence. Neither the Junta Central or the Regency had envisioned it as a constituent congress to draw up a national charter which would change Spain into a limited constitutional monarchy. But that is what it became and what it accomplished.

Once in session the Cortes quickly made itself the supreme arbiter of the affairs of the country. When the Regency objected to what it considered usurpation of its authority, its members were ordered arrested by the Cortes, tried, found guilty, and imprisoned or banished; a new Regency was then appointed. The members of the various ministries were treated likewise. The Cortes, furthermore, quickly arrogated to itself the right to draw up and promulgate a constitution for the Spanish dominions. To do so, this special Cortes, which began its sessions on September 24, 1810, remained continuously at work until September 20, 1813. The special session was followed by the equally revolutionary and liberal regular sessions of October 1, 1813–February 19, 1814, and March 1, 1814–May 10, 1814. These were all hard-working legislative bodies, which met in resolute, painstaking daily session and often in special night sessions until the Cortes was abolished by decree of the king on May 10, 1814, and the constitution and laws were abrogated.

Ferdinand VII, after this abolition of the Cortes and the return to an absolute monarchy, was able to rule Spain and its dominions autocratically until early in 1820. Then the revolt led by General Rafael Riego forced Ferdinand to reproclaim the Constitution of 1812 and the laws implementing it, and to reconvene the Cortes. This newly reconstituted legislative body was, if anything, more radical than the earlier ones of 1810–1814. Its sessions were from June 26, 1820, to November 9, 1820; February 10, 1821, to June 30, 1821; and September 22, 1821, to February 14, 1822 (a special session).

The years 1810–1822 were crucial in the history of New Spain, for during them it began and won the struggle to become the independent Mexican nation. It was no mere coincidence that the struggle was most actively carried on between 1810 and 1814, that it lulled during the period 1814–1820, and that it ended triumphantly in 1821. Yet few developments in the history of the Spanish colonial system have been more carelessly treated or more misinterpreted than the attempt to establish constitutional government under the Spanish monarchy during the 1809–1814 and 1820–1822 periods while Mexico still remained a part of that monarchy.

An example of this misinterpretation is to be found in *The Mexican Nation,* where Herbert Ingram Priestley writes of three distinct events as one: the selection of American representatives to sit as members of the Supreme Central Governing Junta of Spain; the initial election of American deputies to sit in the Cortes which began its sessions on September 24, 1810; and the selection in Spain of substitute delegates to sit in the Cortes until the regularly elected proprietary deputies could arrive from America. Writing of these three events, Priestley says:

> Representation of the colonies in the Cortes was grudgingly provided for. Each viceroy and independent governor was to be allowed to choose one representative for each government in Spanish America. This plan would have provided so scant representation that the number was raised to twenty-eight, to admit one representative from each district instead of each "government." But many of the twenty-eight permissible delegates were never elected. Most of those who were chosen never went, being afraid of the dangerous sea voyage or the political hazard. Finally New Spain was represented by seven substitutes chosen because they were Mexicans living in Spain at the time.[1]

When he states that "each viceroy and independent governor was to be allowed to choose one representative for each government in Spanish America," he is referring to the decree of January 22, 1809, which proclaimed the Spanish dominions in America and the Philippines as integral parts of the monarchy and ordered the immediate election of representatives to the Supreme Central Governing Junta, not to the Cortes as Priestley implies.[2] When he states that "this plan would have provided so scant representation that the number was raised to twenty-eight to admit one representative from each district instead of each 'government'," the "plan" he refers to is that of the aforementioned election of representatives to the Supreme Central Governing Junta as set forth in the decree of January 22, 1809; and the raising

---

[1] Herbert Ingram Priestley, *The Mexican Nation: A History,* p. 204.
[2] These representatives were to be *elected* in each viceroyalty, not appointed by the viceroy or governor, and in most viceroyalties they were elected.

of the number to twenty-eight, which he implies is the number of deputies from the New World to be elected to the Cortes, is actually the number of substitute deputies to be chosen in Spain from Americans then resident there in order that America would be represented in the Cortes even before the regularly elected American deputies arrived. Finally, when he states that "many of the twenty-eight permissible delegates were never elected," his statement becomes virtually inexplicable, for here he is obviously referring to the deputies elected in the New World, specifically Mexico. But the figure of twenty-eight was not established as a limit to the number of deputies Mexico or any part of America was to elect. No specific number was set for Mexico or the New World other than that one deputy should be elected in each *capital cabeza de partido* of the provinces—a rather vague expression that received different interpretations in different regions.[3] One must deduce that Priestley's "twenty-eight permissible delegates" refers to that specified number[4] of substitute deputies who were to be elected in Spain from Americans resident there. Priestley to the contrary, they were definitely elected; also they were resident in Spain and did not have to make the long, dangerous sea voyage. Not all were to represent Mexico, however; only seven of them were supposed to and did, as Priestley, in his only accurate statement so far, says: "Finally New Spain was [temporarily] represented by seven substitutes chosen because they were Mexicans living in Spain at the time."

With this paragraph, Priestley disposes of the subject of Mexican representation in the Cortes and the manner of election and the significance of it. There is no mention of the five different elections held in Mexico to select its deputies to the Spanish Cortes or of the fact that actually more than 160 Mexicans were elected to that body between 1810–1814 and 1820–1822, of which number over 70, not including the substitute deputies, actively participated and thereby gained valuable parliamentary experience.

In *A History of Mexico* Henry Bamford Parkes, in three lines of total misinterpretation, says:

So the American town councils were invited to elect delegates. Mexico was allowed seven representatives, the most prominent of whom was a

---

[3] See Chapter I.
[4] This number was first set at twenty-six and later raised to twenty-eight.

stout, loquacious, aggressive, and self-confident priest from Nuevo León, Miguel Ramos Arizpe.[5]

It is easy to dismiss Parkes' treatment, for obviously he did not attempt to learn anything about the subject, but Priestley's account, so compounded of errors, demands that we know its source. A careful comparison of Priestley's account with Hubert Howe Bancroft's treatment of the subject in *History of Mexico*[6] quickly convinces one that Priestley is an excellent synthesis of Bancroft. The misinterpretation obviously began with Bancroft, and has been carried down to the present—in Priestley one finds the same errors as in Bancroft. The earlier writer, apparently anxious to emphasize Spain's mistreatment of her colonies, presents the events in greater detail and seems to fully document his statements, or so it appears until one really studies the sources offered. But Priestley accepted Bancroft's account without looking into the sources; in his synthesis he omits only a few of Bancroft's errors, or slightly changes them. Both imply erroneously that elections in Mexico were not held widely and that most of those elected declined to go "to Spain in the expectation that some new order would exclude them from the Cortes on their arrival," or because of fear "of the dangerous sea voyage or the political hazard." Both leave their readers with the idea that, as a result, New Spain was represented by only seven substitute deputies chosen in Spain, and this is the single idea that Parkes caught and further distorted by naming Miguel Ramos Arizpe as one of the seven substitute deputies in the period 1810–1813, when in fact he was a regularly elected proprietary deputy.

With this compounding of errors at the very beginning of the story of the Spanish Cortes, these authors prepare the reader for the acceptance of their thesis that that body and the Constitution of 1812 and the laws subsequent to it had little impact on institutional and political developments in Mexico. Bancroft (on pages 465–466), Priestley (on pages 229–230), and Parkes (on pages 167–168) all emphasize the supposedly quick suspension of the Constitution by Viceroy Francisco Javier Venegas in December of 1812, when, in fact, it was not suspended until it was revoked by Ferdinand VII upon his return to Spain in May, 1814. Venegas did suspend that sec-

[5] Henry Bamford Parkes, *A History of Mexico*, p. 166.
[6] Hubert Howe Bancroft, *History of Mexico*, IV, 85–88.

tion of the Constitution granting freedom of the press and did not
allow the completion of the municipal elections in Mexico City during his brief term in office after the promulgation of the Constitution,
but he did not suspend the Constitution, and both municipal elections
and those of deputies to the Cortes of 1813 and 1814 were held in
some parts of Mexico while he was in office.

All three authors—Bancroft, Priestley, and Parkes—mention the
fact that the promulgation of the Constitution helped the rebel cause
and weakened the Spanish colonial authorities but not even Bancroft
seemed to realize fully the seriousness of the situation which the
promulgation of the Constitution created for Viceroy Francisco Javier Venegas and his successors Félix Calleja and Juan Ruíz de
Apodaca. It placed each of them in turn in a peculiar situation. Each
had been named viceroy of a colonial kingdom with full regal power,
but under the new government's Constitution and the laws passed by
the Cortes the position of viceroy did not and could not exist, for it
was replaced by the much more limited position of political chief.
The question each "viceroy" had to face in the midst of rebellion was:
What, then, is my position? Venegas faced it by calling a *real acuerdo*
in December, 1812, at which, because of the exigencies of the time, it
was decided to ignore the Constitution in so far as possible and to
continue the old order of things. Calleja, who under the Constitution
became the Political Chief of New Spain, faced it when he began to
implement the Constitution in Mexico City, and especially when he
realized the meaning of the powers granted the other political chiefs,
of Nueva Galicia, Yucatán, San Luis Potosí, the Eastern Interior
Provinces, and the Western Interior Provinces. His political power
was no greater than theirs, they too could read the Constitution and
the laws, and some challenged his authority over them. To solve his
dilemma Calleja appealed to his council, his government attorney,
and his military attorney, explaining his actions and his difficulty in
carrying on the fight against the rebels since under the new order
he apparently was not granted the authority that the viceroy had enjoyed. He asked for confirmation of viceregal authority and received
it, of course, from his advisers, but not from the Constitution or the
Cortes.

That Calleja found it necessary to explain his use of authority as
late as early 1814, and to seek confirmation of it, shows that he was
having difficulty asserting it, even though the Regency then governing Spain, had on July 24, 1813, approved his actions as captain gen-

eral of New Spain, and a committee of the Cortes had subsequently recommended that a military regime be authorized there. Since the Constitution had been proclaimed in Mexico and was being read and put into effect by the other political chiefs, it was only natural that they would use it to their own advantage and would question Calleja's authority over them. Not even the Regency, or for that matter the Cortes, foresaw what the Constitution would mean to administrators in the New World. When the Constitution of 1812 was reproclaimed by Ferdinand VII in 1820, he had to appeal to his council to interpret it in regard to the position to which he was to appoint Juan O'Donojú. At that time the council stated specifically that the position of viceroy no longer existed or could exist and that as far as political appointments were concerned, as opposed to military appointments, the king could appoint O'Donojú only to the position of political chief of the provincial deputation of New Spain, the jurisdiction of which the Cortes had already reduced to central Mexico and which it shortly thereafter reduced to solely the province of México itself.

If this is what happened to the position of the viceroy under the Constitution, and if the aforementioned error-filled writings of Bancroft, Priestley, and Parkes are illustrative of what has been written about the Spanish Cortes and the Constitution of 1812 in Mexico, the question arises as to what did really occur there. What was the extent of Mexican participation in the Spanish Cortes and what was the impact of it and the Constitution of 1812 on developments in Mexico during the period 1809–1822 and possibly later?

To find out from primary sources what really transpired was the assignment given a group of graduate students in a one-semester seminar on Mexican historiography. Among the topics suggested for investigation were: local, provincial, or national government; military, economic, educational, land, press, or judicial reform; the Inquisition; methods proposed for restoring peace; and constitutional principles. Each student was instructed to choose one of these topics, look into it broadly, then limit it as he thought best for a thorough treatment in a paper of not over thirty typewritten pages. The following chapters are the product of that seminar. It is felt that although they do not represent a definitive and complete treatment of the historical significance of the Spanish Cortes to Mexico, they do cast a new light on it and are worthy of consideration by those interested in Mexican history of that and subsequent periods.

1. The Election of the Mexican Deputies to the Spanish Cortes, 1810–1822

Charles R. Berry

The significance of the Spanish Cortes of the period 1810–1814 and 1820–1822 and their effect on initiating democratic processes in the New World have been largely overlooked. Especially has the establishment of procedures to choose the American representatives in the congresses been overlooked, although the procedure worked smoothly for eight years. On the contrary, the tendency in the past has been to discount or ignore almost completely the role the Cortes played in early political activities in the Western Hemisphere. Perhaps this tendency may be largely attributed to the lack of consideration devoted to the Peninsular legislature by Spanish American writers contemporary with that epoch. Unconsciously or consciously, writers have minimized this political milestone in Spain because of their bitter anti-Spanish feelings, produced by the trade policies of the metropolis prior to the wars for independence and by the destructive wars themselves.

A close study of the elections for deputies to the Cortes held in Mexico and some other parts of the Spanish empire between 1810 and 1822 dispels the general impression that the congresses of this period produced no results beneficial to the American colonies in the way of democratic processes. Not only were these elections held in New Spain at the required times, but the provisions of the laws were strictly adhered to in most cases.

The abdication of Charles IV and Ferdinand VII demanded by Napoleon at Bayonne in early 1808, and Joseph Bonaparte's ascension to the throne of Spain a few months later provided the catalyst which set in motion certain democratic machinery in the Spanish empire. A popular outburst against the French usurpation followed in the Peninsula. Juntas to assume the direction of the government sprang up in various localities, and toward the end of the year a central governing body was established to direct affairs until the deposed Spanish monarch should return to his throne. This central junta in turn gave way to a regency of five men. In 1810 the Regency announced the convocation of the Cortes, which had not been summoned for many years past. For the first time the overseas provinces were to be treated equally with those on the European continent and were to be represented in the congress. The regents issued a decree on February 14 to the dominions in America calling for the election of representatives to attend the Cortes in Spain. That decree, which contained instructions for holding the elections, reached Mexico City on May 16 and was printed in the official newspaper on May 18.[1]

According to its provisions, one deputy was to be chosen for each of the Mexican provinces. The procedure in this first election was to be relatively simple. The municipal council of each capital would meet and name three men, native to the province, who were endowed with integrity, talent, and education. The names would be placed in a container from which one would be drawn. The man so chosen would be the deputy to the Cortes. If any disputes arose over the procedure, they were to be resolved quickly and absolutely by the viceroy or the captain general of the province in cooperation with the audiencia. The municipal council would then certify the election and give the deputy instructions on matters which he should present before the Cortes. When he received these instructions, the representative was to leave for Europe by the shortest route. He was told to proceed to the island of Mallorca, where all the American delegates were to assemble to await the opening of the Cortes. Each municipal council had the power to fix the traveling and per diem expenses of its deputy, but was cautioned that once he reached Mallorca, he should receive no more than six *pesos fuertes* per day, the same amount that the delegates from the Spanish provinces would receive.

The Audiencia of New Spain, exercising viceregal powers, in May, 1810, ordered elections to be held without the slightest delay by the

---

[1] Spain, Council of Regency, Decree of February 14, 1810, issued on the island of León and signed by Xavier de Castaños, Francisco de Saavedra, Antonio de Escaño, and Miguel de Lardizábal y Uribe, published in the *Gaceta del gobierno de México*, Tomo I, Núm. 56 (May 18, 1810), pp. 419–420; México, Archivo General de la Nación (hereinafter cited as AGN, Historia), Ramo de Historia, Vol. 446, exp. 2, fol. 1.

municipal councils of the capitals of the provinces of México, Puebla, Veracruz, Yucatán, Oaxaca, Michoacán, Guanajuato, San Luis Potosí, Guadalajara, Zacatecas, Tabasco, Querétaro, Tlaxcala, Nuevo León, and Nuevo Santander.

At the time of the 1810 elections, Coahuila, Sonora, Sinaloa, Chihuahua, Durango, Nuevo México, and Texas were not subject to the viceregal authority and were therefore not mentioned in the addendum to the February 14 decree. These areas formed the Interior Provinces and were under the commandant general, Nemesio Salcedo, who, like the Audiencia, received the decree directly from Spain. Salcedo, on May 28, 1810, sent printed copies of the decree to the commanding officers of the provinces under his control and ordered them to proceed at once with the balloting.[2]

Elections were held throughout the Mexican provinces: in Puebla on June 26, in Texas on June 27, in Tlaxcala in late June or early July, in Veracruz on July 3, and in Nuevo México on August 11. Yucatán selected its representative sometime before November.[3] Generally, these elections were held with enthusiasm and were occasions for festivities; it is reported that in Veracruz the event was followed by a Te Deum and a popular celebration. In Puebla the festivities lasted until late at night and were accompanied by the firing of artillery and bands playing. The chosen deputy, Antonio Joaquín Pérez, a canon of the cathedral and later bishop of the Puebla diocese, was carried

[2] The Interior Provinces were organized in 1776 and subsequently modified in area and political structure by royal decrees in 1793 and 1804, the latter of which was not put into effect until 1812. In 1810 the Californias were controlled by the viceroy, and since he mentioned neither Alta nor Baja California in the addendum, the omission meant that these two areas were not entitled to hold elections. The remaining area of present-day Mexico not accounted for in the addendum was Chiapas, which at the time was considered a part of Guatemala and will therefore not be treated in this paper. See Nettie Lee Benson, "Texas' Failure To Send a Deputy to the Spanish Cortes, 1810–1812," *Southwestern Historical Quarterly,* LXIV (July, 1960), 5; Herbert Eugene Bolton, *Guide to the Materials for the History of the United States in the Principal Archives of Mexico,* pp. 75–77; Edmundo O'Gorman, *Breve historia de las divisiones territoriales: Aportación a la historia de la geografía de México,* pp. xxxvi–xlii, 16–17.

[3] For the election in Puebla, see *Diario de México,* Tomo XIII, Núm. 10736 (July 4, 1810), 13–14; for Texas, see Benson, "Texas' Failure To Send a Deputy," p. 6; for Tlaxcala, *Diario de México,* Tomo XIII, Núm. 10745 (July 13, 1810), p. 52; for Veracruz, *ibid.,* Núm. 10740 (July 8, 1810), p. 32; for New Mexico, H. H. Bancroft, *History of Arizona and New Mexico, 1530–1888,* in *The Works of Hubert Howe Bancroft,* XVII, 287–290; for Yucatán, AGN, Historia, Vol. 446, exp. 1, fols. 29–30.

through the streets on the shoulders of the members of the municipal council.

Not all the elections were held according to the strict letter of the instructions issued by the Regency. The deputy from Nuevo México, Pedro Bautista Pino, described the procedure followed in that province in a report that he presented to the Cortes after he was seated as a delegate. Since Nuevo México did not have a municipal council, the governor invited all the towns under his jurisdiction to participate in choosing their representative.[4] Texas also did not conform with the prescribed procedures. The municipal council of San Fernando de Béjar met and elected the governor of the province, Lieutenant Colonel Manuel de Salcedo, as its deputy, because the province was too poor to support a representative in the Cortes. It was reasoned that Salcedo could rely on his salary as an official of the government for his support while in Spain. In the correspondence that passed between the officials of Texas and the commandant of the Interior Provinces it was also stated that there were not three men, natives of Texas, who met the qualifications and that there was an insufficient number of men on the municipal council in Texas. The Audiencia of Guadalajara, to which the Interior Provinces were attached for legal purposes, ruled the Texas election invalid and ordered a new one to be held. Suffice it to say that throughout the next twelve years Texas never successfully elected its own deputy to the Cortes, although an earnest attempt was made to choose a representative and the electoral process was repeated several times.[5]

The Regency's concern that the elections be held in the overseas provinces is shown by a decree issued in the name of Ferdinand VII on June 26, 1810, urging that the electoral process be carried out immediately so that when the Cortes convened in September, the deputies from America would be present. That decree did not reach Mexico City until September, after the congress had already opened.

---

[4] Pedro Bautista Pino, *Noticias históricas y estadísticas de la antigua provincia del Nuevo-Méjico presentadas por su diputado en cortes D. Pedro Bautista Pino en Cádiz el año de 1812, adicionadas por el Lic. D. Antonio Barreiro en 1839; y ultimamente anotadas por el Lic. Don José Agustín de Escudero para la Comisión de Estadística Militar de la república mexicana*, pp. 35–36.

[5] Benson, "Texas' Failure To Send a Deputy," *passim*. An extensive search has failed to turn up details of the 1810 elections in provinces other than those indicated. The October 12, 1810, issue of the *Gaceta del gobierno de México*, Tomo I, Núm. 120, pp. 856–857, contains a list of seventeen deputies elected, indicating that by that date most of the provinces had chosen their representatives.

Mexico and the Spanish Cortes

Viceroy Venegas had it printed and copies distributed on September 25.[6]

To insure that the overseas dominions were represented in the Cortes from the moment it opened its sessions, the decree that established the Regency on January 28, 1810, and which announced the convocation of the Cortes, had made provision for such representation until the overseas deputies should arrive in Spain. On March 1, 1810, six American natives resident in Cádiz were to draw forty names from a container filled with names of Americans living in the Peninsula. From these forty, a second drawing of twenty-six names would be held, these last to serve as alternate deputies in the Cortes, representing America until the arrival of the regularly elected delegates from the overseas provinces.[7] At this drawing, seven men were selected to represent the Mexican provinces. All of them were present when the congress opened and were destined to sit in that body until 1814. Some of them served in later Cortes and played active roles in the deliberation (see Table I).

As a result of the elections of 1810 in the Mexican provinces, fifteen deputies finally arrived in Spain and were seated in the Cortes. One, Pino of Nuevo, Mexico, who had the farthest to travel, did not arrive until August, 1812. The delay is indicative of the determination of the provinces to have their representatives in the Cortes. A few of the Mexican delegates failed to reach Spain (see Table II).

Although the first selection of overseas representatives to the Cortes could be called an election only by a broad interpretation of the word, since only municipal council members of the provincial capitals participated, certain significant aspects of the process as first established merit comment. Most important, of course, was the fact that the deputies had to be natives of the provinces that they were chosen to represent. This provision insured that ultramarine interests were truly upheld by men born in the colonies. The arrange-

---

[6] Decree issued from Cádiz, dated June 26, 1810, signed by Silvestre Collar, AGN, Historia, Vol. 446, exp. 1, fol. 1.

[7] Decree of January 29, 1810, "El rey, y á su nombre la suprema Junta Central Gubernativa de España e Indias," Art. 4, quoted in Modesto Lafuente y Zamolloa, *Historia general de España desde los tiempos primitivos hasta la muerte de Fernando VII*, V, 117. There is some disagreement among historians contemporary with the events concerning the number of substitute delegates chosen in Cádiz; a thorough discussion may be found in James F. King, "The Colored Castes and American Representation in the Cortes of Cádiz," *Hispanic American Historical Review* (hereinafter referred to as HAHR), XXXIII (February, 1953), 35–36, n. 5.

Table 1

Substitute Deputies Selected in Cádiz in 1810

Name	Offices Held in Cortes[1]
Couto, José María	Vice-President, April 24, 1813
Fernández Munilla, Francisco	
Gutiérrez de Terán, José María	Secretary, Nov. 24, 1811
	Vice-President, Mar. 24, 1812
	President, April 24, 1812
Maldonado, Máximo[2]	
Obregón, Octaviano	
Samartín, Salvador	
Savariego, Andrés	

[1] According to the rules governing the organization of the Cortes, the principal offices were those of the president, vice-president, and two secretaries. The first two were elected on the twenty-fourth of each month. Their duration of office was for one month and they could not be re-elected until an interim of six months had passed. The secretaries were also elected on the twenty-fourth, but were to hold office for two months, with the election of each secretary staggered so that only one was chosen each month. Secretaries could not be re-elected until two months had elapsed. Spain, Cortes, *Reglamento para el gobierno interior de las Córtes* [dated November 24, 1810], (Cádiz: La imprenta real, 1810). The dates given in the table above are those of election.

[2] Died June 20, 1813.

ment for a group of substitute deputies to sit in the congress until the regularly chosen delegates should arrive is also noteworthy. The seven alternates selected for the Mexican provinces were able men who performed their duties conscientiously, and who, despite provisions that they were to give up their seats when the proprietary delegates arrived, managed to remain accredited as representatives throughout the duration of the first Cortes, thereby increasing the strength of the Mexican delegation.[8]

[8] The numerical strength of the American deputation in the Cortes, both in regard to the proprietary representatives and the substitutes chosen in Spain, was a source of constant debate in the Cortes. For a full discussion of the question of increasing the deputation, see Demetrio Ramos, "Las Cortes de Cádiz y América," *Revista de estudios políticos*, Núm. 126 (November–December, 1962), pp. 511–538. The question of allowing the substitutes to remain in the Cortes after the arrival of the regularly chosen deputies was very important, but unfortunately it falls outside the framework of this paper, although it will be alluded to in a few places. There is abundant material on the topic in the body of debates in the Cortes and also in the propagandistic literature written by Mexicans in Spain, revolutionary in purpose and nationalistic in tone. The question

Table 2

Deputies Elected in Mexican Provinces for Cortes, 1810–1813

Those Who Attended

Name	Province	Date Seated	Offices Held in the Cortes
Beye Cisneros, José	México	3/1/1811	
Cárdenas, José Eduardo de	Tabasco	2/27/1811	
Foncerrada, José Cayetano de	Michoacán	3/4/1811	
González y Lastiri, Miguel	Yucatán	3/12/1811	
Gordoa, José Miguel	Zacatecas	3/4/1811	Vice-President, 8/24/1812
			President, 8/24/1813
Güereña, Juan José[1]	Durango	4/8/1811	President, 7/24/1811
Guridi y Alcocer, José Miguel	Tlaxcala	12/10/1810	President, 5/24/1812
Maniau, Joaquín	Veracruz	3/1/1811	Vice-President, 7/24/1811
			President, 2/24/1813
Mendiola Velarde, Mariano[2]	Querétaro	1/15/1811	Vice-President, 2/24/1811
Moreno, Manuel María[3]	Sonora	3/26/1811	
Obregón, Octaviano[4]	Guanajuato	12/23/1810	
Pérez, Antonio Joaquín	Puebla	12/23/1810	President, 1/24/1811
Pino, Pedro Bautista	Nuevo México	8/5/1812	
Ramos Arizpe, José Miguel	Coahuila	3/21/1811	
Uría, José Simeón de	Guadalajara	3/4/1811	Vice-President, 6/24/181

Those Who Did Not Attend[5]

Name	Province
Barragán, José Florencio[6]	San Luis Potosí
Garza, Juan José de la[7]	Nuevo León
Ibáñez de Corvera, Juan María[8]	Oaxaca
Mexía, Manuel María[9]	Oaxaca
Villamil, Bernardo[10]	San Luis Potosí

---

[1] Died October 9, 1813.

[2] Also served as a member of the Permanent Deputation between the close of the special sessions of the 1810–1813 Cortes and the beginning of the regular session in October, 1813.

[3] Death announced on September 4, 1811.

[4] Obregón was seated on September 24, 1810, as an alternate deputy, one of those chosen in Cádiz. He was also elected to represent Guanajuato, and in December was recognized as a proprietary deputy.

[5] Taken from *Gaceta del Gobierno de México*, Tomo I (October 12, 1810), pp. 856–857.

[6] Became incapacitated.

[7] Died en route.

[8] Certified to take Mexía's place.

[9] Refused to accept position after being elected.

[10] Alternate who was certified to represent San Luis Potosí when Barragán could not fulfil the position.

Many tasks presented themselves before the 1810 congress, but perhaps the most important was the adoption of a constitution. Soon after the Cortes was officially opened on September 24, 1810, a committee was appointed to begin work on writing the fundamental law. The result of this long and arduous task was the promulgation on March 19, 1812, of the Political Constitution of the Spanish Monarchy. In great detail, it provided for elections of deputies to future Cortes.[9] The sessions of the congress were to convene on March 1 of every year and were to last for three months (Article 106); deputies were to be chosen every two years, and thus would sit for two consecutive sessions; and the entire body was to be renewed every two years (Article 108).

The electoral procedures established were elaborate and somewhat complicated. The choosing of deputies to the congress was to be indirect and to take place in three stages on three different levels of government: the parish, the district, and the province. The parish elections were to be held in the overseas provinces on the first Sunday of December, fifteen months before the convening of the biennial Cortes.

On the appointed day, those entitled to vote in the parish were to assemble in a body to choose men from among them who, in turn, would select the parish electors. Voter qualifications as set forth in the Constitution were vague. Only male citizens could cast ballots. Men who could trace their lineage on both sides to Spanish dominions in either hemisphere and who resided in any part of the empire were citizens and had the right to vote. Sons born in any of the provinces to aliens, who had reached the age of twenty-one, who had some useful profession, and who had never left the provinces without the government's permission also were considered Spanish citizens. Provision was made for naturalization, which could be granted by the Cortes to certain foreigners who had either rendered some service to Spain or who were property-holders, and who were married to Span-

---

arose to plague every new Cortes that met between 1810 and 1821, and frequently led to long and heated discussions on the floor. There is also ample evidence that Mexicans resident in Spain, including some of the delegates to the congresses, carried on an active lobby to get the numerical strength of the Mexican deputation greatly augmented.

[9] Of a total of 384 articles, 113 directly or indirectly concerned the holding of elections. See Spain, Constitution, *Constitución política de la monarquía española.*

ish women. Men of African origin could obtain citizenship only by special acts of the Cortes, which would be passed in the case of those who rendered service to the nation or distinguished themselves in other ways. Written into the Constitution was a provision stating that, beginning in 1830, those who had newly acquired citizenship must know how to read and write. It is to be noted that no age limit is mentioned except in the case of sons born in the Spanish Empire to aliens resident there; probably, by extension, this same age limit of twenty-one years applied to all as the minimum age required for casting ballots. The main voting qualification seemed to center on who was an *avecindado* of the parishes.

It is practically impossible to define *avecindado* today as it could be defined in an 1810 context. The general connotation is a kind of local citizenship, and to acquire it, certain conditions had to be met.[10] These conditions were constantly undergoing change. For example, in 1845, a law was passed in Spain setting forth some four stipulations, such as that one must be the head of a household and must have resided in the pueblo at least a year and a day. Apparently it was the intent of the Cortes to let the voting qualifications remain vague so as to permit local interpretation of the constitutional provisions.

Such an interpretation was given in Mexico by the junta established to prepare for the Cortes elections that were to commence in December, 1812. In the instructions issued by that body, under the section entitled "Concerning the Parish Juntas," three articles discussed the persons who had the right to vote. The qualifications applied only to males, for no woman could vote. Spanish citizens (including pure Indians or mestizos) who were married, widowers, or bachelors, if they had a place of residence and an honest occupation, and were not disbarred by the Constitution from the privileges enjoyed by citizens, could vote. Domestic servants who received wages or who rendered personal service and who were considered lackeys, coachmen, stable boys, porters, cooks, chamberlains, messengers, or the like, could not vote. Day laborers, muleteers, shepherds, herdsmen, and men with similar occupations, even though they lived on estates

10 For a discussion of the word, see the *Enciclopedia Universal Ilustrada Europeo-Americana*, LXVII (1929), s.v. "vecindad." 410 ff., which states, in part: "En cuanto a los requisitos necesarios para adquirir la vecindad, son innumerables las disposiciones de nuestra antigua legislación, adoleciendo algunas de ellas de gran confusión: decían la calidad de vecindad que, unidos al domicilio, ofrecían formal propósito de permanecer en un pueblo."

or ranches, were not to be considered as domestic servants and could not be denied the right to vote.[11]

The size of the population of each parish determined the number of representatives to be chosen. The general rule provided for one elector for each two hundred citizens and residents of the parish. If the parish was entitled to have one elector, each citizen allowed to vote must name eleven men of the parish, and the eleven so named who received the highest number of votes would then choose the elector; if the parish was entitled to two electors, twenty-one would be chosen who would vote for the two; if entitled to three, then each citizen must name thirty-one men of the parish, who in turn would choose the three electors. In no case would more than thirty-one be selected to choose the representatives, even though the parish might be entitled to more than three electors. In thickly populated parishes, this procedure put a heavy burden on the citizens, for each had to walk up to a table presided over by the judges of the election and name thirty-one qualified men without hesitation.

Provisions were also included in the Constitution for holding a mass before each parish election, for choosing the officials, and for settling any disputes that might arise concerning who had the right to vote. No citizen was to be excused from the obligation of voting; no one would be allowed to bear arms at the polling stations; and a Te Deum was to be offered after the process was completed.

Those men chosen to select the parish electors would proceed immediately to name the parish representatives. Each man would vote for the designated number of electors and those receiving the highest number of votes would be the parish representatives entitled to participate in the next-higher stage of the election.

In America on the first Sunday in January following the December parish elections, the representatives were to meet at the seat of each district to name district electors, this time by secret ballot. Much the same procedure was observed at this level as at the parish level. A solemn high mass was celebrated before the voting, the constitutional provisions regarding the election were read to the participants, and they selected the judges for the occasion.

---

[11] "Instrucción que para facilitar las elecciones de Diputados para las próximas Cortes generales del año de 1813 ha formado la Junta Preparatoria de México" in Rafael Alba (ed.), *La constitución de 1812 en la Nueva España*, I, 163; AGN, Historia, Vol. 445, exp. 1, fols. 27–80.

The third and final stage of the electoral process took place in the provincial capital on the second Sunday of March following the district balloting. There the electors chose the deputies to the Cortes, roughly on the basis of one for every seventy thousand people in the province. The process to be followed on the provincial level differed from that of the district. The electors met together to hear read to them the four chapters of the Constitution detailing the procedures for selecting deputies, then had their credentials examined by a board of election judges whom they chose from among themselves. Following this, the electors then went in a body to the cathedral to hear a solemn mass and a sermon by the bishop. After these preliminaries, the voting was held. Each elector approached a table presided over by the officials and named one man as his choice for deputy. After every elector had voted, the judges tabulated the results and declared elected the man receiving an absolute majority. If no one received a majority, a run-off was held between the two receiving the highest number of votes. In case of a tie, a drawing was held and the first name drawn was the elected deputy. This process was repeated until the designated number of deputies was selected. Next, following the same method, alternates were chosen at the ratio of one to every three regular deputies. Even if a province were entitled to only one deputy, it also selected one alternate. These substitutes were authorized to attend the Cortes only upon the incapacity or death of the regular deputy.[12]

It is to be noted that there were no provisions in the Constitution regarding nomination of candidates for parish or district electors or for the deputies who were chosen to represent the province in the Cortes. The electors merely named the men who met the qualifications established by the Constitution and who they considered would best represent their interests. It is not inconceivable that within such a framework, partisan feelings and activities could develop, and perhaps certain groups did offer candidates for the various positions. But any discussion of political maneuvering to dominate the electoral juntas or to get candidates elected as deputies lies outside the scope of this paper.

The qualifications for deputies were set forth in the Constitution. A man so chosen must be a citizen in the full exercise of his rights, at least twenty-five years of age, and a native born in, or resident for at

---

[12] The parish election provisions are detailed in Title III, Chap. I of the Constitution; those of the district in III, ii; and those of the province in III, iv.

least seven years in, the province which selected him as its representative. He could be either a private citizen or a member of the secular clergy (Article 91). Furthermore, he was required to have an annual income from his own interests, but this provision was not to be effective until the Cortes stipulated the amount of the income and the type of sources from which it should be derived (Articles 92 and 93). Excluded from being deputies were certain special government employees (Article 95) and any naturalized citizen (Article 96). No public employee could represent the province in which he held his office (Article 97). Provision was also made to resolve the situation which might arise, and in fact did arise, whereby a man could be selected to represent two provinces—the one in which he was born and the one in which he resided. In such a case, he must represent only the province of which he was a resident, and his duly elected alternate would be authorized to represent the province in which the deputy in question was born (Article 94).

Since the Constitution was not adopted until mid-March, 1812, the Cortes foresaw that elections in the overseas provinces could not possibly be held in time for the deputies to arrive in Spain by the following March, the date established by the Constitution for the convening of the regular session of the congress. Therefore, on May 23, a decree was issued which stated that, because of the chaotic times and the distances involved, the regular session would not convene until October 1, 1813.[13]

Some preliminary work also had to be done in the provinces to determine the number of deputies each was entitled to have and the number of electors each parish and district should name; so on May 23, 1812, the Cortes issued a second decree, supplementing the instructions contained in the Constitution. According to this document, preliminary meetings would be held in Mexico City, Guadalajara, Mérida, Monterrey, and Durango to prepare for the elections in the respective kingdoms of New Spain, Nueva Galicia, Yucatán, and the Eastern and Western Interior Provinces. On the basis of the latest or most accurate census available, these bodies were to determine the number of deputies each province was entitled to elect, to divide the

---

[13] Spain, Cortes, "Decreto CLXII de 23 de Mayo de 1812: Convocatoria para las Cortes ordinarias de 1° de Octubre de 1813," in *Colección de los decretos y órdenes que han expedidos las Cortes generales y extraordinarias*, II (1820), 210–211. The 1814 session, then, would meet as scheduled in the Constitution; that is, on March 1.

area into districts if this had not been done previously, and to provide for any difficulties that might arise during the balloting.[14]

Venegas presided over the preparatory junta in Mexico City. For purposes of the election, New Spain was divided into the provinces of Oaxaca, Puebla, Tlaxcala, Querétaro, Veracruz, Valladolid de Michoacán, Guanajuato, San Luis Potosí, and México.[15] The population of New Spain, using the census taken during Revilla Gigedo's administration in 1792, was fixed at 2,886,238 persons. The allotment of deputies to each province was established as follows:

Province	Deputies	Alternates
México	14	4
Puebla	7	2
Michoacán	3	1
Guanajuato	5	1
Oaxaca	6	2
Veracruz	2	1
San Luis Potosí	2	1
Tlaxcala	1	1
Querétaro	1	1

The dates for holding the elections in parishes and districts were left up to the various political chiefs of each territorial division, but the junta specified that the district representatives were to meet in the provincial capitals on February 1, 1813, to choose the deputies to the Cortes.

On Sunday, November 28, 1812, in Mexico City, the machinery as set forth in the Constitution was put into operation for the first time with the parish elections. There were complaints concerning the

[14] Spain, Cortes, "Instrucción conforme a la cual deberán celebrarse en las provincias de Ultramar las elecciones de Diputados de Cortes para las ordinarias del año próximo de 1813," in Alba, *La constitución de 1812 en la Nueva España,* I, 151–154; *Diario de México,* Tomo XVII, Núm. 2567 (October 11, 1812), pp. 422–424, and Núm. 2568 (October 12, 1812), pp. 425–426; AGN, Historia, Vol. 445, exp. 1, fols. 5–7.

[15] The decisions of the junta in Mexico City were adopted on November 27, 1812, and are embodied in the Bando cited by Francisco Xavier Venegas and José Ignacio Negreiros y Soria, in Alba, *La constitución de 1812 en la Nueva España,* I, 155–161; *Diario de México,* Tomo XVII, Núm. 2617 (November 30, 1812), pp. 637–638; Núm. 2618 (December 1, 1812), pp. 645–646; Núm. 2619 (December 2, 1812), pp. 648–650; Núm. 2620 (December 3, 1812), pp. 652–653; and AGN, Historia, Vol. 445, exp. 1, fol. 26. Also on November 27, the junta issued a set of instructions meant to govern the election (see note 11).

duplications of votes, the use of written ballots which the Constitution had not authorized, and the celebrations that followed. All the electors chosen in Mexico City were creoles, and in this fact lay the basis for all the criticisms. For these and other reasons, Venegas suspended the electoral process in the province of Mexico. Not until Calleja became the superior political chief of New Spain the following spring was the process resumed.[16]

With Section III, Articles 34–103, of the Constitution again in effect, the parish balloting was held without incident on Sunday, July 4, 1813. A week following, the parish electors met in the seats of the districts and selected their representatives, who on July 18 met in a body as called for in the Constitution and voted for the men who would attend the Cortes.[17]

In these 1812–1813 elections, Puebla, Tlaxcala, Querétaro, Guanajuato, and San Luis Potosí succeeded in choosing representatives to the Cortes, but no record of the deputies from the latter province has been found.[18] Neither did a search reveal any mention of elections being held in Veracruz. In Oaxaca and Michoacán, under the control of Morelos in this period, no balloting was held.

The suspension of the electoral process applied only to the province of México in New Spain, but a delay was also experienced in holding the Cortes elections in Nueva Galicia, Yucatán, and in the Interior Provinces because of the time that elapsed before these distant areas received the Constitution and the decrees of the Cortes concerning establishing juntas to prepare for the balloting. Nueva Galicia held its Preparatory Junta in June and on June 21 called for the holding of the Electoral Junta on September 4, 1813. The allotment of deputies for its two provinces was: Guadalajara, six proprietary deputies and two alternates, and Zacatecas, three proprietary deputies and one alternate. The electors for the province of Guadalajara met on

[16] For an analysis of the 1812 parish elections in Mexico City, see Nettie Lee Benson, "The Contested Mexican Election of 1812," *HAHR*, XXVI (August, 1946), 336–350.

[17] For the results of the parish elections, see *Diario de México*, Tomo II, Núm. 7 (July 7, 1813), Núm. 8 (July 8, 1813), Núm. 11 (July 11, 1813), Núm. 12 (July 12, 1813). For the results of the provincial elections, see *ibid.*, Núm. 20 (July 20, 1813), and "Noticia de los que salieron electos Diputados (propprietarios y suplentes) á Cortes por la provincia de México," dated July 18, 1813, Mexico City, and signed by Ramón Gutiérrez del Mazo, in Alba, *La constitución de 1812 en la Nueva España*, I, 172–173.

[18] Spain, Cortes, 1813–1814, *Actas de las sesiones de la legislatura ordinaria de 1813*, p. 378.

Table 3

Partial List of Men Chosen in the 1813 Elections for the 1813–1814 Cortes

Guadalajara¹	*Alternate*
Proprietary	Yllescas, José Manuel de
Aldama, José María de	**Guanajuato⁴**
Aranda, Diego	*Proprietary*
Cañedo, Juan de Dios	Espinosa de los Monteros, Juan José
Cordón, Juan José	Fuentes, Dr. Victorino de las
Sánchez Resa, Domingo	San Juan de Rayas, Marqués de
Velasco, Francisco Antonio de	
Alternates	**México⁵**
García Cárdenas, Serafín	*Proprietary*
Rosa, José Cesareo de la	Alfaro, Miguel
	Alvarado, Ignacio
Yucatán²	Assorey, Juan Manuel
Proprietary	Cortazar, Manuel
Alonso y Pantiga, Angel	Gil, José María
Cárdenas, Juan Nepomuceno	Gómez de Navarrete, Juan
Martínez de la Pedrera, José	Lope Vergara, Félix
Quijano, José Miguel	López Salazar, José Antonio
Regil, Pedro Manuel de	Molinos, Francisco
Rivas y Vértiz, Juan	Obregón, Juan
Villamil, Eusebio	Posada, Manuel
Alternates	Salgado, Tomás
Pérez, Raimundo	Sánchez Carrasco, Ignacio
Solís, Diego	Villaseñor, Juan Ignacio
	Alternates
Tlaxcala³	Apartado, Marqués del
Proprietary	Gama, Antonio
Roxano y Mudarra, Agustín	Lejarza, José Simón de
	Valdovinos, Agustín

¹ AGN, *Historia*, Vol. 445, exp. 10, fol. 9; Alba, *La constitución de 1812 en la Nueva España*, I, 172–179.

² Manuel A. Lanz, *Compendio de historia de Campeche*, p. 505.

³ AGN, *Historia*, Vol. 445, exp. 2, fols. 10–12.

⁴ Alba, *La constitución de 1812 en la Nueva España*, I, 195–199.

⁵ *Ibid.*, p. 172. Lillian Estelle Fisher, *The Background of the Revolution for Mexican Independence*, p. 334, mentions three other delegates chosen in this election: Ignacio Adalid, Fagoaga, and José María Alcalá, but adds that the first two were tried for conspiracy and were not permitted by Calleja to go to Spain. Alcalá, however, did travel to the Peninsula. Fisher cites as authority the "Informe del Exmo. Sr. Virrey D. Félix Calleja sobre el estado de la N.E. dirigido al Ministerio de Gracia y Justicia en 18 de Agosto de 814" [*sic*]. The present writer has examined this report, and Calleja does mention Alcalá as being a deputy to the Cortes, as well as the other two men's having been elected but prohibited from attending.

Querétaro[6]	Puebla[8]
Proprietary	*Proprietary*
Cabeza de Baca, Antonio	Alvarez, Ramón
Alternate	Estévez Ravanillo, Juan
López Secada, Manuel	Nepomuceno
	Fernández Almanza, José María
Zacatecas[7]	Franco de la Vega, Tomás
Proprietary	García Paredes, Juan Miguel
Apezechea, Fermín Antonio de	Oller, José María
Larrañaga, Pedro	Rosas, Antonio
Sánchez Resa, Domingo	*Alternates*
Alternate	Morón, José María
Rosa, José Cesareo de la	Zapata, José María

---

[6] AGN, Historia, Vol. 445, exp. 2, fols. 5–6.
[7] *Ibid.*, exp. 10, fol. 21.
[8] *Ibid.*, exp. 1, fol. 88.

September 4, 1813, and on the following day, the six deputies and two alternates were chosen.[19] In Yucatán the Cortes elections were completed on March 14, 1813, with seven deputies and two alternates being chosen to represent the provinces of Yucatán, Campeche, and Tabasco.[20] The Eastern Interior Provinces did not hold the final election for its deputies until March 20, 1814.[21] A search has failed to reveal any details concerning elections in the Western Interior Provinces (see Table III).

Because of the delay in the voting in New Spain and the adjacent territories, as well as the chaotic political conditions, the military disturbances created by the rebel army, and, most important, the lack of funds in the treasuries of the various provinces, it was not propitious for the deputies to make an attempt to reach Spain to sit in the Cortes. Only seven, or possibly eight, of the delegates ever reached the Peninsula to participate in either the 1813 or 1814 sessions of the congress (see Table IV).

It is noteworthy that some of the provinces of Mexico made an attempt to conform to the provisions of the Constitution by holding

[19] "Actas de la Junta Electoral de la Provincia de Nueva Galicia," and "Aviso," both dated September 5, 1813, in Alba, *La constitución de 1812 en la Nueva España*, I, 173–179; *Diario de México*, Tomo II, Núm. 115 (October 23, 1813); AGN, Historia, Vol. 445, exp. 10, fols. 1–9.

[20] Nettie Lee Benson, *La diputación provincial y el federalismo mexicano*, p. 25.

[21] *Ibid.*, p. 30.

Table 4

Deputies Who Attended the 1813–1814 Sessions of the Cortes

Name	Province	Date Seated 1813 Cortes	1814 Cortes	Offices Held in the Cortes 1813	1814
*Alonso y Pantiga, Angel	Yucatán	Nov. 14	Mar. 1		
*Cárdenas, Juan Nepomuceno de	Yucatán	Nov. 17	Mar. 1		
Couto, José María	Nueva España	Oct. 1	Mar. 1		
Fernández Munilla, Francisco	Nueva España	Oct. 1	Mar. 1		
Foncerrada, José Cayetano de	Michoacán	Oct. 1	Mar. 1	Vice-Pres., 11/1	
*Franco de la Vega, Tomás[1]	Puebla	Feb. 19, 1814	Mar. 1		
*García Paredas, Miguel	Puebla	Oct. 1	Mar. 1		
Gordoa, José Miguel	Zacatecas	Oct. 1	Mar. 1	Sec'y, 11/1	
Gutiérrez de Terán, José María	Nueva España	Oct. 1	Mar. 1		
Maniau, Joaquín	Veracruz	Oct. 1	Mar. 1		
*Martínez de la Pedrera, José	Yucatán	Nov. 14	Mar. 1		
Mendiola, Mariano	Querétaro	Oct. 1	Mar. 1		
Obregón, Octaviano	Nueva España	Oct. 1			Sec'y, 2/16
Pérez, Antonio Joaquín	Puebla	Oct. 1	Mar. 1	Vice-Pres., 1/16 Pres., 2/16	Vice-Pres., 4/1 Pres., 5/1
*Quijano, José Miguel de	Yucatán	Oct. 1	Mar. 1		
Ramos Arizpe, José Miguel	Coahuila	Oct. 1	Mar. 1		
*Rivas y Vértiz, Juan	Yucatán	Feb. 18, 1814			
Savariego, Andrés	Nueva España	Oct. 1	Mar. 1		
Samartín, Salvador	Nueva España	Oct. 1	Mar. 1		
Sánchez Resa, José Domingo	Guadalajara		Apr. 29		

* One of the seven deputies chosen in the delayed elections in Mexico in 1812–1813 who arrived in Spain to take their seats in the congress. Of the fifteen regularly elected deputies and six substitutes (one of whom, Obregón, was later chosen as a regular deputy) chosen in Spain who represented the Mexican provinces in the 1810–1813 Cortes, six returned home and three died, leaving twelve who reappeared in the 1813 Cortes (regular session). To supplement this number, seven were chosen in the delayed elections in Mexico. One of the seven died before taking his seat, leaving eighteen to represent Mexico.

In the next session of the Cortes, which commenced on March 1, 1814, sixteen of the eighteen from the previous session remained. Unaccounted for are Obregón and Rivas y Vértiz, who were absent at this session. But Sánchez Resa, representing Guadalajara, made his appearance and was seated in late April, 1814, only a few days before Ferdinand VII dissolved the body. His arrival brought the strength of the Mexican delegation to seventeen.

[1] On January 21, 1814, the Cortes formally approved the credentials of Franco de la Vega. There is no notice in the official gazette, however, that he was ever seated or that he swore to uphold the Constitution, the next two steps in the formal recognition of a deputy. During the next session of the Cortes, that which convened on March 1, 1814, notice is given of Franco's death, and he is spoken of as a deputy-elect. Probably he never was seated, but his name is listed since he was in the process of being recognized formally. Spain, Cortes, 1813–1814, *Actas de las Sesiones de la Legislatura Ordinaria de 1813*, Núm. 76 (January 21, 1814), p. 358; *ibid.*, 1814, *Actas de las Sesiones de la Legislatura Ordinaria de 1814*, Núm. 52 (April 12, 1814), p. 241.

elections on the three levels in December, 1813, and January and March, 1814, for the 1815–1816 sessions of the Cortes.[22]

Even in the provinces under the control of the rebels, the electoral process was not unknown, for according to the provisions of the Constitution of Apatzingán, drawn up by those in revolt, deputies were to be elected to a congress. Although in the end no elections were held, significantly enough the form of balloting called for followed very closely that used in the other provinces subject to the Constitution of 1812 for the selection of deputies to the Cortes. Under the rebel plan, the minimum age for voting was eighteen years. The elections were to be conducted on three levels before the delegates were finally chosen, and the same provisions prevailed regarding the holding of a mass, bearing of arms at the voting places, choosing the electoral judges, settling disputes concerning who was enfranchized, and compulsory voting.[23]

The deputies selected in the 1813–1814 elections soon found that there was no Cortes for them to attend. Events had begun to move rapidly in Spain, and in May, 1814, when Ferdinand VII returned, the conservatives prevailed upon him to dissolve the Cortes, abolish the Constitution of 1812, and resume his autocratic control over the Spanish empire. The King was only too willing to comply with such a policy. He declared the Constitution null and void on May 11, dissolved the Cortes, and threw into prison many of its liberal leaders, among whom were the Mexican delegates Ramos Arizpe, Maniau, and Gutiérrez de Terán.

For almost six years Ferdinand continued his autocratic rule. Meanwhile, the revolt in various parts of the Western Hemisphere gained impetus. In late 1819, in an effort to halt its spread, the King ordered the concentration of Spanish troops in Cádiz preparatory to their being sent to America. There was much dissatisfaction in the army, and a few of the officers rebelled. The liberals joined with the soldiers; Riego emerged as the leader; and on March 6, 1820, Ferdi-

[22] Reports of the elections in Guanajuato, San Luis Potosí, México, Zacatecas, Guadalajara, Puebla, and Veracruz can be found in AGN, Historia, Vol. 445, exp. 10. Puebla did not hold its final balloting, the provincial level, until June 13, 1814, and Veracruz on June 27, 1814, but all the other provinces for which reports were found maintained the schedule established by the Constitution.

[23] "Decreto constitucional para la libertad de la América mexicana sancionado en Apatzingán a 22 de octubre de 1814," in Juan A. Mateos, *Historia parlamentaria de los congresos mexicanos de 1821 a 1857*, I, 42–58. See particularly Chaps. V–VII of the Constitution of 1812.

nand was forced to issue a call for the Cortes. The following day, the Spanish rebels compelled him to re-establish the Constitution of 1812.[24]

For both the peninsular and overseas provinces to choose delegates to attend this congress, it was obvious that the December–January–March pattern of elections as called for in the Constitution could not be followed. A provisional junta in Spain was established to prepare for the opening of the sessions, and, following the precedent of the 1810 Regency, on March 22, 1820, it issued a set of instructions designating July 9 as the opening date for the Cortes and providing for the selection of substitute delegates, to be chosen in Madrid on Sunday, May 28, from among the Americans resident in Spain. Seven substitutes were to be selected for the Mexican provinces. As in 1810, these alternates would serve until the regularly elected deputies from America should arrive.[25] The selection was made, though not without controversy.[26] Again New Spain was fortunate to have outstanding men as its representatives (see Table V).

To provide for the election of the deputies in the ultramarine dominions, Ferdinand VII issued a set of instructions from Madrid on March 24, 1820. The same procedure as that set out in the Constitution was to be used, with the exception of the timetable. Preparatory juntas meeting in México, Guadalajara, Mérida, Monterrey, and

[24] Lafuente, *Historia general de España*, V, 341.

[25] *Decreto de 22 de marzo de 1820, convocando a Cortes ordinarias para los años de 1820 y 1821*, signed by José María de Parga. A copy of this decree is in the Alejandro Prieto papers, the Latin American Collection of The University of Texas Library. It is also quoted in Lafuente, *Historia general de España*, V, 343–344, n. 1.

[26] The controversy centered around the procedures observed at the selection of the alternates and the small number of men designated to represent America in general and the Mexican provinces in particular. Several broadsides were published in which the authors urged that the selection, which was made by drawing names from a container, be nullified and a new drawing held. See, *e.g.*, Juan de Dios Cañedo, *Manifiesto a la nación Española sobre la representación de las provincias de ultramar en las próximas Córtes, por el Lic. D. Juan de Dios Cañedo, diputado suplente por la Nueva España*; Cristóbal Lily, Juan Manuel Ausel y Domínguez, José Joaquín Ayesterán, and José Mariano Michelena, *Representación presentada a la Junta Superior de Galicia por los Americanos residentes en esta Provincia*; M. [L. de] V[idaurre y Encalada?], *Manifiesto sobre los representantes que corresponden a los americanos en las inmediatas Córtes*; and *Representación que los Americanos Españoles, residentes en Madrid, han entregado a S.M. por medio de los Sres. Marqués de Cárdenas de Montehermoso, D. Manuel Inca Inpanqui, y D. Gabriel Señero, el dia 4 del presente mes de abril* [dated March 31, 1820, and signed by 146 individuals].

Table 5

Substitute Deputies Selected in Madrid in 1820[1]

Name	Offices Held in Cortes
Cañedo, Juan de Dios	
Cortazar, Manuel[2]	
Couto, José María	Secretary, March, 1821
Fagoaga, Francisco[3]	
Michelena, José Mariano[4]	
Montoya, José María	
Ramos Arizpe, José Miguel	

[1] List taken from Lucas Alamán, *Historia de Méjico desde los primeros movimientos que prepararon su independencia en el año de 1808 hasta la época presente*, V, 47.

[2] Cortazar not only was selected as an alternate in the drawing in Madrid, but was also elected as a regular deputy from both Guanajuato and México. The Committee on Credentials of the Cortes ruled that he was a native of Guanajuato and was therefore to be seated as one of that province's deputies. It is to be noted that this ruling was in contradiction to the constitutional provisions regarding such a situation. See Spain, Cortes, 1821, *Diario de las Sesiones de Cortes. Legislatura de 1821*, I, Núm. 30 (March 27, 1821), 717 (hereinafter cited as *Diario de Sesiones de 1821*); *Gaceta del Gobierno de México*, Tomo XI, Núm. 126 (September 19, 1820), pp. 971–972, and Núm. 130 (September 26, 1820), p. 993.

[3] Also elected as a regular deputy from the province of México and recognized as such rather than as a substitute, once the election certificates from America were examined by the credentials committee. *Gaceta del Gobierno de México*, Tomo XI, Núm. 126 (September 19, 1820), 971–972.

[4] Also elected as alternate deputy from Michoacán. When one of the regular deputies from that province, Manuel Diego Solórzano, notified the Cortes from Cuba that he was returning to Veracruz, Michelena asked that he be recognized as the regular deputy from Michoacán, to take Solórzano's place in the delegation. This request was granted. Spain, Cortes, 1821, *Diario de Sesiones de 1821*, III, Núm. 120 (June 27, 1821), 2536.

Durango were to district the provinces, decide how many deputies each area was entitled to have, and set the dates for the elections.[27] The meetings of the junta for New Spain were held in early July and the results were announced on the tenth of that month. The same census as that used in 1812 served as the basis for the 1820 apportion-

[27] Spain, Laws, statutes, 1813–1833 (Ferdinand VII), *Instrucción conforme á la cual deberán celebrarse en las Provincias de Ultramar las elecciones de Diputados de Córtes para las ordinarias de 1820 y 1821*, signed by Ferdinand VII at Madrid, March 24, 1820. A copy of this instruction is in the Bexar Archives, The University of Texas Library, Box A3/62, Printed Decrees 1792–1822.

ment. A breakdown of the population by provinces was listed as follows:[28]

Province	Total Pop.	Pop. with African Blood	Pop. Considered for Electoral Purposes
México	1,134,034	48,864	1,085,170
Oaxaca	411,336	16,767	394,569
Michoacán	273,681	58,593	215,088
Guanajuato	397,924	43,423	354,501
Puebla	618,812	11,979	606,833
Veracruz	120,000	6,095	113,905
San Luis Potosí	145,057	28,885	116,172
	3,100,844	214,606	2,886,238

Tlaxcala was detached from Puebla for electoral purposes and Querétaro was considered as distinct from México, the same as in 1813. Each province was entitled to have the same number of deputies as previously. The parish elections were to be held on August 13, those in the district were to follow a week later, and those of the province were to commence on September 17. An exception was made for Mexico City in that the parochial juntas were to meet on August 6 in the capital.[29]

In the Eastern Interior Provinces, Joaquín Arredondo, the com-

---

[28] Proclamation of the Preparatory Junta, dated July 10, 1820, in *Gaceta del gobierno de México*, Tomo XI, Núm. 91 (July 13, 1820), pp. 638–688; figures taken from *ibid.*, Article 2, pp. 684–685. In 1811 Juan López Cancelada published a different set of statistics for the population of the Kingdom of New Spain and other provinces as of 1808. According to him, México had 1,495,140 inhabitants; Veracruz, 154,286; Puebla, 828,277; Michoacán, 371,975; Oaxaca, 528,860; San Luis Potosí, 311,503; and Guanajuato, 511,616. Since there was to be one deputy elected for every 70,000 people, had López Cancelada's figures been used, or perhaps a census later than that of 1792, the provinces of New Spain might have been entitled to elect more deputies. López did not cite the source of his figures, but undoubtedly he had access to reliable statistics in his official position as editor of the *Gaceta del gobierno de México*. Juan López Cancelada, *Ruina de la Nueva España si se declara el comercio libre con los estrangeros*, p. 73.

[29] Bando, dated July 10, 1820, Mexico City, and signed by the Conde del Venadito; Pedro, Arzobispo de México; Ramón Gutiérrez del Mazo; José Ignacio Aguirrevengoa; Juan Ignacio González Vértiz; Lic. Benito José Guerra; José María Fagoaga; Mariscal de Castilla, Marqués de Ceria; and the secretary, Ricardo Pérez Gallardo, in *Gaceta del gobierno de México*, Tomo XI, Núm. 91 (July 13, 1820), pp. 683–688.

mandant general, convoked the preparatory junta on July 6, 1820. Parish elections were held on August 27, and the provincial voting was held in Monterrey on October 1. Even in this political division of the empire, far to the north and on the fringe of civilization, the populace participated in the balloting. The little settlement at Bahía del Espíritu Santo in Texas chose eleven men, who in turn selected one elector from among them. This man met with the two electors from Béjar on September 3 and designated one man to attend the provincial electoral junta in Monterrey in October.[30]

Lucas Alamán, one of the deputies chosen to represent the province of Guanajuato, later wrote in his *Historia de México* that the 1820 elections were "carried out with the same disorder, although with less eagerness, as in the previous constitutional period."[31] He was comparing the 1820 balloting with the November, 1812, parish elections in Mexico City which resulted in the suspension of the electoral process in the province of México until Venegas left office. Neither the 1812 nor the 1820 election was disorderly.[32] In 1820, Venadito, the Superior Political Chief, took great care to insure an absence of disturbances on the appointed day. He issued an instruction on September 14, in which he stated that since the provincial balloting was to be held three days later, all civil authorities and heads of households must maintain the "order, circumspection, and tranquility" necessary and indispensable to the deliberations of the electors.[33]

It must be pointed out, however, that in the 1820 elections, as well as in others of the revolutionary period, some infractions in voting were committed, usually on the parish level where the electorate was large. In reading through the official gazettes of the Cortes, one occasionally comes across decisions of the credentials committee in which such infractions are discussed. Generally the procedure was to accept the results of the election. These infractions never hinted at disorder

    [30] Eugene C. Barker, "The Government of Austin's Colony, 1821–1831," *Southwestern Historical Quarterly*, XXI (January, 1918), 223–224.

    [31] Alamán, *Historia de Méjico*, V. p. 47.

    [32] Alamán was a conservative and based his allegation concerning the 1812 disorders on a report of the balloting written by conservative observers not in sympathy with the electoral process. This report has been shown to be grossly exaggerated. See Benson, "The Contested Mexican Election of 1812," *passim*. Alamán cited no source to verify his allegation regarding the 1820 voting, nor has this writer been able to locate any reports of disorder.

    [33] Bando dated September 14, 1820, Mexico City, signed by the Conde de Venadito, and printed in the *Gaceta del gobierno de México*, Tomo XI, Núm. 124 (September 16, 1820), p. 958.

or civil disturbance and were only minor ones of a technical nature resulting from the complicated process.[34]

Voting was held throughout the provinces in the summer and fall of 1820. As a result, forty-nine deputies from the Mexican provinces were in attendance at the 1821 Cortes (see Table VI).

Since the Constitution was now in effect, the schedule for the electoral process set forth in it was also in effect. This meant that the elections for the session that would convene in March, 1822, as called for in the Constitution, would have to begin on the parish level in December, 1820. Thus, no sooner was the process completed in the autumn of 1820 for the 1820–1821 Cortes than it was begun anew for the 1822–1823 session. Despite the growing chaos in Mexico and the spread of the revolution, this second set of elections was held (see Table VII).

The growth of the rebellion led the American deputies in the 1821 Cortes to urge Ferdinand to convoke a special session for September of that year to consider measures for bringing peace to the Spanish dominions. The forty-eight Mexican delegates present for the regular session in 1821 dwindled to forty-three for the special session, and several of this latter number soon requested and received permission to return home. The delegates elected for the March, 1822, session never arrived in Spain, for by that time Mexican independence had been achieved.[35]

As a direct result of the familiarity which the populace had gained with the electoral form under the Constitution of Cádiz, the same process of a three-level, indirect election, somewhat modified, was used to choose the deputies in Iturbide's first congress in 1822.[36] A year earlier, when opposition to Iturbide was growing because of his

[34] See, e.g., the decision rendered by the committee in the case of the elections of the parish of Malinalco, in the province of México. Spain, Cortes, 1821, *Diario de Sesiones de 1821*, I, Núm. 30 (March 27, 1821), 717.

[35] Two Yucatecan deputies were present, but both were already in Spain when they were notified of their elections. One of them, Miguel Duque de Estrada y Crespi, sympathized with the revolution and requested a passport and permission to return to his province. The other, Augustín de Medina y la Llave, asked the Cortes to grant him funds so that he might remain in Spain to attend the congress, since he did not agree with the course Yucatán had chosen to follow. Spain, Cortes, *Diario de las Sesiones de Cortes. Legislatura de 1822*, I, Núm. 7 (March 2, 1822), 59–60; and Núm. 20 (March 11, 1822), 308.

[36] Alamán, *Historia de Méjico*, V, 367–375, contains a thorough discussion of the adoption of this form by the provisional junta established by Iturbide and the modifications that it underwent as a result of a disagreement between Iturbide and the junta.

Table 6

Deputies Elected to the Cortes of 1821

Name	Deputies Who Attended the Cortes[1] Province	Date Seated (1821)	Offices Held in the Cortes
Alamán, Lucas	Guanajuato	May 2	
Alcaraz, Conde de	Zacatecas	May 18	
Amati, Bernardino	Guadalajara	March 29	
Apartado, Marqués de	México	May 18	
Arroyo, Francisco	Guadalajara	May 14	
Ayesterán, José Joaquín	México	March 17	
Castorena, Luciano	México	May 20	
Cortazar, Manuel	Guanajuato	Feb. 24	
Cristo y Conde, José Antonio del	México	June 22	
Fagoaga, Francisco	México	Feb. 24	
García Moreno[2]	Yucatán	April 4	
García Sosa, Manuel	Yucatán	March 23	
Gómez Navarrete, Juan Nepomuceno de	Michoacán	May 16	

[1] This list contains forty-five names. José Basilio Guerra is included, although he attended only the special session convoked by Ferdinand VII in the autumn of 1821. The list does not include Ramos Arizpe, Cañedo, Couto, and Montoya, who sat in the Cortes as substitute deputies but who were not elected by any province as proprietary deputies. During the special session, the question of the legality of continued recognition of the alternates was raised. After a long and heated debate, it was decided that only the alternates for Peru and the Philippines could continue participating. The four mentioned above soon left. Spain, Cortes, 1821–1822, *Diario de las Sesiones de Cortes, Legislatura extraordinaria*, I, Núms. 1, 2, and 9 (September 22 and 23, and October 3, 1821), 5, 21, and 90 (hereafter cited as *Diario de Sesiones de Legislatura extraordinaria*).

[2] Neither Eligio Ancona, *Historia de Yucatán desde la época más remota hasta nuestros días*, III (1889), 166, nor the *Semanario Político y Literario*, Núm. 10 (September 13, 1820), 252, lists a García Moreno as a deputy from Yucatán, but he is mentioned as such in Spain, Cortes, 1821, *Diario de Sesiones de 1821* ("Indice").

Name	Province	Date	Office
Gómez Pedraza, Manuel	México	May 9	
Guerra, Francisco	México	May 16	
Guerra, José Basilio	Yucatán	Oct. 2	
Gutiérrez de Terán, José María[3]	México	March 28	President, April, 1821
Hernández Chico, José María[4]	?	June 22	Secretary, June, 1821
Jiménez de Castro, José	Guadalajara	March 29	
La Llave y Avila, Pablo de	Veracruz	Feb. 24	
López, Patricio	Oaxaca	April 15	
López Constante, Juan	Yucatán	Feb. 25	
Maniau, Joaquín	Veracruz	Feb. 25	
Martín y Aguirre, Matías de	San Luis Potosí	May 7	
Medina, Joaquín	Guadalajara	March 29	
Michelena, José Mariano[5]	Michoacán	June 27	
Molinos del Campo, Francisco	México	May 9	
Mora, Ignacio	Puebla	March 29	
Moreno, José Mariano	Tlaxcala	March 29	
Murguía, José María	Oaxaca	May 8	
Murphy, Tomás	México	May 9	
Obregón, Ventura[6]	Guanajuato	June 13	

[3] Died sometime after the close of the regular session on June 30, 1821, and before the opening of the special session on September 22, 1821. Spain, Cortes, 1821–1822, *Diario de Sesiones de Legislatura extraordinaria,* I, Núm. 1 (September 22, 1821), 5.

[4] Hernández Chico was reported in the *Gaceta del Gobierno de México* as a deputy from Guadalajara. See Tomo XI, Núm. 130 (September 26, 1820), 993. He presented his credentials as a deputy from Guadalajara but was seated as a deputy from San Luis Potosí. It is a matter of conjecture which province he represented. Spain, Cortes, 1821, *Diario de Sesiones de 1821,* III, Núms. 113 and 115 (June 20 and 22, 1821), 2378 and 2393–2394.

[5] See Table V, note 4.

[6] Obregón was elected as an alternate from Guanajuato. He was in Spain at the time and immediately petitioned the Cortes that he be recognized as a deputy from Guanajuato. Cañedo and others supported him. Spain, Cortes, 1821, *Diario de Sesiones de 1821,* I, Núm. 12 (March 9, 1821), 385–386. In June, he was finally seated, on the basis that word had been received from one of the proprietary deputies from Guanajuato that he had become ill in Cuba and that another deputy from the same province

Table 6 (Continued)

Name	Province	Date Seated (1821)	Offices Held in the Cortes
Puchet, José María	Puebla	April 15	
Quioy y Tehuanhuey, Félix	Puebla	March 29	
Quirós y Millan, José María	Sonora and Sinaloa[7]	May 29	
Ramírez, Francisco María	Oaxaca	May 21	
Ramírez, José Miguel	Guadalajara	May 12	
Río, Andrés del	México	May 20	
Sánchez Pareja, Eusebio	México	May 16	
Sánchez Resa, José Domingo	Guadalajara	March 29	
Savariego, Andrés[8]	México	March 28	
Uraga, Antonio María	Michoacán	May 16	
Valdés, Juan Bautista	Nuevo León	May 25	
Vargas, Tomás[9]	San Luis Potosí	May 4	
Zavala, Lorenzo de	Yucatán	Feb. 25	

Deputies Elected in 1820 Who Did Not Attend the Cortes

Conde de S. Mateo Valparaiso	México		
García Cantarenas, Francisco[10]	Puebla		

had returned to Veracruz. Therefore, according to Art. 90 of the Constitution, Obregón was entitled to be seated. *Ibid.,* III, Núm. 106 (June 13, 1821), 2219.

[7] Sonora and Sinaloa were joined for purposes of the election.

[8] When Cortazar was recognized as a deputy from Guanajuato, the vacancy in the delegation from the province of Mexico was filled by the first alternate, Savariego. See Table V, note 2.

[9] Vargas was elected from San Luis Potosí, but he is listed as being seated from Guadalajara. Spain, Cortes, 1821, *Diario de Sesiones de 1821,* II, Núm. 74 (May 12, 1821), 1562.

[10] Cantarenas got as far as Cuba and turned back. *Ibid.,* III, Núm. 122 (June 29, 1821), 2608.

Torres, Gabriel de	Puebla
Díaz de Luna, José Ignacio[11]	Puebla
González Angulo, Bernardo	Puebla
Sosaya Bermudez, ?	Guanajuato
Solórzano, Manuel Diego[12]	Michoacán
Iturribarría, Pedro Ignacio de	Nueva Vizcaya[13]
Estrada, Francisco	Nueva Vizcaya
Delgado, Francisco	Sonora and Sinaloa
Fajardo, Domingo	Yucatán[14]
Milanés, Manuel	Yucatán
Campiña, Nicolás	Yucatán
Pino, Pedro Bautista[15]	Nuevo México
Castillejos, Mariano[16]	Oaxaca
Flores Alatorre, Juan José[17]	Zacatecas

[11] Díaz de Luna wrote the Cortes from Cuba that he was returning to his home because of ill health. *Ibid.*

[12] See Table V, note 4.

[13] Durango and Chihuahua were joined for purposes of the election.

[14] Two lists of the Yucatecan delegates, neither of which agrees, were found by this writer. Ancona, *Historia de Yucatán*, names only six men, whereas the *Semanario Político y Literario*, Núm. 10 (September 13, 1820), 252, lists seven. Ancona correctly states that only three attended the Cortes, "perhaps because the treasury of the colony was so exhausted that the expenses of the journey could not be met" (III, 166).

[15] Pino made an effort to attend, and traveled as far as Veracruz. But he was forced to return to his home because of a lack of funds for financing the remainder of the trip to Spain. See Spain, Cortes, 1821–1822, *Diario de Sesiones de Legislatura extraordinaria*, I, Núm. 27 (October 21, 1821), 331, and also Bancroft, *History of Arizona and New Mexico, 1530–1888*, pp. 289–290.

[16] Castillejos died en route to the Cortes. Spain, Cortes, 1821, *Diario de Sesiones de 1821*, II, Núm. 74 (May 12, 1821), 1565.

[17] Flores Alatorre, also spoken of as Juan José de la Torre, sent word to the Cortes that he was too ill to make the trip to Spain. Spain, Cortes, 1821, *Diario de Sesiones de 1821*, II, Núm. 42 (April 8, 1821), 964, and Núm. 54 (April 22, 1821), 1149.

Table 7

Deputies Chosen in the March, 1821, Provincial Elections for
the 1822–1823 Sessions of the Cortes

México[1]

Proprietary
Azorrez, Juan Manuel
Baz, Bernardo
Bustamante, José María
Espinosa de los Monteros, Manuel
Garza, Simón de la
Gual, Manuel
Monteagudo, Matías
Noriega Cortina, Manuel de
Posadas, Manuel
Quintana Roó, Andrés
Ribas, Antonio
Segura, Estanislao
Velázquez de la Cadena, José
   Manuel
Zubicueta, Manuel
Alternates
Anaya, Rafael
Arrillaga, Basilio
Gallegos, José María
Peñasco, Conde del

Puebla[2]

Proprietary
La Llave, José María de
Luciano Becerra, José María
Mendizabal y Zubialdea, Luis
Oller, José María
Otero, Juan Nepomuceno
Ovando y Para, José María
Piñeiro, Pedro
Alternates
Castillo Rosete, José
Enciso, Joaquín Luis

Tlaxcala[3]

Proprietary
Rojano [Roxano y Mudarra?],
   Agustín
Alternate
Carvajal, Manuel María

Querétaro[4]

Proprietary
Osores, Félix
Alternate
Llaca, Pedro de

Provincias Internas de Oriente[5]

Proprietary
Cevallos, José Manuel
Fernández, José Eustaquio
Alternate
Garza Leal, Francisco de la

Veracruz[6]

Proprietary
La Llave, José María de
Quiroz, José María
Alternate
Lobo, Manuel

Oaxaca[7]

Proprietary
Esteves, Francisco
Garfías, Domingo
Irigoyen, Cristóbal
Mantecón, Antonio
Ortiz de la Torre, José
Valentín, José Miguel

[1] *Gaceta del gobierno de México*, Tomo XII, Núm. 33 (March 13, 1821), 256.
[2] *Ibid.*, Núm. 34 (March 15, 1821), 262–263.
[3] *Ibid.*, Núm. 36 (March 20, 1821), 280–281.
[4] *Ibid.*, Núm. 43 (April 3, 1821), 332–333.
[5] *Noticioso general*, Núm. 50 (April 25, 1821), 1.
[6] Manuel B. Trens, *Historia de Veracruz*, III (1948), 312, n. 4.
[7] *Gaceta del gobierno de México*, Tomo XII, Núm. 43 (April 3, 1821), 332–333.

Table 7 (Continued)

Alternates
Campo, Francisco del
Recoz, Domingo

Nueva Galicia[8]

Proprietary
Caballero, Juan Manuel
Cañedo, Juan de Dios
García Monasterio, José
González, Toribio
Maldonado, Francisco Severo
Ruíz de Cabañas, Juan Cruz

Alternates
Huerta, José de Jesús
Nogueras, José Manuel

San Luis Potosí[9]

Proprietary
Cendoya, Francisco

Martínez de los Ríos, Ramón
    Esteban

Alternate
Guillén, José María

Zacatecas[10]

Proprietary
Gómez Farías, Valentín
González Peredo, Juan
Iriarte, Agustín de

Alternate
Ferrer, Juan Manuel

Sonora and Sinaloa[11]

Proprietary
Iribarren, Francisco de
Salido, José Salvador

Alternate
Riesgo, Juan Miguel

---

[8] *Ibid.*, Núm. 36 (March 20, 1821), 280–281.
[9] *Ibid.*, Núm. 41 (March 29, 1821), 313–314.
[10] *Ibid.*, Núm. 72 (May 31, 1821), 546.
[11] *Ibid.*, Núm. 69 (May 24, 1821), 522.

delay in calling for congressional elections, José Joaquín Fernández de Lizardi published a pamphlet posing fifty questions which were meant to embarrass the strongman; one of the questions asked was, "When will the towns hold free elections in conformity with the Spanish system?" This serves to indicate the confidence placed in the electoral process as established by the Constitution of 1812.[37]

The deputies to the Cortes elected by the citizenry gained valuable experience that would aid them in their subsequent careers as participants in the affairs of state of independent Mexico. Many of the former deputies held important positions in the government, both on the state and national levels, after independence was won.

Lucas Alamán, Pablo de la Llave, Manuel Gómez Pedraza, Francisco Fagoaga, Juan de Dios Cañedo, Ignacio Mora, José Mariano Michelena, José Miguel Ramos Arizpe, and Lorenzo de Zavala frequently filled cabinet posts in the period between 1823 and 1853,

[37] José Joaquín Fernández de Lizardi, *Cincuenta preguntas del Pensador a quién quiera responderlas*, p. 3, question 5.

some serving in several different ministries.[38] Some of the ex-deputies, among them Tomás Murphy, Zavala, Michelena, Cañedo, Ramos Arizpe, and Llave, filled diplomatic posts and did great service for Mexico in that capacity.

Many of them continued their careers in politics and sought and gained election to the various congresses in the early years of independence. Tomás Vargas, José Miguel Guridi y Alcocer, Ramos Arizpe, Ignacio Mora, Luciano Castorena, and José Hernández Chico were among those in the constitutional congress of 1823. Ramos Arizpe, the "Father of Mexican Federalism," was the principal author of the Constitution of 1824. Gómez Pedraza, Fagoaga, and José María Couto were only a few of the former delegates to the Cortes who sat in the national legislature of the republic as deputies and senators. Gómez Pedraza reached the highest office of the nation when he served as President in 1832–1833.

Several of the ex-deputies were military figures. Patricio López, José Joaquín de Ayesterán, Mora, and Michelena all held important commandancies or positions in the War Ministry.

On the state level, Manuel Cortazar was the political chief of Guanajuato, Molinos del Campo held the same position in the state of México, Zavala was a later governor of the state of México; and José María Murguía served as governor of Oaxaca. José Martínez de la Pedrera held various minor positions in the government of Yucatán. José Domingo Sánchez Resa and Francisco Arroyo served many terms in the legislature of Jalisco.

José Miguel Gordoa became Bishop of Guadalajara and Antonio Joaquín Pérez was made Bishop of Puebla. In addition, Pérez signed the Act of Independence and was a member of the Council of Regency in the turbulent Iturbide period. Juan Nepomuceno de Gómez Navarrete was another of Iturbide's strong supporters and remained close to the family after Iturbide was deposed.

These men represent only a small percentage of the deputies from the Mexican provinces who served in the Cortes from 1810 to 1814 and 1820 to 1822. The activities attributed to them are by no means complete, nor, in some cases, are they remembered for the posts they held and the political roles they played after independence. Alamán

[38] Secretarios de Estado del Gobierno Mexicano [covers the period 1810–1876; ms. drawn up by Genaro García]. The Genaro García Papers, Latin American Collection, The University of Texas Library.

is best known for his multivolume *Historia de Méjico*; Francisco Fagoaga, a member of a wealthy family whose income was derived from mining interests, is remembered as a great and magnanimous philanthropist, one of the earliest of his kind and one of the few such benefactors produced by all of Latin America; Pablo de la Llave is perhaps best recalled as a linguist and a botanist, whose scientific studies made his name famous throughout the scholarly world; Zavala gained renown for his last act, the most dramatic of his career—that of signing the Texas Declaration of Independence.

It might be argued by some that only the well-educated men attended the Cortes as Mexican representatives and that their education and backgrounds would have propelled them into positions of leadership even if they had not participated in the series of congresses in Spain. This is only a supposition, and it would be equally valid to postulate that had not the Cortes given these men the opportunity to discover their qualities of leadership, such a person as Ramos Arizpe might have served out his life as a priest in a dusty frontier town in the northern reaches of Mexico; Llave might have remained buried in his studies in the Botanical Gardens in Madrid; and Gómez Pedraza would probably have been only a lawyer in Mexico City.

In the period between 1810 and 1822, the Mexican provinces experienced five elections for deputies to the Spanish Cortes, each being held on three different levels and each involving all citizens who had the right to vote. In the same period, the populace was also electing members to the provincial deputations and the municipal councils. All these elections were held according to the rules set forth in the Constitution of 1812. The Mexican representatives in the Cortes were capable men who learned the intricacies of parliamentary procedure, the value of compromise, and the art of forceful debate, skills that served them well in their later careers. There is evidence that the enfranchized populace participated enthusiastically, taking their obligations as citizens seriously, despite the heavy burden placed upon the voters by the rather cumbersome electoral procedures. It would be another matter, impossible to ascertain, to assert that they cast their ballots intelligently; probably they were as enlightened and knowledgeable an electorate for their time and place as the great majority of men and women who participate in popular elections today. Furthermore, the electoral procedures as established by the Spanish constitution were practiced so widely and became so familiar that they were adopted in modified form by the abortive Congress of Chilpancingo and later by Iturbide's first legislature. Despite tendencies among historians to minimize the effects of the Constitution of 1812, it has been seen that in the areas of modern Mexico, the revolutionary years provided considerable experience in civil education and representative government.

2. Mexican Constitutional Expression in the Cortes of Cádiz

David T. Garza

In September of 1810, when the first general and extraordinary sessions of the Cortes of Cádiz were convened, Spain and her empire faced total collapse.[1] Respect for the crown had been seriously undermined by the ignominious reign of Carlos IV, whose naive trust in the Francophile policies of his first secretary, Manuel Godoy, finally led to the invasion and occupation of almost all of Spain by the armies of Napoleon. To make matters worse, "El Deseado," King Fernando VII, who had displaced his father in a popular coup, had fallen into French captivity, and lost his throne to the usurper Joseph Bonaparte. Confronted with these calamitous developments in the motherland and fearful lest Napoleon should decide to extend his influence to the Americas, several colonial provinces began to initiate movements for emancipation, and self-determination. To prevent the loss of these territories, Spain's prime source of economic sustenance, and to preserve the sovereignty of the empire, the governing revolutionary council in Spain, the Supreme Central Junta, realized fundamental reforms in the political system were in order; thus the Cortes was assembled in Cádiz, and empowered with the mission "to restore and improve the fundamental Constitution of the Monarchy."[2]

[1] For general history of the period see Conde de Toreno, *Historia del levantamiento, guerra y revolución de España*; Federico Suárez, *La crisis política del antiguo régimen en España*; F. Jiménez de Gregorio, "La convocatoria de Cortes Constituyentes en 1810: Estado de la opinión española en punto a reforma constitucional," in *Estudios de historia moderna*, V; L. Sánchez Agesta, *Historia del constitucionalismo español*.

[2] Powers were conferred upon the deputies, as cited by Pedro Canel Acevedo, *Reflexiones sobre la Constitución Española, Cortes nacionales, y estado de la presente guerra*, p. 41, Adolfo de Castro y Rossi, *Cortes de Cádiz*, p. 127, and Conde de Toreno, *Historia del levantamiento*, III, 379.

To both the Spanish and American deputies elected to the Cortes, the drafting of a written constitution which would incorporate traditional features of Spanish law, yet correct the abuses of absolute monarchy, became the overriding objective of that assembly. Perhaps the Americans, even more than the Spaniards, were to rely most heavily on the Constitution, for it was the instrument they hoped would bring to an end the arbitrary colonial rule of the provinces and establish officially, as had been conceded in the decree of October 15, 1810,³ the equal right and status of the Americas with the Peninsular provinces. The importance given to the elaboration of this charter by the overseas deputies is strikingly revealed in the words of the Mexican representative, José Miguel Guridi y Alcocer, who in justifying his criticism of one of the articles to the Constitution, stated: "Since the Constitution—for whose formation we are principally congregated—is the most important work of the Cortes, the greatest endeavor should be made to see that it turns out perfect."⁴

This solicitous attitude expressed by the Tlaxcalan deputy was shared by the entire Mexican delegation. Indeed, the twenty-one Mexicans in attendance were to demonstrate their singular concern in the positive role which they played during the deliberations and debates affecting the composition of the fundamental charter. Among the most active participants were Miguel Ramos Arispe of Coahuila, Mariano Mendiola of Querétaro, the Tlaxcalan Guridi y Alcocer, José Beye Cisneros of Mexico City, José Miguel Gordoa from Zacatecas, Antonio Joaquín Pérez of Puebla, and the Guadalajaran deputy, José Simeón de Uría.⁵ Of note is the fact that of the five Americans who composed the constitutional committee charged with drafting a plan of the constitution for debate, two⁶ were Mexican—Pérez and Mendiola.

A study of the constitutional debates in which these deputies from Mexico participated affords an important insight into the constitu-

---

³ Spain, Laws and statutes, 1810–1822, *Colección de los decretos y órdenes que han expedido las Cortes generales y extraordinarias*, Decreto V, I, 10.

⁴ Spain, Cortes, 1810–1813, *Diario de las discusiones y actas de las Cortes*, VII (August 28, 1811), 15 (hereinafter cited as *Diario de las Cortes*).

⁵ For a complete list of the Mexican deputies attendant at the Cortes, see Chapter I, *supra*.

⁶ The other three Americans represented on the committee were Vicente Morales Duárez (Peru), Joaquín Fernández de Leyva (Chile), and Andrés de Jáuregui (Habana). Spain, Cortes, 1810–1813, *Diario de las Cortes*, VII (July 8, 1811), 68.

tional attitudes and convictions that they, as Americans, professed, particularly with relation to the political doctrines prevalent at the time. Primary among the revolutionary concepts which they courageously espoused were the doctrine of popular or national sovereignty, the separation of powers, equal representation, equality of rights and privileges, and semiautonomous local government. These liberal tenets, set loose by the Age of Enlightenment and the North American and French revolutions were the standards for political reform advocated most frequently by the overseas deputies. In articulating them openly in the Cortes of Cádiz for the first time, they outlined the pattern of constitutionalism that was later to have widespread effect throughout the Americas.

Debates on the Constitution began in the Cortes on August 25, 1811, and from the very inception the Americans showed their determination to be heard. Mendiola and Fernández Leyva, both members of the constitutional committee, spoke out in defense of the proposed preamble, comparing its "sublime brevity" to the beginnings of the great sacred texts.[7] Matters of greater import were raised, however, by Guridi y Alcocer with regard to the wording of Article 1, which read: "The Spanish Nation is the reunion of all Spaniards of both Hemispheres." Insisting upon a less ambiguous definition of what was meant by the "Spanish Nation" and Spaniard," he pointed out that in a strict physical sense, the Spanish nation was no more than the peninsula called Spain, and the Spaniard the equivalent of those born or originated therein. Considered as such, the Americans would definitely have been excluded from the category of "Spaniard," with its inherent rights and privileges. The ambiguity of the word "reunion," moreover, left wide room for distortion and exclusion. As defined in the dictionary, the word implied the reuniting of two objects that had separated from their original union. This meaning might have encompassed Spaniards living in the Americas, but whether it included the American-born Spaniard was not explicitly clear to Guridi y Alcocer. What he sought to arrive at in his discussion was a wording that could leave no loopholes by which the equal status of the Americans could be circumscribed, for as the article read, accurate differentiation between a peninsular Spaniard, a territorial Spaniard, and a foreigner merely resident within Spanish territory was lacking.

The nation is not just the union of its members, Guridi y Alcocer

---

[7] *Ibid.*, VIII (August 25, 1811), 10–11.

suggested, but the aggregate that results from such union. Thus, he advised that a political definition of the nation should contain three elements: the composite or aggregate that results in the union (the nation), the objects united (the people), and the objective for which they are united (government). Such a distinction was important in the debates to follow, centering on the doctrine of popular sovereignty. With regard to Article 1, however, he proposed that the article be altered to read: "The Spanish Nation is the collection of the inhabitants of the Spanish peninsula and the other territories of the Monarchy united in a government and subjected to a sovereign authority."[8]

By offering this definition, perhaps he also hoped to avert the controversy that was to develop between the Americans and the European Spaniards concerning the requirements for citizenship, that is, precisely who could legally be considered as a "Spaniard." More significantly, the matter reflected upon a principle vital to all the overseas delegates—that their political rights and privileges be maintained on a par with those of the Peninsular deputation, as had been proclaimed in the decree of February 9, 1811.[9]

In the debates to follow, from Article 3 to Article 171, the doctrine of national sovereignty in almost every instance acted as the underlying tenet upon which the Americans based their contentions. Again the pattern was set by Guridi y Alcocer in the misgivings he expressed regarding the choice of words in Article 3, which as proposed declared that sovereignty resided *essentially* in the nation, and therefore the nation had the exclusive right to establish its fundamental laws and to adopt the form of government best suited to it. His objection was not to the spirit of the article, but to the letter. Sovereignty, he asserted, results from the willful submission of each person to an authority to which he voluntarily subjects himself thereafter. According to the principles of public law, sovereignty resides in that same authority, but, he insisted, its source and root is the consent of each person in the society. That being the case, he proposed to rephrase the article to read that sovereignty resides "fundamentally" or "originally" in the nation (that is, in the collection of all the citizens united in a government). Either word, he felt, would make impossi-

---

[8] *Ibid.*, VIII (August 25, 1811), 15–16.
[9] Spain, Laws and Statutes, 1810–1822, *Colección de los decretos,* Decreto XXXI, I, 72–73.

ble the future despotic centralization of authority in one body or person who could then coerce the rights of the individual citizen.[10] Exactly who was to qualify for Spanish citizenship, however, was to become the subject of the longest (August 31 to September 24, 1811) and most heated of the constitutional debates. As stated above, the question involved again the definition of the term Spaniard, but in a new sense; that is, the distinction now made was between a Spaniard generally protected by the civil code by virtue of his residence in the empire, and the Spaniard endowed with the political right to exercise a representative voice in the government. The entire issue hinged, as far as the Mexicans were concerned, on the larger question of equal rights and proportional national representation in the Cortes. The sanctioning of these rights in the Constitution was foremost among the objectives they sought. In defense of these rights a bitter cleavage broke out between the Peninsular and overseas deputies that was to belie the original purpose of unity in the Cortes. Precipitating this controversy was Article 22, which proposed to exclude from Spanish citizenship all those Spaniards who from whichever hereditary line descended from Africa, with the exception that the Cortes could confer a letter of citizenship upon those who distinguished themselves by eminent services, industry, or good conduct, provided, of course, that they had been legitimately sired by freeborn, legally wed parents resident in Spanish dominions. Finally, they had to have a profitable profession, office, or useful industry, sufficient to maintain their house and educate their children.[11]

Unequivocally, the motive behind this measure was the intention of the Spanish deputies to contain the American quest for greater political voice in government and equal representation, for to grant either would have been to weaken the central authority and control of the motherland. The exclusion of the colored castes (as the Americans referred to those Spaniards of African descent) from citizenship rights at once disenfranchised and eliminated from the census in ap-

[10] Spain, Cortes, 1810–1813, *Diario de las Cortes,* VIII (August 28, 1811), 62–63.

[11] Spain, Cortes, 1810–1813, *Diario de sesiones de las Cortes generales y extraordinarias,* III (September 4, 1811), 1761 (hereinafter cited *Diario de sesiones de las Cortes*).

For a more specialized study of the controversy over Article 22, see James F. King, "The Colored Castes and the American Representation in the Cortes of Cádiz," HAHR, XXXIII (February, 1953), 33–64.

portioning representation perhaps the largest lineal group in the Americas.[12] Instead of the possible representational majority the overseas provinces might have warranted if the castes, as citizens, had been included in the basis for apportionment, they faced continued subordination of rights and interests to the central government.

Provoked and insulted, the Mexican deputies once again assumed the role as leading spokesmen for the American sentiments. In arguments often brilliant in their logic, as well as in the application of liberal ideals, they sought to demonstrate that discrimination against the castes was in direct contradiction to Articles 1 and 3, which deposited sovereignty in the nation, defined as the reunion of *all Spaniards* of both hemispheres; of Article 6, part 4, which proclaimed the freedman a Spaniard upon his acquisition of liberty in Spanish territory; Article 18, which conferred citizenship upon those Spaniards who from both lines of heredity originated from Spanish dominions in both hemispheres, and were therein resident; and Article 20, which granted citizenship at age twenty-one to sons born in Spanish territory of foreigners.[13]

Deputy Uría of Guadalajara was the first to point out the basic conflict between Article 22 and Article 3, the latter which, by virtue of having declared every Spaniard on Spanish soil to be an integrant of the nation, rendered him as such an agent of the national sovereignty. Thus, in Uría's opinion, it was inconceivable to declare one to be a determinant of the nation's sovereignty—which a member of a caste was, owing to his status as a Spaniard in the dominions of Spain—but not to be a citizen of the nation.[14] In a variation on the same theme, Ramos Arispe argued that the right to participate in the legislative function flowed from the character of popular sovereignty which encompassed the castes. It therefore followed that to share in the above function, the castes required representation, a privilege belonging to citizens. Thus justice demanded that they be granted this personality.[15]

From a more legalistic standpoint, Guridi y Alcocer established

[12] Quoting population figures compiled by Humboldt, the Mexican deputy Beye Cisneros, for example, asserted that of the sixteen million residents of Mexico, at least ten million had Negro blood. Spain, Cortes, 1810–1813, *Diario de las Cortes,* VIII (September 6, 1811), 223.

[13] Spain, Cortes, 1810–1813, *Diario de sesiones de las Cortes,* III, 1761–1798.

[14] *Ibid.,* III (September 9, 1811), 1761–1762.

[15] *Ibid.,* III (September 5, 1811), 1773–1775.

that no previous article, decree, or law had ever explicitly excluded the castes from citizenship. Reaching back for precedent to the laws of the Siete Partidas, he further pointed out that citizenship as such had never before been granted under Spanish law, but that instead "letters of naturalization" were conferred. In the latter case, however, the criteria required for naturalization were already supplied by the castes—native birth, subjection, military service, marriage, Spanish heritage, residence, and even Christian conversion.[16]

Since the castes were already native-born freemen and nowhere specifically excluded from Article 21, which conferred citizenship on the sons of foreigners, Deputy Gordoa of Zacatecas insisted they qualified for citizenship under the terms of that article. After all, most of the colored castes had five or six generations of ancestors born on Spanish soil, and in many cases three lines of parental descent that were non-African. As for their eminent services to the nation, these were a proven fact. The castes formed the major part of the veteran regiments and militias in the Americas; they were the artisans and miners of silver, upon which Spain's wartime economy depended heavily; they were farmers; they professed the Catholic religion and often were distinguished members of the clergy.[17]

Ramos Arispe returned to the theme of equality of rights, and in answer to allegations that not all the Americans had favored citizenship for the castes, reminded his opponents that as early as the second session of the Cortes (September 25, 1810), the overseas deputies had submitted a draft proposal demanding equality of rights between European Spaniards and the native free residents of America. They had also urged that the basis for alloting deputies should be the census composed indiscriminately of all the free subjects of the king. Finally, he said, this plea had been repeated the twenty-ninth of September in behalf of *all free men* (my italics). While in none of the instances cited, had the castes been expressly designated as being qualified for citizenship, neither had they been specifically excluded, but in fact were understood to be the subject of the American demands.

Aware that only a strong appeal might sway the Spaniards from their stand, the Mexican representative forewarned them that what was actually at stake was the unity and integrity of the monarchy.

[16] *Ibid.*, III (September 4, 1811), 1762–1764.
[17] *Ibid.*, III (September 4, 1811), 1766–1767.

To sanction the article would be, he admonished, to cause directly the separation of the Americas.[18]

Perhaps it was Guridi y Alcocer who summed up best the attitude of the Americans to Article 22. The distinction between civil rights and political rights in this case, he declared, was one of pure theory and metaphysics, since to separate civil from political rights, ascribing only to the latter the rights and privileges of citizenship, was to set apart that which pertains to the citizen from that which in nature is civil—an action entirely foreign to man. Continuing, he asserted that to equate legal rights with the civil code, and political rights with the Constitution, was tantamount to saying the latter was not a law, whereas actually it was "more law than all others, since it is both original and fundamental." With eloquent simplicity, he concluded that laws which are not consistent with justice cease to be laws and become expedients or caprices.[19]

Despite the justice of their objections to Article 22, which was basic to the Spanish design to deny them equal rights, the Americans failed to secure the article's repeal. Moreover, the revision that resulted was worse in content than the original. Substituted for the phrase "Spaniards descended by whatever line from Africa," were the words, "Spaniards by whatever line held or reputed to be of African descent."[20] Although ostensibly intended as a concession that would avoid embarrassing those respectable old families in the Americas, Ramos Arispe protested that the idea that one's family honor would be subjected to pure opinion and repute was a greater personal insult to the Americans than the first draft. In an effort to eliminate the concept of ancestry as a criterion of citizenship and to gain some concessions for the castes, he proposed that citizenship be granted to all those who were sons of freeborn fathers or grandchildren of free grandparents, resident in the territories.[21] But this motion also failed.

Exclusion of the castes continued to be the subject of debate in Articles 28 through 33. Increasingly it became clear that the Peninsular deputies in reality did not believe the castes were morally irresponsible or intellectually unprepared to accept and perform the duties of citizenship, as was unconvincingly claimed; barring the

[18] *Ibid.*, III (September 5, 1811), 1773–1775.
[19] *Ibid.*, III (September 10, 1811), 1813.
[20] *Ibid.*, III (September 10, 1811), 1807.
[21] *Ibid.*, III (September 10, 1811), 1808–1809.

castes from rights of citizenship was simply an expedient means to entrench domination of the colonies from Spain. Although Article 28 confirmed the same basis for national representation in both hemispheres, Guridi y Alcocer was quick to expose the latent dishonesty and inequality of the article's wording. Posing his question rhetorically, he inquired if the article accorded equal representation or the same basis for representation, that is, if each hemisphere would claim the same number of deputies, or if deputies were to be apportioned according to increases and decreases on a general basis.[22] Obviously he was alluding to the previously mentioned fact that on an unrestricted basis of census alone, the Americas would be entitled to more congressional seats than the peninsula. Not unaware of this, the Spaniards contrived in Article 29 to set the basis for apportionment as the population composed only of those natives descended on both sides from Spanish origins, or those who had obtained a letter of citizenship from the Cortes, and native-born children of foreigners.[23]

Drawing upon much the same arguments directed against Article 22, the Mexican deputies launched their attack upon this proposal. Once again the doctrine of popular sovereignty supported the weight of their theoretical arguments, illustrating how strongly imbued these men were with the liberal thinking of the era. Surely the most succinct and lucid statement of this tenet was offered by Mariano Mendiola. The substance of all political and civil rights, he reasoned, is the sovereignty that resides essentially in the nation; he who is part of this sovereignty also participates proportionally in the total aggregate of rights of which it is composed. Therefore, having declared that sovereignty resides essentially in the nation, composed of the union of all Spaniards in both hemispheres, it was a contingent and indomitable truth, he asserted, that "Spaniards" as well as "citizens" were participants in both civil and political rights. The latter, consequently possessed the political right to be represented in the Cortes.[24]

Since the Cortes had declared itself to be the depository of the national sovereignty, and thus the representative of the entire nation, Ramos Arispe admonished the assembly that to exclude six or

[22] Spain, Cortes, 1810–1813, *Diario de las Cortes*, VIII (September 14, 1811), 330.
[23] *Ibid.*, VIII (September 14, 1811), 301.
[24] *Ibid.*, VIII (September 14, 1811), 314.

seven million Americans from the basis for apportioning representation was to render the congress imperfect and illegitimate. Besides
this, he found it odious that although the insane and criminals and
idiots as well as debtors and vagabonds were also denied citizenship,
they nevertheless could be counted in the basis for representation.
Yet the same right was denied millions of honorable and industrious
colored castes.[25]

It seemed unrealistic to Guridi y Alcocer to deny the castes representation when in fact, as he asserted, the American deputies at
the Cortes acted in behalf of all the people in their constituencies
as well as in the nation as a whole, regardless of descent. If they
had been meant to represent only the elite or a particular class, then
the Cortes would have been established in the traditional order of
Estates. But since they were set up in behalf of the entire nation,
every Spaniard in the empire participated through his representative. Indeed the very definition of the word "representative," the
Mexican deputy pointed out, stipulated that the deputy speak for
the rest of the nation in Congress, and seek to promote the general
will.[26]

One extremely practical consideration which all these Mexican
deputies appreciated was that the elimination of the castes from the
basis of representational apportionment would also mean that many
provinces would no longer meet the requirement that seventy thousand citizens were needed for a congressional seat. Therefore, not
only would they lose their right to send a deputy to Cortes, but they
would be forced to join themselves to the neighboring province, which
in the Americas meant municipal governments would often be separated by some two hundred leagues, making a just representation
of interests impossible.[27]

Having lost their fight in behalf of the castes, the American and
Mexican deputies were determined to continue to resist all further
encroachments on the so-called equality granted them by the decree
of October 15. Thus a major target for assault was Article 91 which
stipulated that a deputy to the Cortes, besides being at least twenty-
five years old and having seven years' residence in the province from
which elected, need simply be an inhabitant therein, and not neces-

[25] *Ibid.*, VIII (September 14, 1811), 303–306.
[26] *Ibid.*, VIII (September 15, 1811), 335–336.
[27] Spain, Cortes, 1810–1813, *Diario de sesiones de las Cortes,* III (September 23, 1811), 1902–1903.

sarily a native. As far as the Mexican deputies were concerned, this constituted another means by which the European Spaniards could curtail the number of native-born American deputies to the Cortes, since those more powerful and rich *peninsulares* living in the Americas would surely seek to elect themselves to such office, for reasons of personal interests and the desire to return home to Spain covered with honor.[28]

Well acquainted with the unreliability and fickleness of European Spanish representatives, who failed to sustain territorial interests against those of the motherland, the Mexicans insisted that only a native-born resident of a province qualify as a deputy to the Cortes. Since both the Central Junta and the Regency had employed this same criterion in the election of deputies to those bodies and to the Cortes itself, it seemed to Guridi y Alcocer that it could be applied equally well under the present circumstances. Perhaps in frustration from so many defeated attempts to secure any concessions from the overwhelming Spanish majority in the Cortes, he offered as a compromise the proposal that each province in America elect two sets of deputies to the Cortes: one group would constitute the native-born deputies, apportioned according to the basis set in the Constitution; the other group, whose number could double or triple that of the first, would be made up of European Spaniards resident in the same province. Under such a system, the Spaniards could maintain their precious majority in congress, while at the same time, he chided, the Americans would not be denied their legitimate number of deputies.[29]

A more subtle measure was offered by Mendiola, who submitted that the qualifications for a deputy include, besides residence, that he be a local farmer, manufacturer, or founder of some factory, or, in the Americas, that he be a registered miner, or worker of some mine, or a laborer, builder, or manufacturer. Obviously the logic behind this proposal was the assumption that if a deputy was tied to his province by particularistic economic interests, he would be far less likely to favor Spanish policies prejudicial to the Americas. Moreover, with respect to the miners, practically all were native Americans, and many of them were castes.[30]

[28] Spain, Cortes, 1810–1813, *Diario de las Cortes*, IX (September 27, 1811), 1–16.
[29] *Ibid.*, IX (September 27, 1811), 8–10.
[30] *Ibid.*, VIII (September 26, 1811), 456–458.

Territorial interests or narrow parochial objectives were surely not the only factors that encouraged the Mexicans to bear part in the constitutional discussions. Indeed they frequently espoused the cause of instituting comprehensive, fundamental political reforms. Particularly, they supported the principle of separation of powers, professed by so many of the Spanish liberals. Having declared that sovereignty no longer centered in the king but sprang from the consent of the nation, the king was held to be a constituted agent, established and delimited by the constitution. The Cortes, on the other hand, as the representative of the nation, assumed the greater authority to legislate in behalf of the general will. Only two legislative functions were conceded to the king: the right to propose laws and the power to veto.

Under the terms of Article 148 the king might veto the same bill two years in succession, despite continued support of the Cortes. Moreover, once vetoed, the same bill could not be reintroduced during the same year. Considering this imperial prerogative ruinous to the interests of the nation, especially in those cases where the defeated bill was meant to reform an existing bad law, Guridi y Alcocer opposed its adoption. To entrust that much power to one person, he cautioned, was to invite its abuse. It was his opinion that since the Cortes were responsible to the nation as a whole, but the king to no one, the Cortes knew better than he what laws were in the best interest of everyone. The Cortes were envisaged to correct national ills and to act as a check or safeguard against the executive power, he declared; thus, to invest the king with the power of a double veto was to rob that body of its regulatory function. As the seat of legislative power, the Cortes was obligated to legislate energetically and actively; to do less, according to the Tlaxcalan deputy, was to deny the very tenet of limited monarchy and to return to the abuses of absolutism. Citing as precedent the practice of the United States, he recommended that any bill reintroduced by the Cortes for the second time, after it had been vetoed, should become law if it received the approval of at least two-thirds of the deputies of the same Cortes. In any instance when a bill was recommended for passage a second time by a completely new Cortes, this too would constitute the abrogation of a second veto.[31]

Although his proposal was not accepted, Guridi y Alcocer was not

[31] *Ibid.*, IX (October 6, 1811), 130–131.

disheartened in his effort to further restrict executive powers. In particular he spoke out strongly against the right of the king to declare
war and to make and ratify treaties of peace without the prior notification or consent of the Cortes, as conceded by Article 171, part 3.
Since the Constitution granted the Cortes the right to provide for
military appropriation, arms, and soldiers, as well as the powers to
ratify treaties of offensive alliance and to permit or prohibit the entry
of foreign troops into the kingdom, Guridi y Alcocer insisted it
should also exercise the authority to declare war. Again citing the
practice of the United States Congress and its right to declare war,
he proposed that the king be allowed to participate in this function
only with the prior instruction and approval of the Cortes.[32]

Consonant with the desire to limit the absolutism of monarchical
rule was the Mexican resolve to secure an end to indiscriminate Peninsular domination over the American provincial governments and
economic interests. Uppermost among overseas grievances was the
failure of Spain to take account of the distinct personality of the provinces, of the diversity of their politico-economic interests, or of the
vastness of the territories concerned—a vastness which gave rise to
complex administrative needs. A striking example of this shortsighted
policy manifested itself in the draft proposal of Article 222, which
provided six government ministries for the Peninsula—those of State,
Justice, Treasury, War, Navy, and the Home Office—but allowed
only two universal or general ministries for the whole of the Americas—one for the northern portion and one for the southern.

Appealing to the Cortes on the grounds that it had already established the principle of separation of powers for the branches of government, and now established it for the different metropolitan ministries, Ramos Arispe questioned why the same rule had not been applied to the Americas and why they had been divided in terms of
territory instead of ministerial functions. It was to him inconsistent
and unjust that concern for the diverse affairs and enterprises of
these territorial provinces should fall into the hands of one or two
individuals. As he demonstrated, while Spain merited six ministries
to manage the Peninsular provinces, wherein resided only eleven
million people, the vaster territorial area of the Americas, with its
fifteen million people, was inexcusably kept in an inferior and subordinate position of having to depend upon the Peninsular ministries

[32] Spain, Cortes, 1810–1813, *Diario de sesiones de las Cortes,* III (October 10,
1811), 2037–2038.

to handle its affairs.[33] To correct this inequality he asked that two extra Home Offices be created for the overseas territories, specifically to handle their concerns separately from those of the motherland. Moreover, he proposed that these offices include and be responsible for the affairs of the Ministry of Justice in the Americas.[34]

As with many of his other proposals in the past, this measure too failed to be approved. In defense of the right of the Americas to have the same number of ministries as those allotted to the central government, Guridi y Alcocer exposed the real complaint of the Americans—that without such offices the territories could never escape the stigma of colonialism.[35] Despite their protests, the Mexican deputies failed to secure their demands. But the battle was not yet over, nor was the resolve of the Mexicans to win local governmental autonomy a closed issue. Their major stand was to come on December 26, 1811, when the section of the Constitution dealing with the internal government of the provinces and towns came up for discussion.

Once again the major role was to be played by the Mexican deputation, and in particular by Ramos Arispe, probably the most ardent defender of local autonomy. It was he who first introduced the proposed new form of provincial government for the Americas—the "provincial deputation"—in a dissertation he presented to the Cortes concerning the geographical, historical, economical, political, and judicial conditions of the four Eastern Interior Provinces of Mexico.[36]

Most of the American representatives viewed this proposed institution as the best possible instrument for acquiring more political independence for the provinces. In the words of Guridi y Alcocer, the provincial deputation was to be a local legislature whose power would come from the people and which would exclusively represent the will and interests of its province.[37] Led by Ramos Arispe, the Americans sought to increase not only the powers and the membership of the deputations but at the same time they proposed limiting the

[33] Spain, Cortes, 1810–1813, *Diario de las Cortes,* IX (October 22, 1811), 366–367.
[34] *Ibid.,* X (December 14, 1811), 376.
[35] *Ibid.,* X (December 17, 1811), 398.
[36] Miguel Ramos Arispe, *Memoria que . . . presenta á el augusto congreso sobre el estado natural, político, y civil de su dicha provincia, y las del Nuevo Reyno de León, Nuevo Santander y los Texas,* pp. 40–41.
[37] Spain, Cortes, 1810–1813, *Diario de las Cortes,* XI (January 13, 1812), 261–262.

powers of the political chief and the intendant, vassals of the king, by denying them a vote and a voice in the deputations.[38]

The Spanish deputies were immediately aware of the implications of federalism in these deputations and strongly argued that they were intended only as administrative councils with advisory capacity but not legislative function. The Conde de Toreno, an astute Peninsular deputy, pointed out with reason that the very vastness of the Spanish nation urged it forward, under a liberal system, toward federalism, which if not avoided would result in a federation, particularly in the overseas provinces, like that of the United States and which unconsciously would come to imitate the most independent of the ancient Swiss cantons, and end by constituting separate states.[39] Paradoxically, other Spanish deputies supported the American proposal for increasing the size of the deputation, alleging that if there were to be federalism it would not stem from the number of, but the institution of, the provincial deputation itself.[40]

These were to be prophetic words indeed, for the very origins of the seed of Mexican federalism adopted by the Mexican Constitution of 1824, were sown by the creation of the provincial deputation in that country. As one student of the period has written, it is quite possible that Ramos Arispe, the so-called father of Mexican federalism, may have advocated this institution expressly for the purpose of laying a foundation for the system that took form in the 1824 charter.[41]

The significance of Mexican constitutional expression is important, therefore, not only in terms of its effect on the making of the Spanish constitution adopted in 1812, but also with respect to the effects that the ideas and proposals presented had in developing the political history of that period throughout the Americas. By virtue of the widespread circulation of the *Diario de Cortes* in the Americas, plus the coverage of the constitutional debates in many of the newspapers of the day,[42] the liberal doctrines and principles articulated by men like

[38] *Ibid.*, XI (January 12, 1812), 239–240, 242–244.
[39] *Ibid.*, XI (January 12, 1812), 241.
[40] *Ibid.*, XI (January 12, 1812), 244–245.
[41] Nettie Lee Benson, *La diputación provincial y el federalismo mexicano,* p. 21. See also Benson, "The Provincial Deputation in Mexico, Precursor of the Mexican Federal State" (unpublished Ph.D. dissertation, The University of Texas).
[42] See, for example, *El Español* (London, 1810–1814), *El Conciso* (Cádiz,

Ramos Arispe and Guridi y Alcocer were to become actual standards for American constitutionalism. In particular, the Mexican charters of 1814 and 1824 bear a marked resemblance to the 1812 Spanish document, not only in content and organization, but to a large extent in phraseology.[43] Much of this similarity can be attributed to the fact that the principle author of the *Acta constitutiva* was Ramos Arispe and that *Acta* formed the basis of the 1824 Constitution.

1810–1812), *Diario de México* (1805–1816), *Semanario patriótico americano* (*México*, 1812–1813), *El Telégrafo americano* (Cádiz, 1811–1812); see also Jaime Delgado, *La independencia de América en la prensa española.*

[43] See, for example, James Q. Dealey, "The Spanish Sources of the Mexican Constitution of 1824," *Quarterly of the Texas State Historical Association,* III, No. 3 (January, 1900), 161–169, and David T. Garza, "Spanish Origins of Mexican Constitutionalism: an Analysis of Constitutional Development in New Spain, 1808 to Independence." (unpublished Master's thesis, The University of Texas, 1965.)

3. Mexican Municipal Electoral Reform, 1810–1822

Roger L. Cunniff

The attempt by a liberal Spanish Cortes to install popularly responsible institutions in Mexico during the upheaval of the independence
movement has been one of the most neglected facets of Mexican history. Because responsibility for much of the reform ultimately de-
volved upon the municipalities, and because of their importance in
Mexican tradition, the installation of popularly elected town councils
was one of the key measures ventured by the Cortes. Students of the
Mexican municipality have hitherto either ignored completely or
touched only very lightly on the changes in the institution under the
Cortes and the Constitution of 1812.[1] This essay can pretend to be no
more than a beginning toward understanding the transformation of
the municipality during this period from a closed corporation to a
popularly elected body. The purposes here are to show what influence Mexican delegates to the Cortes had on constitutional provisions
for electoral reforms, what those reforms were, and to what extent
and under what conditions they were implemented in Mexico from
1812 to 1821.

Towns in the Spanish colonies were primarily transplantations of
the medieval Castilian municipalities. These had been popularly
elected institutions with considerable local autonomy. By the time of
the Spanish conquest of America, however, the municipal councils
were reduced to closed corporations whose members were appointed
by incumbent councilmen or directly by the crown. The chief officials
of a municipal council (*ayuntamiento*) were one or two magistrates

---

[1] See, for example, M. C. Rolland, *El desastre municipal en la república mexicana,* and Gustavo Carvajal Moreno, *El municipio mexicano.*

(*alcaldes ordinarios*), several aldermen (*regidores*), and one or more syndics (*síndicos procuradores*). The magistrates presided over the council and municipal affairs in general, and they also usually had first-instance judicial authority. Aldermen exercised general supervision of the city under the direction of the magistrates and usually held other minor posts as well. The syndic was the city attorney, with the particular trust of safeguarding the rights of the local citizens before the council. As early as 1523, Charles V had provided that aldermen in America be popularly elected and not eligible for re-election for two years. This attempt to re-establish the traditional Spanish system in America was short-lived; in 1525 that same monarch began granting municipal offices in perpetuity, and Philip II hastened the decline of the popular council by introducing the practice of selling municipal offices to the highest bidder.[2]

Although there has never been an adequate study of the Mexican municipality, those historians who have touched on its condition in the late eighteenth century are agreed that it was greatly deteriorated. Control of councils in large cities usually rested in the hands of a few wealthy creoles who were less concerned with the responsibilities of their positions than with the prestige they carried. In many small villages, municipal councils dried up for lack of officeholders. The famous royal visitor, José de Gálvez, recognized that the internal development of the viceroyalty was being seriously limited through lack of efficient government on the local level. The system of intendants established in 1786 as a result of his recommendations brought more uniformity than had earlier existed but, by placing each municipality directly under the control of a royal official, tended to diminish still further its strength and efficiency.[3]

The Ordinance of Intendants failed to solve the problems besetting the Mexican municipality, which by 1812 was badly in need of reform. Municipal councils were most notable for their scarcity, especially in the frontier regions. In his famous *Memoria* to the Cortes, Miguel Ramos Arizpe, delegate from Coahuila, declared that

    [2] Constantino Bayle, *Los cabildos seculares en la América Española*, pp. 101–113; Clarence Haring, *The Spanish Empire in America*, pp. 162–176; T. Esquivel Obregón, *Apuntes para la historia del derecho en México*, II, 207–249; J. H. Parry, *The Sale of Public Office in the Spanish Indies under the Hapsburgs*, pp. 33–47.
    [3] Lillian E. Fisher, *The Background of the Revolution for Mexican Independence*, p. 271; Herbert I. Priestley, *José de Gálvez, Visitor-General of New Spain* (1765–1771), pp. 301–310.

in his entire home province there was only one municipal council, which was in Saltillo, a city of ten thousand. Monclova, with a population of over six thousand, had only a "half-council" of two magistrates and a syndic, as did Santa María de las Parras. There were no others among the twelve Spanish towns of the province. The province of Nuevo León had only three, while Tamaulipas had none in any of its twenty-six Spanish towns; each settlement there was governed by a captain of militia, with his two lieutenants serving as aldermen and his first sergeant being the syndic.[4]

Of the three towns in Texas only San Fernando de Béjar had a council, and this was not fully constituted, having only two magistrates, two aldermen, and a syndic in December, 1810.[5] Nuevo México in 1812 had no complete council, although Santa Fe, Albuquerque, and La Cañada had half-councils.[6] There were no formal councils among the three Spanish villages in California; Los Angeles and San José had half-councils, and Branciforte had only a magistrate.[7]

The more heavily populated areas of central Mexico also were short of *ayuntamientos*. Josef Eduardo de Cárdenas, delegate from Tabasco to the Cortes, complained in 1811 that there was only one properly constituted municipal council in his province and that the administration of justice suffered accordingly.[8] Lucas Alamán attested that in the years just prior to 1812 the councils in most small towns in central Mexico were vacant due to the small prestige attached to the positions.[9]

There was good cause for this lack of prestige. The actual powers of *ayuntamientos* had deteriorated to such an extent that a municipal

[4] Miguel Ramos de Arizpe, *Memoria que Dr. Miguel Ramos de Arizpe . . . presenta a el augusto congreso, sobre el estado natural, político, y civil de su dicha provincia, y las del nuevo reyno de León, Nuevo Santander, y los Texas, con exposisción de los defectos . . . y de las reformas . . . que necesitan para su prosperidad*, pp. 8–30.

[5] Don Manuel Salcedo, Governor of Texas, to Senior Magistrate of Béjar, Béjar, December 28, 1810, MS in Bexar Archives, University of Texas Library; José María Guadiana to Salcedo, Béjar, January 4, 1810, *ibid.*

[6] Pedro Bautista Pino, *Noticias históricas y estadísticas de la antigua provincia del Nuevo-México, presentadas por su diputado en Cortes D. Pedro Bautista Pino, en Cádiz el año de 1812*, pp. 1–27.

[7] Irving S. Richman, *California under Spain and Mexico, 1535–1847*, p. 175.

[8] Josef Eduardo de Cárdenas, *Memoria a favor de la provincia de Tabasco . . . presentada a S.M. las Cortes generales y extraordinarias por el Dr. D. Josef Eduardo de Cárdenas*, pp. 6, 55.

[9] Lucas Alamán, *Historia de Méjico*, pp. 167–168.

officeholder was little more than a ceremonial functionary. Every formally constituted municipal council was headed by a royal official. In Mexico City it was the Corregidor for the province of México; in Campeche, it was a *teniente del Rey*, who was directly responsible to the captain general of Yucatán in Mérida. Intendants and governors presided over the councils in their capitals and appointed subdelegates to preside over those which might exist in other towns.[10]

There was less uniformity in the ways councils were chosen and perpetuated. In apparently all cases the magistrates were chosen by vote of the incumbent councilmen, as the syndics frequently were. In some places, Parral for example, the council remitted a yearly fee to the royal treasury for the retention of this privilege. The mode of selecting aldermen, however, varied widely from place to place. In Mexico City the fifteen permanent aldermen held office by virtue of heredity, their families having held the positions for over a hundred years. In many other places the posts were hereditary but they were often sold at public auction as well.[11] An interesting development in the late eighteenth and early nineteenth centuries was that councils in some places were choosing honorary aldermen from among the leading local citizens. In Mexico City these honorary members were generally of superior nature to the complacent hereditary councilmen; hence, they exercised great influence on the council.[12]

Only in small villages with no formal *ayuntamientos* do we find any trace of popularly elected councilmen. Some such places, often small, transitory fishing and mining villages, regularly elected informal municipal councils. Recognizing that this practice existed in Tépic, Nueva Galicia, the Cortes implied in 1811 that it was widespread among such settlements.[13]

It is apparent that the prestige and authority of municipal government was at a low point in 1812. Although a form of popular government seems to have existed in some small and remote localities, most

[10] *Ibid.*; Francisco Alvarez, *Anales históricos de Campeche, 1812 a 1910,* I, 10.

[11] *Ibid.*; Alamán, *Historia de Méjico,* III, 167; José Ramón Royo, *Escribano* of Nueva España to the Ayuntamiento of San José del Parral, Durango, December 3, 1808, microfilm in El Archivo de Hidalgo del Parral (hereinafter cited as Archivo del Parral), Año 1812, G-3; *Actas* of Ayuntamiento of Parral, September 1, 1810, *ibid.*, Año 1810, G-2.

[12] Alamán, *Historia de Méjico,* III, 168; Ramos Arizpe, *Memoria,* p. 14.

[13] Spain, Cortes, 1810–1813, *Diario de las discusiones y actas de las Cortes,* VII, 158 (hereinafter cited as *Diario de las Cortes*).

municipal councils were manned by self-perpetuating or hereditary oligarchies content to rest on the prestige of their positions and leave the governing to crown officials. Especially in the northern areas, *ayuntamientos* were scarce and the tradition of popular, responsible local government seemed to be all but extinguished. Nevertheless, it was to be reborn in the midst of a revolution through another long-disused Spanish institution—the Cortes.

Napoleon's capture of Ferdinand VII in 1808 gave rise to a Supreme Junta which presumed to rule in his absence. The principal cities of the Spanish empire were invited to send delegates; Mexico City sent Miguel de Lardizábal y Uribe. As he was to represent the entire colony, all the provincial capitals of Mexico were privileged to send instructions informing him of reforms they wished implemented by the Junta. These instructions are the first indication we have of the feeling of Mexican *ayuntamientos* just prior to the revolution. Although some of the instructions were quite elaborate, none of the councils complained of the lack of popular representation on the local bodies, nor did they protest the power held by royal officials in each town.[14] It is readily understandable why hereditary municipal officials would not want to reinstate the tradition of popular elections. That they did not protest the presence of royal officials indicates an apathy in the face of royal power and a lack of desire for responsibility in their prestigious positions.

This impression is reinforced by the instructions given by municipal bodies to delegates to the Cortes a few years later. That given to Antonio de Larrazábal, delegate from Guatemala, was liberal to a high degree, but it proposed no change in the makeup of the *ayuntamiento* or the mode of electing it.[15] More significantly, the instructions of the municipality of Saltillo to Miguel Ramos Arizpe gave no sign of dissatisfaction with the current mode of perpetuation, yet Ramos Arizpe

---

[14] "Instrucción que en cumplimiento de la Rl. órden de 22 de enero del presente año de 1809 . . . dirige el Ayuntamiento de San Luis Potosí," San Luis Potosí, October 24, 1809, in México, Archivo General de la Nación, Ramo de Historia, Vol. 417, exp. 323; "Instrucción . . . de la Ciudad de Puebla," March 3, 1809, *ibid.*, exp. 179; "Instrucción que la Ciudad de Arizpe . . . remite," March 28, 1810, *ibid.;* "Instrucción del Ayuntamiento de Guanajuato," October 23, 1809, *ibid.*, exp. 118 (hereinafter cited AGN, Hist., 417).

[15] Guatemala, Ayuntamiento, *Instrucciones para la Constitución fundamental de la monarquía española y su gobierno . . . dadas por el M.I. Ayuntamiento de la . . . Ciudad de Guatemala a su diputado el Sr. Dr. D. Antonio de Larrazábal.*

was to be the person most responsible for municipal reform provisions in the forthcoming constitution.[16] Further, none of the eleven demands presented to the Cortes in December of 1810 as the nucleus for the American deputies' program of reform referred to *ayuntamientos.*[17] On the basis of the available evidence, then, we must conclude that there was no widespread demand for municipal reform in Mexico, despite the scarcity of *ayuntamientos* and the lamentable condition of those existing.

The most energetic among the Mexican delegates to the Cortes of 1810 to 1813 was Miguel Ramos Arizpe, and perhaps his most cherished project was the establishment of municipal councils where they were lacking in America; to him, responsible and democratic local government seemed the best means of improving the economic and social welfare of Mexico. There can be little doubt that he was the chief instigator of actions taken by the Cortes regarding municipal councils. On October 11, 1811, he placed a formal proposition before the Cortes in which the beginnings of many of the constitutional provisions on municipalities can be seen, although his proposals related specifically to the Eastern Interior Provinces. The proposition was remitted for study to the committee on the Constitution, as later was his *Memoria*, which incorporated most of the thoughts of this earlier project.[18]

On January 10, 1812, the Cortes began discussion of constitutional provisions relating to *ayuntamientos*, and almost immediately there arose a heated debate over the philosophy of government under which they would be established. Liberal American deputies, led by Ramos Arizpe and Florencio del Castillo, of Costa Rica, were determined to free the municipalities from control by the central government. They argued that Spanish tradition based municipal power in the citizens of the villages, that the presence of a royal official as chief municipal official usurped the legitimate rights of the people. The Conde de Toreno answered that municipalities derived their only power from the king and Cortes, whatever the manner of their elec-

[16] Reproduced in Tomás Berlanga, *Monografía histórica de la ciudad de Saltillo*, pp. 68–75.

[17] Spain, Cortes, 1810–1813, *Proposiciones que hacen al Congreso Nacional los diputados de América y Asia, Isla de León, 31 de diciembre de 1810.*

[18] Spain, Cortes, 1810–1813, *Diario de las Cortes*, IX, 220; Ramos Arizpe, *Memoria*, pp. 37–47.

tion. Despite the opposition of many American deputies, that viewpoint prevailed and was incorporated into the Constitution.[19] Article 309 provided that municipal councils be composed of magistrates, syndics, and aldermen in the familiar manner, and that the Political Chief, if present, should preside.[20] Thus the autonomy of the municipality remained limited and the liberal reformers failed to achieve one of their principal goals.

Article 310 provided that municipal councils were to be established where they were lacking and needed. The influence of Ramos Arizpe on this provision is evident. In his October 11, 1811, report to the Cortes he had proposed that settlements consisting of more than thirty property-owning residents should be allowed to establish *ayuntamientos* and that smaller places should also have them if they could show necessity. Towns with insufficient population or resources to support a council should join with others of the same status.[21] Article 310 in its final form required *ayuntamientos* in villages of over one thousand, but did not prohibit them in smaller ones.[22] This provision was directed specifically to the situation in America. Towns of under one thousand population were not required to establish councils because the American deputies had convinced the constitutional committee that many such places would be unable to support them.[23] Because some Spanish deputies feared that the provision might eliminate municipal government in many small villages in Spain, the matter was clarified in the implementing decree of May 23, 1812, which provided that places of less than one thousand persons could establish local governing bodies if they could demonstrate their need to their provincial deputations and show means to support the councils.[24] This distinction between villages of more than one thousand population and those of less was insisted upon by Ramos Arizpe, who

[19] Spain, Cortes, 1810–1813, *Diario de las Cortes*, XI, 210.

[20] Spain, Constitution, *Constitución política de la monarquía española promulgada en Cádiz a 19 de marzo de 1812*, Title VI, Chap. I, Art. 309. This article was first debated as Article 307; each article here cited was first numbered two digits lower than when it appeared in the last draft of the Constitution.

[21] Spain, Cortes, 1810–1813, *Diario de las Cortes*, VII, 158.

[22] Spain, Constitution, Title VI, Chap. I, Art. 310.

[23] Spain, Cortes, 1810–1813, *Diario de las Cortes*, XI, 213.

[24] Spain, Laws and Statutes, 1810–1822, *Colección de los decretos y órdenes que han expedido las Cortes generales y extraordinarias*, II, Decreto CLXII, May 23, 1812, "Formación de los Ayuntamientos Constitucionales," pp. 221–225 (hereinafter cited as *Decretos*).

wished to eliminate all possible obstacles to the establishment of *ayuntamientos* in the larger towns of Mexico.[25]

Under the May 23 decree, villages of under two hundred population were to have one magistrate, two aldermen, and a syndic. The numbers of members then increased in proportion to village size to the point where provincial capitals containing over ten thousand property-owning residents should have two magistrates, sixteen aldermen, and two syndics. The principle of this division followed one of the proposals made by Ramos Arizpe on October 11, 1811, although the proportions varied.[26]

In his *Memoria,* Ramos Arizpe had argued that Spanish tradition recognized the right of free men to choose their own leaders, that the prevailing mode of perpetuating municipal councils in Mexico violated that tradition, and that popularly elected local offices should be revived by the Cortes.[27] Opponents of the proposal did not deny the tradition, but objected to popularly chosen councils on other grounds. José Ignacio Beye de Cisneros, deputy from Nueva España, introduced a complaint from the perpetual aldermen of Mexico City claiming that any move to abolish their positions was a violation of their contract with the crown. Antonio Larrazábal from Guatemala, supported by the Conde de Toreno, argued that elected councilmen would be unable to remain in office long enough to gain the experience necessary for efficient service.[28] Ramos Arizpe and the liberal viewpoint prevailed: Article 312 of the Constitution provided that municipal officials would thenceforth be selected by popular election, and that all perpetual offices would immediately cease.[29] The liberals seem to have taken little cognizance of the difficulties of implementing such elections in the midst of a violent revolution.

Having decided on popularly elected *ayuntamientos,* the Cortes established a complicated and imperfect formula of indirect elections. It is important to note that the parish elections for municipal councils were not the same as those preliminary to the choosing of provincial deputations and deputies to the Cortes. They were entirely separate sets of elections, involving electoral groups of different proportions.[30]

[25] Spain, Cortes, 1810–1813, *Diario de las Cortes,* XII, 125.
[26] Spain, Laws and Statutes, 1810–1822, *Decretos,* II, Decreto CLXII, p. 222.
[27] Ramos Arizpe, *Memoria,* p. 45.
[28] Spain, Cortes, 1810–1813, *Diario de las Cortes,* VIII, 87; XI, 217–219.
[29] Spain, Constitution, Title VI, Chap. I, Art. 312.
[30] *Ibid.,* Title I, Chaps. II–III, Title VI, Chap. I, Arts. 313–314; Spain, Laws and Statutes, 1810–1822, *Decretos,* II, CLXIII, Arts. III–XI.

Election procedures involved Articles 18–23 and 313–319 of the Constitution and the subsequent decrees of May 23 and September 21, 1812, and June 23, 1813. As soon as each town in America received and published the Constitution and the implementing decree of May 23, 1812, the citizens of each parish were to meet in parish juntas presided over by the political chief, a magistrate, or an alderman to select a number of electors in proportion to the population of the parish. In towns of less than fifty citizens there were to be no separate parish elections. Towns of less than one thousand population were to select nine electors, those between one and five thousand population seventeen, and those larger than five thousand were to elect twenty-five. Once chosen, all the electors of a particular town were to meet in a junta as soon as possible, where, under the chairmanship of the political chief, senior magistrate, or senior alderman, they were to select the members of the municipal council. Those towns able to conclude the elections four months before the end of 1812 were again to hold elections in December of that year; otherwise, the first-elected council members would hold office until the end of 1813.[31]

There were some important oversights in the provisions for municipal election procedures. Although the Constitution stipulated that village curates should aid in parish elections leading to selection of provincial deputations and deputies to the Cortes, this was overlooked in the election instructions for municipal councils. However, the committee on the Constitution declared that it was the duty of clerics to aid in the elections, a fact that should not have to be explained in the Constitution.[32] More important was the Cortes' failure to specify the exact procedure villages were to follow in the popular voting for parish electors and in the electoral juntas. When this was called to the attention of the chairman of the committee on the Constitution, he gave assurances that it would be taken care of in future legislation.[33] The May 23 implementing decree, however, contained no further clarification, an oversight which was to be a large factor in the 1812 election disorders.

Spanish citizens possessing the quality of *vecino* could vote. Under the Constitution, all persons tracing their descent through both lines

[31] Spain, Constitution, Title VI, Chap. I, Arts. 313–314; Spain, Laws and Statutes, 1810–1822, *Decretos*, II, CLXII, Arts. III–XI.

[32] Spain, Constitution, Title III, Chap. II, Art. 46; Spain, Cortes, 1810–1813, *Diario de las Cortes*, VIII, 429.

[33] Spain, Cortes, 1810–1813, *Diario de las Cortes*, XI, 220.

to the Spanish domains in either hemisphere were citizens. Foreigners who were especially skilled, were married to Spaniards, or had been born on Spanish soil could become citizens. Indians were citizens but Negroes were not, although individuals of that race could gain citizenship by special dispensation of the Cortes.[34] Violent protest to this exclusion, notably by Ramos Arizpe and Larrazábal, led the Cortes to allow villages composed mainly or entirely of non-citizens to elect their own local councils following constitutional procedures.[35]

Other persons excluded from citizenship were criminals, debtors, vagrants, domestic servants, and persons who had long lived in or given service to foreign countries.[36] In addition to being a citizen, a voter had to be a *vecino*. This quality traditionally pertained to the head of a family possessing a permanent residence in a town, but was subject to widely varying interpretations in actual practice.[37] The failure of the Cortes to define this term for electoral purposes was to be a source of much future confusion. There was no age qualification as such, but sons of foreigners could not be allowed to citizenship until the age of twenty-one.[38]

Once elected, magistrates would hold office for one year; the aldermen were to hold office for two years, and one-half of their number was to be replaced yearly. Similarly, syndics were elected to two-year terms, and if a village possessed two, one was to be replaced each year. Where there was a large enough population to allow it, a person who had held one municipal office was ineligible to hold that or any other local office until two years had elapsed. Citizens twenty-five years of age and resident for at least five years in the town could hold office, but royally appointed public employees, with the exception of militia, were ineligible. Clerics could vote but could not hold municipal office.[39]

[34] Spain, Constitution, Arts. 18–23.

[35] Spain, Laws and Statutes, 1810–1822, *Decretos*, II, CLXII, Art. XII; Spain, Cortes, 1810–1813, *Diario de las Cortes*, XI, 220–221.

[36] Spain, Constitution, Art. 24.

[37] Spain, Cortes, *Recopilación de leyes de los reinos de las indias*, Libro IV, Título 10, ley vi. See the discussion of this problem in Chapter I, *supra*.

[38] Spain, Constitution, Art. 21.

[39] *Ibid.*, Arts. 315–318; Spain, Laws and Statutes, 1810–1822, *Decretos*, III, Decreto CXCIII, September 21, 1812, "Los eclesiásticos seculares tienen voto en las elecciones de los ayuntamientos, pero no pueden obtener en ellos ningún oficio," pp. 87–88. Many of these regulations showed strong influence from previous royal legislation for colonial municipal government. Under the *Recopilación*, magistrates could hold office for one-year terms and were ineligible for re-election

The powers and responsibilities of the municipalities derived from Article 321 of the Constitution and were more specifically enumerated in a special instruction of June 23, 1813. In general, the *ayuntamientos* were given local police powers and charged with maintaining the health, education, and welfare of their communities. They were to build and maintain hospitals, schools, roads, and jails, maintain the health of the population by assuring sanitary conditions in the streets and markets and by providing an adequate supply of good food and water. They were to keep an accurate record of vital statistics in their area. Councils were given the responsibility of promoting local industry and commerce by providing good rural roads and any other public works to that end. To do all this, they were to form municipal ordinances subject to approval by their Provincial Deputation. All of this would seem to be conducive to the improved state of internal affairs which Ramos Arizpe envisioned for Mexico. But having made a detailed list of the ends they wished to pursue, the Cortes refused to supply the means; municipalities were refused the right to levy taxes without special permission from the Cortes; their only independent income was from municipally owned property and licensing fees, which in many cases were quite meagre.[40]

Ramos Arizpe repeatedly protested that the small villages which he championed would be virtually helpless under these conditions, since they had very little property income. In an attempt to remedy the situation he proposed that those towns having little or no income be subsidized from a special fund, and that municipalities be given the right to sell and administer the vacant crown lands in their immediate neighborhoods. Both these proposals were studied by the committee on the Constitution but were ultimately rejected as infringements on the power of the Cortes.[41]

Thus the liberals failed in their aim to make the municipality an autonomous political and economic unit; they succeeded, however, in

---

until two years had passed. Only *vecinos* of the area could serve on local councils, and royal officials, with the exception of militia, could not be magistrates. Under the intendant system, magistrates served for two years, with one being chosen each year. See Spain, Cortes, *Recopilación*, Lib. V, Tit. III, leyes iii–ix; Lillian Fisher, *The Intendant System in Spanish America*, p. 278.

[40] Spain, Constitution, Art. 321; Spain, Cortes, *Instrucción para los ayuntamientos constitucionales, juntas provinciales, y gefes políticos superiores decretada por las Cortes generales y extraordinarias en 23 de junio de 1813*, Chap. I, Arts. 1–21.

[41] Spain, Cortes, 1810–1813, *Diario de las Cortes*, II, 229–232, 239–241, 468.

providing for local government freely elected and responsible to the citizenry. The next, and more difficult, task was to put these reforms into practice in revolt-rent Mexico.

On September 9, 1812, Francisco Venegas, Viceroy of Mexico, received from Ignacio de la Pezuela, Minister of Grace and Justice for the Regency, three hundred copies of the Constitution, with orders to publish it. Hostile to the liberal document, Venegas delayed its publication in Mexico City until September 30, when he forwarded copies and publishing orders to intendants and municipal councils throughout Mexico.[42] The decree of May 23 relative to installation of popular *ayuntamientos* was received by Venegas on September 24. After receiving the advice of his attorneys, the Viceroy published the decree on October 15, and ordered that it be complied with throughout the realm.[43]

The evidence indicates that those areas near the viceregal seat not occupied or isolated by the insurgents received the Constitution from Venegas and quickly installed popular *ayuntamientos*. The province of Tabasco seems to have been the first to take advantage of the new Constitution; Villahermosa, the capital, established a popular *ayuntamiento* on November 3, 1812, the same day on which the copy of the Constitution sent by Venegas arrived. The nine other Spanish towns in Tabasco quickly followed, as did other central Mexican places able to correspond with the viceroy. Oaxaca, Guanajuato, and Michoacán were still dominated by insurgents, which prevented the citizens in those places from implementing the Constitution.[44]

Popular councils were installed with conspicuous rapidity in seaboard areas open to direct communication with Spain. These areas, notably Veracruz and Yucatán, were marked by strong liberal sentiment; although cut off from direct contact with the viceroy, hence lacking official sanction for institutional changes, they early had access to unofficial copies of the Constitution and put pressure on

[42] Ignacio de la Pezuela to Francisco Venegas, Cádiz, June 8, 1812, AGN, Hist., 402; "Lista de los cuerpos a quienes se circuló el bando anunciando el día en que se publicó la Constitución," *ibid.*; *Gaceta del gobierno de Mexico,* October 1, 1812.

[43] "Acuerdo del Virrey y Parecer Fiscal" in Rafael de Alba, *La Constitución de 1812 en la Nueva España,* I, 226–227; *Diario de México,* October 16, 1812.

[44] Ayuntamiento of Villahermosa to Viceroy, Villahermosa, March 2, 1813, AGN, Hist., 402; *Gaceta del gobierno de México,* November 17 and 28, 1812; Alba, *La Constitución de 1812,* I, 70–76; Alamán, *Historia de Méjico,* III, 273.

provincial officials to implement it immediately. Success in each case depended on the character of the local governor. In Veracruz liberal Spanish merchants, saying the Constitution would serve to mollify the rebels and restore peace, were able to persuade Governor María Soto to publish the unofficial copy he had received from Spain. Soto allowed a popular *ayuntamiento* to be established, then abolished it. His successor proved more malleable, and councils were elected throughout the province by the end of 1812.[45] Captain General Manuel Artazo y Barral of Yucatán was made of sterner stuff, but he governed what was perhaps the most liberal area in New Spain. At first refusing to implement the Constitution without viceregal orders, he yielded on the advice of his attorneys and of Miguel González y Lastiri, deputy from the province to the Cortes, and allowed *ayuntamiento* elections in Mérida in mid-November, although he still had received neither Constitution nor implementing decrees through official channels. Having yielded to pressure in Mérida, Artazo tried in vain to withhold the Constitution from the rest of the province. The quick installation of the council in Campeche was aided by Artazo's lieutenant, Miguel de Castro y Aráoz, one of the few royal officials to cooperate openly in implementing the Constitution.[46]

In sharp contrast was the attitude of José de la Cruz, the unyieldingly conservative intendant of Nueva Galicia. Although the commander at the port of San Blas received a copy of the Constitution directly from Spain early in January, 1813, Cruz, supported by his Audiencia, adamanantly refused to publish it without orders from the viceroy, despite the fact that he had the official implementing decrees in his possession. The Constitution was not implemented in Nueva Galicia while Venegas was viceroy.[47]

Meanwhile in Mexico City the Constitution had slowly gone into

[45] Don José Quevedo, Governor of Veracruz, to Viceroy Calleja, Veracruz, March 5, 1813, AGN, Hist., 403; Spain, Cortes, 1810–1813, *Diario de las Cortes*, XVII, 243, 482–483; Alamán, *Historia de Méjico*, III, 438–439.

[46] Governor of Yucatán to Secretaría del Despacho de Estado, Mérida, December 1, 1812, in Spain, Cortes, 1810–1813, *Diario de las Cortes*, VIII, 55–56; Governor of Yucatán to Governor of Presidio of Carmen, Mérida, December 23, 1812, AGN, Hist., 402; Spain, Cortes, 1810–1813, *Diario de sesiones de las Cortes generales y extraordinarias dieron principio el 24 de setiembre de 1810 y terminaron el 20 de setiembre de 1813*, VII, 5279 (May 15, 1813) (hereinafter cited as *Diario de sesiones de las Cortes*); Juan Francisco Molina Solís, *Historia de Yucatán durante la dominación española*, III, 395, 415.

[47] Vicente Alonso Andrade, Fiscal of the Royal Audiencia of Guadalajara, to Viceroy Venegas, Guadalajara, January 7, 1813, in Alba, I, 77–78.

effect. On November 29 the citizens of each parish chose electors who were to elect the members of the *ayuntamiento*. The elections were characterized by confusion on the part of election officials and jubilation on the part of liberals, as creoles gained unanimous possession of the electoral junta. The lack of specific electoral instructions in the Constitution and the May 23 decree gave rise to many questions. As the Constitution failed to describe how parish electors in municipal elections should be chosen, the election officials followed the provisions for parish-level elections for provincial deputations, but these in themselves were far from explicit. The confusion was compounded by lack of certainty as to what constituted a citizen and *vecino* for voting purposes.[48] Despite this inexactness, and considerable noisy campaigning by the jubilant liberals, the election was reasonably honest and orderly.[49] Viceroy Venegas, however, fearing that the creole electors would elect a creole *ayuntamiento* and that the forthcoming parish elections leading to selection of the provincial deputation would fan revolutionary aspirations, suspended the election process in Mexico City at the end of December and ordered the old *ayuntamiento* to stay in office.[50] Only those areas near Mexico City not occupied by insurgents, and the seacoast areas of Veracruz and Yucatán, elected *ayuntamientos* in 1812.

It should not be assumed, as it often has, that Venegas' ban on popular elections applied to all of New Spain.[51] Under the Constitution, the viceroy was political chief of the province of México, with jurisdiction over only that province; politically, therefore, he had legal rights only in that area. Whether or not Venegas accepted the limitation placed on the range of his powers by the Constitution, it is clear that he did not intend the ban to extend outside Mexico City, much less outside the province of México. While elections were prohibited in Mexico City, towns in the surrounding province continued to re-

---

[48] "Bando del Corregidor . . . de la Ciudad de México en que se convoca a los vecinos . . . para que el día de 29 de noviembre designen a los electores que deberán proceder al nombramiento de alcaldes, regidores, y procuradores síndicos," in Alba, *La Constitución de 1812*, I, 226–227; Ramón Gutiérrez del Mazo to Venegas, Mexico, December 3, 1812, AGN, Hist., 447; José María de Echabe to Gutiérrez del Mazo, December 15, 1812, *ibid.*

[49] For a detailed study of the election, see Nettie Lee Benson, "The Contested Mexican Election of 1812," HAHR, XXVI (August, 1946), 336–350.

[50] Alamán, *Historia de Méjico*, III, 278.

[51] See Fisher, *Background*, p. 329; Herbert H. Bancroft, *History of Mexico*, IV, 465–467; Alamán, *Historia de Méjico*, III, 278; Wilbert H. Timmons, *Morelos, Priest, Soldier, Statesman of Mexico*, p. 89.

port the establishment of popular *ayuntamientos,* and Venegas approved them.[52] There is no evidence that councils earlier established ceased to function due to Venegas' action.

Venegas did not further hinder the progress of the Constitution by any positive action; however, by the negative act of simply not sending official copies to the northern provinces, he greatly delayed its implementation there. Whether or not this was deliberate, present evidence does not reveal. The residents of the north were fully aware that a new Constitution was in effect—delegates to the Cortes from those regions had sent copies to their constituents soon after it was formulated, and these were circulating freely. Nueva Viscaya received at least one copy from its delegate, Guereña, in October, 1812; Miguel Ramos Arizpe supplied copies to several villages in the Eastern Interior Provinces, including at least Santa María de las Parras, Saltillo, and Aguayo.[53] Only the provinces of California, Nuevo México, and Texas seem to have been ignorant of the provisions of the new Constitution at the beginning of 1813, and this is not certain.

Despite the currency of the Constitution, royal officials steadfastly maintained that they would publish only official copies sent directly by the viceroy. Had they been of liberal persuasion, provincial officials might well have used the constitutional limitations on viceregal powers as justification to proceed under their own authority. However these limitations derived from the Constitution itself, the only available examples of which had arrived through what conservative royal officials chose to regard as unorthodox channels. Although their actual purpose was probably to block implementation of the Constitution until, hopefully, a conservative reaction should abolish it, they were faced with a very real jurisdictional dilemma. This attitude, coupled with Venegas' unwillingness, or inability, to assert his authority over the northern provinces, goes far to explain why there were no legal Constitutional *ayuntamientos* established in that area during his term of office.[54]

---

[52] Venegas to Fiscal Civil of Mexico City Audiencia, Mexico, February 9, 1813, AGN, Hist., Ramo de Guerra, Vol. 30, Ayuntamientos, fol. 236; Alcalde Primero of Coyoacán to Gutiérrez del Mazo, Coyoacán, February 29, 1813, *ibid.,* fol. 246; Subdelegate of Malinalco to Venegas, Malinalco, January 20, 1813, *ibid.,* fol. 271.

[53] Spain, Cortes, 1810–1813, *Diario de sesiones de las Cortes,* VII, 5283 (May 15, 1813); *ibid.,* 5329; *ibid.,* VIII, 5761–5762 (July 21, 1813).

[54] *Ibid.,* VIII, 5761–5762 (July 21, 1813); Intendant of San Luis Potosí to Viceroy Calleja, San Luis Potosí, May 18, 1813, AGN, Hist. 402. This jurisdictional puzzle needs further study. The situation was particularly confusing in the

In such places as Yucatán, Veracruz, and Mexico City, liberal elements had been strong enough to persuade authorities to implement the Constitution, but they had made no effort to proceed with reforms on their own initiative. Neither did the citizens of the northern provinces attempt, in most cases, to take the law into their own hands. The available evidence indicates that they were frustrated and anxious to test the liberal new laws, but at the same time unwilling to act without the sanction of royal officials—in short, they lacked revolutionary spirit. Their protests took the form of petitions to the intendant, as in the case of Durango, or complaints to their delegates at the Cortes, as in the cases of Parras, Saltillo, and Aguayo, who complained to Ramos Arizpe.[55] Only in the Western Interior Provinces did some settlements install *ayuntamientos* without the consent of their governor. Chihuahua City took advantage of the absence of the subdelegate to publish the Constitution and elect a new council late in 1812. At least three small villages in Nueva Viscaya established *ayuntamientos* on their own initiative after waiting in vain for the Constitution to be published officially. All these abortive *ayuntamientos* were quickly extinguished by Commander General Bernardo Bonavía.[56] In the overwhelming majority of cases,

---

Interior Provinces, where repeated administrative changes over a period of thirty-six years had reduced authorities and residents to a state of baffled confusion. Since being established in 1776 the Interior Provinces had alternately been dependent and independent of the viceroy, and administered at different times as one, two, or three units. They were organized as one Commandancy-General independent of the viceroy from 1793 to 1811, when the Regency ordered them returned to viceregal control under the terms of an 1804 *cédula* which had never been enforced. Venegas had scarcely gotten the Commandant General, Nemesio Salcedo y Salcedo, to adhere to this order in principle, if not in fact, when the Constitution of 1812 separated the area from viceregal authority once again. Although subsequent viceroys made attempts to draw the area into their jurisdiction, they acted on uncertain legal grounds, and for the most part, with little success. The question remained unsettled for the remainder of the period of the wars for independence. See Herbert E. Bolton, *Guide to Materials for the History of the United States in the Principle Archives of Mexico*, pp. 75–77; see also viceregal correspondence relative to this problem in AGN, Ramo de Provincias Internas, Vol. 129.

[55] Spain, Cortes, 1810–1813, *Diario de sesiones de las Cortes*, VII, 5283 (May 15, 1813); *ibid.*, VIII, 5761–5762 (July 21, 1813).

[56] Bonavía to Secretaría de la Gobernación de Ultramar, Durango, March 16, 1814, Archivo General de Indias, Legajo 297, no. 4, fol. 1 (typescript copy in the possession of Nettie Lee Benson, Austin, Texas—hereinafter cited as AGI typescript); Spain, Cortes, 1810–1813; *Diario de sesiones de las Cortes*, VII, 5281–5282 (May 15, 1813).

however, the citizens waited with a patience bordering on apathy for the Constitution either to be instituted or abrogated. For example, the members of the Parral *ayuntamiento* themselves chose their new magistrates for 1813 even though they had been familiar with the Constitution for two months. Monterrey did likewise, despite the fact that the town and province had been under the control of a popularly elected junta since the desertion of the governor and that the Constitution had been known there since October, 1812.[57]

Félix Calleja replaced Venegas as viceroy of Mexico in March of 1813. Although from this distance it seems clear that the great majority of Mexicans were not willing to revolt in order to gain the benefits of the new Constitution, to Calleja it apparently seemed that they were. Accordingly, he resolved to implement the document in the hope that it would bring some of the revolutionary elements back into the fold.[58] On April 4, 1813, on Calleja's orders, the electors of the previous November chose Mexico City's first constitutional *ayuntamiento*.[59] Although unsure of the extent of his authority under the Constitution, Calleja gradually asserted his power over the entire country. Early in April he began sending copies of the Constitution to those areas where it was yet unpromulgated. Throughout the spring and summer of 1813 governors of the northern provinces began to allow municipal elections, but some continued to resist. Bernardo Bonavía, in the Western Interior Provinces, stubbornly refused to institute the charter until the syndic of the Durango *ayuntamiento* wrote directly to Calleja, petitioning him, as ruler of all Mexico (sic), to order that the Constitution be put into effect. The viceroy then decided to expand his authority over the northern areas. On August 1 he ordered Bonavía to hold elections without further delay.[60] The

---

[57] José Ramón Royo de Iberri to Ayuntamiento of Parral, Durango, December 22, 1812, Archivo del Parral, Año 1812, G-3; Israel Cavazos Garza, *El muy ilustre ayuntamiento de Monterrey desde 1596*, p. 81; Vito Alessio Robles, *Coahuila y Texas en la época colonial*, p. 659.

[58] "Proclama de D. Félix María Calleja al encargarse del gobierno como virey 26 de marzo de 1813" in J. E. Hernández y Dávalos, *Colección de documentos para la historia de la guerra de independencia de México de 1808 a 1821*, V, 6–10.

[59] *Diario de México*, April 6, 1813.

[60] Fernando de Obregón, Síndico Procurador of Durango, to Calleja, Durango, June 14, 1813, AGN, Hist., 402; Alba, *La Constitución de 1812*, I, 82; Calleja to Durango Ayuntamiento, México, August 1, 1813, AGN, Hist., 402; Calleja to Bonavía, México, August 1, 1813, *ibid*. As political chief of the province of México under the Constitution, Calleja had no political authority over this region, but as captain general, he did have military authority over Bonavía.

commander general then reluctantly complied, but moved so slowly that most villages in Nueva Viscaya and Nuevo México did not establish *ayuntamientos* until well into 1814, just a few months before the Constitution was abolished.[61] Due to similar intransigence on the part of the governor of Coahuila, the Constitution was not put into effect there until mid-February, 1814.[62] Although Monterrey established a constitutional council in May, 1813, most other places in the Eastern Interior Provinces were scarcely able to elect *ayuntamientos* before the abrogation of the Constitution snuffed them out.[63]

As insurgent-held areas yielded to the Viceroy's forces, constitutional local government was established. Michoacán held municipal elections in June of 1813, Oaxaca and Guanajuato not until mid-1814, by which time constitutional *ayuntamientos* had been established in almost all parts of Mexico.[64]

Only in Texas and California were no popular *ayuntamientos* established in this period. There is no evidence in the Bexar Archives that the royalist junta which controlled the village from March 1, 1811, to March 29, 1813, attempted at any time to establish a popular *ayuntamiento* or that it possessed a copy of the Constitution.

[61] Subdelegate of Parral to Governor of Nueva Viscaya, Parral, February 14, 1814, Archivo del Parral, Año 1812, G-3; Electors of Chihuahua to Bonavía, Chihuahua, January 18, 1814, AGI typescript; Francisco R. Almada, *Apuntes históricos de la región de Chínipas*, p. 247; Ignacio Bustamante, Intendant of Sonora, to Calleja, Arispe, November 8, 1813, AGN, Hist., 402; Francisco Almada, *Diccionario de historia, geografía, y biografía sonorenses*, p. 18; Ralph E. Twitchell, *The Spanish Archives of New Mexico*, II, 582, 584, 594.

[62] "El Intendente de San Luis avisa de ni haberse recivida ni publicada en la Provincia de Coahuila la Constitución Política de la Monarquía," AGN, Hist., 403; Intendant of San Luis to Governor of Coahuila, San Luis, November 14, 1813, *ibid.*; Governor of Coahuila to Calleja, Saltillo, February 28, 1814, *ibid.*

[63] "Extracto de las actas de acuerdo y operaciones que ha tenido el Ayuntamiento Constitucional del Presidio de Río Grande," Archivo General del Estado de Nuevo León, Monterrey, typescript copy in possession of Nettie Lee Benson, Austin, Texas; Juan Bautista de Arispe to Ayuntamiento of Monterrey, Monterrey, May 14, 1814, *ibid.*, "Oficios y Contestaciones de la Diputación Provincial desde el día 1° de Mayo de 1814," *ibid.*; Provincial Deputation to Antonio Cordero, Monterrey, June 23, 1814, *ibid.*

[64] Constitutional Ayuntamiento of Valladolid to Calleja, Valladolid, July 30, 1813, AGN, Hist., 403; "El Intendente de Oaxaca remitió a V.E. los documentos que accreditan la publicación de la Constitución Nacional, la Junta Popular para votación de Electores de Ayuntamiento Constitucional, y la votación para instalación deste cuerpo," Antequera, June 1, 1814, *ibid.*; Military Commander of Salamanca to Viceroy, Salamanca, February 27, 1814, *ibid.*; "Testimonio liberal de las diligencias que acaecieron la publicación hecha en la villa de San Miguel el Grande de la Constitución . . . y las correspondientes elecciones," *ibid.*

When Joaquín de Arrendondo recaptured the settlement from the rebel Gutiérrez de Lara in August, 1813, he refused to implement the document on the grounds that so many people had fled the province during the revolution that insufficient qualified persons remained to fill an *ayuntamiento*.[65] Although there is some evidence that the Constitution was published in California during this period, it seems to have had little or no effect, due to confusion as to whether the Californias were under the jurisdiction of the Audiencia of Nueva Galicia or that of México.[66]

While Calleja believed that the popular *ayuntamientos* might channel some revolutionary energy into less troublesome pursuits, he was apprehensive of the possible results of leaving them to creole control. He accordingly attempted to assure the placement of at least some Europeans on councils within his reach. There is no doubt that he attempted to influence the 1813 elections in Mexico City. Of the twenty-five electors chosen in parish elections the previous November, eleven were clerics. Seeing in them a possible conservative force in the April, 1813, election, Calleja asked the Bishop of Mexico to prevail upon them to select some Europeans to the municipal council. The effort failed, and creoles dominated.[67] It is interesting to note that none of those clerics were on the electoral junta chosen for the municipal election in December of 1813.[68] Calleja's efforts were equally futile in Querétaro, where he asked Ecclesiastical Visitor José Mariano Beristáin to keep the forthcoming elections in hand. Beristáin called all clergy in the city together and instructed them to use their influence to keep creoles, which he equated with insurgents, from being elected. He was forced to report to Calleja that his labor was for nothing and that all *ayuntamiento* positions had been captured by creoles.[69]

[65] "Memorial Petitioning that the Spanish Constitution be Published in Texas," May 18, 1814, translation in University of Texas Library, Nacogdoches Archives, Archive 185, Vol. 17, pp. 128–29; Joaquín de Arredondo to Governor Don Benito de Armiñán, Béjar, March 8, 1814, in *ibid.*, Bexar Archives; Arredondo to Armiñán, Monterrey, September 3, 1814, *ibid.*

[66] Calleja to Governor of Upper California, Mexico, March 31, 1814, AGN, Hist., 403; "Superior decreto de 15 de marzo sobre no haberse comprendido específicamente la Península de California en las providencias dictadas . . . para las nombramientos de Diputados de Cortes y Vocales de las juntas provinciales de este Reino," *ibid.*, 448.

[67] *Diario de México*, December 2, 1812; Alamán, *Historia de Méjico*, III, 412.

[68] *Diario de México*, December 28, 1813.

[69] "Oficio del Visitador Eclesiástico a varios individuos del clero de Querétaro,

On June 23, 1813, the Cortes issued a long and detailed list of instructions for the internal government of the realm. The electoral confusions of the previous year were recognized by a clause requiring election inspectors, to be elected by voters in each step of the municipal voting procedure, to check voter qualifications and prevent fraud. One previous oversight was corrected by instructions that municipal parish elections were thenceforth to follow the procedures in Articles 46 to 52 of the Constitution, referring to the first step of Provincial Deputation elections.[70] This instruction arrived in time to be applied to the December, 1813, election in Mexico City, which proceeded in an orderly manner,[71] whether due to more experience on the part of voters and officials, more explicit instructions, or the firm hand of Viceroy Calleja, evidence does not reveal.

That Calleja's generals were less concerned with observance of election laws than with maintenance of strict order is indicated by the election in Antequera de Oaxaca. Shortly after recapturing the city from the rebels, Melchor Álvarez met with the bishop and two other leading clerics to decide on the manner of holding elections. This group decided which citizens were eligible to vote, then called them together to choose the electoral junta. After aiding the governor in conducting the election, the same clerics found themselves members of the electoral junta. Each member of the junta informed Álvarez separately and orally of his selections for the *ayuntamiento*. In violation of the 1813 instruction, no inspectors were chosen to check the actions of the governor. The municipal council revealed a suspiciously fine impartiality: exactly half of the aldermen were Europeans and half creoles, and one of the two alcaldes was a European.[72]

The election in San José del Parral, Nueva Viscaya, affords an example of a small town far removed from immediate viceregal influ-

---

con motivo de las elecciones de Ayuntamiento . . . diciembre 18 de 1813," in Hernández y Dávalos, *Colección de documentos*, V, 368–369; "El Dr. Beristáin da parte al Virrey de las medidas que tomó para las elecciones, del resultado de éstas y de la derrota de D. Rafael Rayón . . . diciembre 23 de 1813," *ibid.*, 369.

[70] Spain, Cortes, *Instrucción para los ayuntamientos constitucionales, juntas provinciales, y gefes políticos superiores . . . 23 de junio de 1813*, Chap. I, Art. 23.

[71] *Diario de México*, December 23, 28, 1813.

[72] "El Intendente de Oaxaca remitió a V. E. los documentos que acreditan . . . la Junta Popular para votación de Electores de Ayuntamiento Constitucional, y la votación para instalación deste cuerpo," Antequera, June 1, 1814, AGN, Hist., 403, fol. 302.

ence and from the military activities of the revolution. After receiving orders to proceed with the election, the subdelegate called the citizens of the village together on January 30, 1814, to choose the electoral junta. Following the spirit and letter of the Constitution as closely as he could, he ordered all citizens, whether Indian, mestizo, or white, whether rich or poor, to vote in this first election. Each citizen brought two sheets of paper to the plaza, on one of which was written his choice for the secretary of the citizen's junta. After the secretary had been chosen, each citizen then brought the secretary his second sheet of paper containing the names of seventeen electors. The secretary, the subdelegate, and the village curate acted as election judges. No inspectors were chosen from among the citizens, an indication that the instruction had not yet reached the area. The curate received the largest number of votes for the position of elector. If not proof of the curate's influence on the first step of the election, it is at least an indication of his importance in the community, and it may be assumed that he exercised his prestige in the selection of the new municipal council. Only one of the seventeen electors had been on the council in previous years, and only four were elected to the new one.[73] If the election had been dominated by any one element, it seems likely that this would have resulted in its controlling the junta and choosing the councilmen largely from among its group. As a whole, the Parral election was a good first step in the direction of popular government on the municipal level.

Local clerics were the greatest single influence in the elections for Mexico's first constitutional *ayuntamientos*. Virtually every account reveals clergy in a guiding role. The importance of the clergy in the Mexico City, Querétaro, Antequera, and Parral elections has been noted. Other examples are not difficult to find: in San Miguel el Grande at least five of the seventeen members of the electoral junta were priests; in the Western Interior Provinces clerical influence was so strong that Commander General Bernardo Bonavía characterized the elections as being more ecclesiastical than popular.[74] This influ-

[73] Proclamation of Gregorio de San Martín to the Citizens of Parral, January 23, 1814, Parral Archives, Año 1812, G-3; Record of the selection of the electoral junta, January 30, 1813, *ibid.*; Record of the election of the Constitutional Ayuntamiento, February 2, 1814, *ibid.*
[74] "Testimonio liberal de las diligencias . . . en San Miguel el Grande," AGN, Hist., 403; Bonavía to Secretaría de Estado y del Despacho, Durango, March 16, 1814, AGI, Leg. 297, no. 4, fol. 1 (typescript copy in the possession of Nettie Lee Benson, Austin, Texas).

ence is understandable; the clergy were often the only educated persons in a parish and they had access to church records testifying to citizenship qualifications. Practically speaking, their assistance in elections could hardly be dispensed with, particularly in the smaller villages.

The most frequently violated constitutional provision was that prohibiting members of previous *ayuntamientos* from continuing on the new councils. Large settlements such as Mexico City, Campeche, and Veracruz, having a sufficiency of both educated men and liberals anxious to follow the Constitution, were not guilty of this. But in such smaller towns as Parral, Antequera, San Miguel, and Monterrey, old aldermen appeared on new *ayuntamientos*, which suggests that such areas suffered from a shortage of persons qualified for the posts.[75] In Monterrey, ten members of the first popularly elected council had served on previous *ayuntamientos*, most frequently as honorary aldermen. There the philosophy of local government changed, but not the personnel.[76]

On May 4, 1814, having reached Valencia on his return from captivity in France, Ferdinand VII issued a royal decree abolishing the Cortes and all legislation fathered by it, including the Constitution of 1812, but he specified that *ayuntamientos* were to continue as they were then constituted. This decree was received by Calleja on August 10, 1814, and on August 17 he ordered the Constitution suppressed. Ferdinand affirmed his earlier inclination to retain popular local government by issuing a decree on May 24 ordering that municipal elections be held in December. To avoid confusion, the parish elections in cities with more than one parish were to be spread out over several days. In this same decree, however, the king ordered that no more new *ayuntamientos* were to be established and that those formed without government approval in places not previously having councils were to be abolished. Acting under this decree, the intendant of Mexico ordered parish elections in the city for the early part of

[75] Álvarez, *Anales históricos*, I, 9–35; Cavazos Garza, *El muy ilustre ayuntamiento*, 70–80; Record of the election of the Constitutional Ayuntamiento, February 2, 1814, Archivo del Parral, Año 1812, G-3; "El Intendente de Oaxaca remitió a V. E. los documentos que accreditan . . . la Junta Popular para votación de Electores de Ayuntamiento Constitucional, y la votación para instalación deste cuerpo," Antequera, June 1, 1814, AGN, Hist., 403; "Testimonio liberal de las diligencias . . . en San Miguel," *ibid.*

[76] Cavazos Garza, *El muy ilustre ayuntamiento*, pp. 70–80.

December.[77] Before the elections could be held, a royal decree abolishing all constitutional *ayuntamientos* arrived and was published in Mexico City on November 8. Municipal councils which had existed previous to the Constitution were to be restored to their 1808 condition, and whenever possible the same men holding office in that year were to be reseated. All councils not existing prior to the Constitution were abolished completely.[78]

There is evidence only in Coahuila of resistance to the abolishment of popular councils.[79] Otherwise, royal officials dominated the abrogation quite as thoroughly as they had the implementation of the Constitution. Owing to the revolutionary condition of the country, the recalcitrance of royal officials, and, despite liberal enthusiasm in some urban centers, the general apathy of the people, the experiment had scarcely begun before it was cut short. Popular *ayuntamientos* in most places were too short lived to prove whether or not they could be responsible agents of municipal government, but removing the Constitution could not remove the fact that dwellers in nearly every corner of the colony had received a taste of popular local government. The situation was to be quite different when the Constitution was restored five years later.

During the next five years the revolution in New Spain was virtually extinguished, while Ferdinand VII again ruled Spain with absolute power. At the beginning of 1820, however, rebellious troops bound for America declared for the Constitution of 1812. The rebellion quickly reached such proportions that on March 9 Ferdinand was forced to swear allegiance to the Constitution of 1812 and to call the Cortes back into session.

The news reached Mexico late in April, but lack of official orders prevented anything's being done immediately. Although the governor of Yucatán published the Constitution in his province on the first of May, he was forced to rescind the order due to conservative

[77] *Gaceta del gobierno de México,* August 11, 13, 14, 15, 16, 18; September 29; October 15, 1814.

[78] *Ibid.,* November 8, 1814. As this decree would have prevented their being held, Bancroft (*History of Mexico,* IV, 599) appears to be in error when he mentions the tumult of the December, 1814, elections.

[79] "El Gobierno Intendente de Nueva Viscaya . . . haberse descubierto una conspiración en Chihuahua," Durango, November 17, 1814, AGN, Provincias Internas, 186.

protests. In the meantime the liberals of Campeche had persuaded the governor's lieutenant to reinstate the popular *ayuntamiento* of 1814. This caused a chain reaction. As the events in Campeche became known, Yucatán's governor was forced to accede to liberal demands and allow the election of a liberal council in Mérida on June 13.[80] Next the merchants of Veracruz learned of the Yucatán happenings and compelled their governor to publish the Constitution and call elections for a new *ayuntamiento*. As the news spread inland, other villages began to establish popular councils.[81] All this was done without the permission of the viceroy. The swift march of events put such pressure on Viceroy Juan Ruíz de Apodaca that on May 31 he found himself obliged to publish the Constitution in Mexico City, although he still had received no official confirmation from Spain. On June 8 he published the royal decree of March 9 ordering immediate municipal elections, and nine days later Mexico City chose her third popular city council.[82]

The speed with which constitutional *ayuntamientos* were re-established in 1820 presented a startling contrast to the 1812–1814 period. During the spring and summer the villages and towns of Mexico hastened to reclaim the privileges granted them by the Constitution.[83] Where it had taken two years to implant elected councils throughout the country during the earlier period, in 1820 the most remote regions elected *ayuntamientos* within three months. Texas, at the extreme north of the colony, received orders to hold its elections in mid-July. Overlooking the fact that the Constitution had not yet been published, the citizens of Béjar quickly held municipal elections, taking care to act in full accord with constitutional provisions. They did not publish the Constitution until September 8. La Bahía del Espíritu Santo established a municipal council in late August.[84]

[80] *El Hispano-Americano Constitutional, periódico filosófico de Mérida de Yucatán,* June 18–22, 1820; Alvarez, *Anales históricos,* 14–15.

[81] *Actas* of the Veracruz Ayuntamiento, May 27–29, 1820, in Alba, *La Constitución de 1812,* II, 172–173; Ayuntamiento of Jalapa to the Viceroy, *ibid.,* 175.

[82] "Bando del Virrey Apodaca en que por haber recibido noticias de que Fernando VII había jurado la Constitución, participa que la jurará," May 31, 1820, *ibid.,* 176–177; *Gaceta del gobierno de México,* June 8, June 9, 1820.

[83] See *Gaceta del gobierno de México,* June 20–September 9, 1820, for announcements of popular *ayuntamientos* established in widely scattered villages.

[84] "Acta de la junta electoral celebrada el día de hoy," Béjar, July 25, 1820, University of Texas Library, Bexar Archives; *Actas* of the Béjar Ayuntamiento, August 31, 1820, *ibid.;* José Encarnación Vásquez to Colonel Don Antonio Martínez, Bahía del Espíritu Santo, September 1, 1820, *ibid.*

Distant Santa Fé, in Nuevo México, held parish elections on August 6.[85]

In contrast to 1812, royal officials made no attempt to block implementation of the Constitution once the viceroy had decided to proceed. The most serious impediment was a shortage of copies of the Constitution and election instructions, as most of them had been destroyed by enthusiastic conservatives in 1814. Especially in the northern provinces, officials complained that elections could not be held in all places until more copies could be obtained.[86] The printing shops of Mexico City turned this need to profit by selling reprints of the Constitution and other official documents.[87] That this practice was allowed in 1820, although strictly forbidden in 1812, is indicative of the changed mood in the colony. Such difficulties were eased in September when the Cortes ruled that as the Constitution had been published throughout New Spain in the earlier period, it was not now necessary for communities to swear allegiance to it before proceeding with elections.[88]

In December, Mexican municipalities held new elections to choose councilmen for 1821.[89] Considering that for the majority of villages this was their third municipal election under the Constitution, and for many their fourth, it is not surprising that there is no evidence of inordinate disorder or confusion. Having gained in experience in the holding of popular elections, and being untroubled by hostile officials and revolutionary conditions, the Mexicans seemed to be fast adapting to a democratic form of local government.

As the beneficiaries of the Constitution were congratulating themselves on its return and growing more experienced in its usage, a new threat developed. Early in January, 1821, Agustín de Iturbide, reflecting the feelings of some Spanish military men and other conservatives who looked with apprehension toward being ruled under the liberal Constitution and Cortes, joined with Vicente Guerrero to

[85] Twitchell, *Spanish Archives*, pp. 630–636.
[86] Governor of Nuevo Santander to Viceroy, San Carlos, August 19, 1820, AGN, Hist., 404; Diego García Conde to Viceroy, Durango, August 9, 1820, *ibid.*; Joaquín de Arredondo to Viceroy, Monterrey, July 28, 1820, *ibid.*
[87] *Gaceta del gobierno de México,* July 29, 1820.
[88] "Gobernación de la Península al Sr. Gefe Político de la provincia de México," Madrid, September 10, 1820, AGN, Hist., 404.
[89] See lists in *Gaceta del gobierno de México,* December 14, 1820, to March 3, 1821; *Actas* of Béjar Ayuntamiento, December 17, 24, 1820, University of Texas Library, Bexar Archives.

give new life to the almost dead revolution. Fearful that Iturbide would deprive them of the constitutional rights to which they were becoming accustomed, town after town pledged aid to the viceroy against the rebel.[90] Iturbide did much to quiet these fears and gain greater popular support when, following his victory at Querétaro on June 28, he announced that all parts of the Constitution not injurious to the independence of Mexico should remain in force until a new organic code was formed.[91] Following Iturbide's sweep to power and the declaration of Mexican independence on September 28, the provisional governing junta reaffirmed the Spanish Constitution as its guide until a Mexican code could be created.[92] On November 18 the Regency called for municipal elections under the provisions of the Constitution of 1812 and the decree of May 23, 1812, as these procedures were now familiar to the citizens.[93] Accordingly, Mexican towns held their elections in December as had been their custom and reported the results to the Regency.[94] A surviving account of the election in Guadalajara indicates that although many of the same issues which had caused so much uproar in 1812 were present, they now were handled in a routine manner. The Constitution and its supporting decrees were followed carefully. As in the 1812 Mexico City election, many citizens brought printed lists of candidates distributed by their partisans, but where this practice had elicited charges of fraud in the earlier period, in 1821 it was recognized as standard practice. The election judges turned away some unqualified voters, but the election as a whole was smooth and orderly.[95]

To follow the course of the *ayuntamiento* further into the history of independent Mexico would be to exceed the scope of this essay. Other than to increase the number of municipal magistrates, the Re-

[90] For example, see the proclamation of the Constitutional Ayuntamiento of Querétaro to its citizens, March 5, 1821, in *Gaceta del gobierno de México,* March 10, 1821; Ayuntamiento of San Miguel el Grande to Viceroy, March 24, 1821, *ibid.,* April 5, 1821; Ayuntamiento of Aguascalientes to Viceroy, March 17, 1821, *ibid.,* March 29, 1821; Ayuntamiento of Mexico City to Viceroy, March 6, 1821, *ibid.,* March 13, 1821.

[91] William Spence Robertson, *Iturbide of Mexico,* p. 96.

[92] *Ibid.,* p. 134.

[93] "La Regencia Gobernadora Interina del imperio a todos sus habitantes," *Gaceta imperial de México,* November 18, 1821, November 27, 1821.

[94] *Ibid.,* December 25, 1821; January 1, 3, 7, 1822.

[95] *Gaceta del gobierno de Guadalajara,* December 12, 22, 26, 1821.

gency did not change the Cortes regulations for municipalities.[96] The Mexican Constitution of 1824 contained no mention whatsoever of municipal councils, allowing the institution as formed by the Cortes to continue into the Republic, where the principle of popularly elected *ayuntamientos* was incorporated into the constitutions of most of the Mexican states.[97]

Just prior to the wars for independence, the Mexican municipality was far removed from the popular institution of Spanish tradition. Self-perpetuating oligarchies with little actual power dominated the councils, leaving the governing to royal officials. Inured to the system, the citizens of Mexico showed little desire to change it, even when the sudden appearance in 1808 of popular government in Spain allowed them to voice their needs. Although the American deputies to the Cortes of Cádiz did not number municipal reform among their most urgent demands, some far-sighted Mexican deputies, led by Miguel Ramos Arizpe, realized that popular, responsible, local government could be a great spur to the internal development of the colony. Failing to achieve local political and economic autonomy, the liberals in the Cortes nevertheless were able to incorporate into the Constitution and subsequent legislation the principle of popularly elected, nonperpetual *ayuntamientos*. The installation of these councils in Mexico from 1812 to 1814 was a slow process, due to the chaos of the revolution and obstruction by most royal officials. Although the ideas of the Constitution were widely current, with few exceptions Mexican towns were content to wait for royal officials to implement them and were as yet unexcited about the unfamiliar, abstract ideas. Elections were generally characterized by order, strict government control, and strong clerical influence. When the popular councils were abolished in 1814 there was little resistance. The experience had aroused a taste for popular government, however, and when the Constitution was re-established in 1820, Mexican cities, towns, and villages rushed to elect new *ayuntamientos*. By the time Agustín de Iturbide declared his Plan of Iguala in 1821, there were few villages which had not established municipal councils and ex-

---

[96] "Bando sobre se duplique el número de alcaldes constitucionales," *ibid.*, February 16, 1822; *Gaceta imperial de México*, February 12, 1822.

[97] Mexico, Constitution, *Constitución federal de los Estados Unidos Mexicanos, sancionada por el congreso general constituyente el 4 de octubre de 1824*; Joaquín de la Llave Hill, *El municipio en la historia y en nuestra constitución*, pp. 64–69.

perienced several elections. Just becoming accustomed to the institution, they voiced fear that Iturbide would abolish it. Recognizing this fear, Iturbide allowed popular *ayuntamientos* to continue through his regime, during which they became even more firmly established. The traditional Spanish popular *ayuntamientos*, brought back to life by the Cortes, became the basis for local government in the Mexican Republic.

It should be re-emphasized that this study presents only the large outline of the great changes introduced by the Spanish Cortes into the political structure of the Mexican municipality. More detailed examinations into the political, economic, and social activities of the *ayuntamientos* would necessitate painstaking research in the numerous municipal archives of Mexico. Scholars willing to undertake such investigations could shed much new light on both the Mexican municipality and the era of the war for Mexican independence.

4. Freedom of the Press in New Spain, 1810–1820

Clarice Neal

Freedom of the press was one of the first matters to be considered by the Spanish Cortes after it convened on September 24, 1810. Three days later a committee was appointed to study the question and recommend action. Only seven of the delegates from New Spain were present and their contribution to the passage of the ninth decree—the law which granted freedom of the press—was negligible. Dated November 10, 1810, its first article, as passed, declared that subject only to the restrictions and responsibilities set forth in the decree, any corporate body or private individual in whatever condition or state was free to write, print, and publish political opinions without necessity of license, revision, or approval prior to publication.[1]

This law abolished the judges of the press, who formerly were charged with censoring all political writing prior to publication, and made writers of libelous, calumnious, and subversive matter personally responsible and punishable for abuse of the new freedom. All writings on religious matters, however, remained subject to censorship of the bishops before publication. To supervise the free press, the Cortes provided for the establishment of a supreme censorship board consisting of nine members, three of whom were to be ecclesiastics. That body was to reside in the main seat of the Spanish government, and a similar board, with five members, including two ecclesiastics, was to be established in each provincial capital. These boards were to examine works denounced by the executive power or justices, decide

[1] Spain. Laws and Statutes, 1810–1822, *Colección de los decretos y órdenes que han expedido las Córtes generales y extraordinarias desde su instalación de 24 de setiembre de 1810 hasta igual fecha de 1811* (hereinafter cited as *Decretos*).

whether they were objectionable and, if so, have the offensive publications collected. A writer was to be given a copy of the objections so that he might defend his publication before the provincial board. If the provincial board rejected his defense, he could make a second and final appeal to the supreme censorship board in Spain.

The supreme censorship board submitted the names of its nominees for the provincial censorship board of Mexico City to the Cortes which, on December 12, 1810, approved the following: Archdeacon José Mariano Beristáin y Souza, José María Fagoaga (a native of Spain believed to be in favor of Mexican independence), Canon Pedro José Fonte (who soon afterwards was named archbishop-elect of Mexico), Agustín Pomposo Fernández de San Salvador (royalist writer who did not favor independence), and Guillermo Aguirre (regent of the Audiencia, who died before taking office).[2] Nominations for a provincial censorship board to be located in Guadalajara were also approved by the Cortes on January 22, 1811, with a membership of José María González Villaseñor, Juan José Cordón of the consulate, Eugenio Moreno Tejada, and Francisco Velasco de la Vara. At the same time the Cortes requested that another name be submitted in place of Juan Fernández de Munilla, who had been nominated but had subsequently died.[3]

Although the Law of Freedom of the Press became effective in Spain in November, 1810, it was not immediately promulgated in New Spain by Viceroy Francisco Xavier Venegas, who feared that such freedom would be used to promote the revolution which had begun on September 16, 1810. The death of Aguirre and the failure of the Cortes to name a successor also provided an excuse for delaying the installation of the Mexico City board. Furthermore, Venegas was advised by his attorneys to ask the views of the bishops and political chiefs of the provinces on a free press in Mexico. The bishops of Puebla, Valladolid, Guadalajara, Mérida (Yucatán), Monterrey, and Mexico City, and the intendants of the provinces of México, Oaxaca, San Luis Potosí, Guanajuato, Mérida, and Zacatecas replied that the free press would be an easy and certain means of fomenting the revolution, gaining for it many new adherents, with resulting great

---

[2] Spain, Cortes, 1810–1813. *Diario de las discusiones y actas de las Córtes,* (hereinafter cited as *Diario de las Cortes*), I, 135; Lucas Alamán, *Historia de Méjico,* III, 265.

[3] Alamán, *Historia de Méjico,* III, 49.

damage to the country. According to their collective advice, only disorder and anarchy would ensue.[4]

In contrast, the archbishop-elect of Mexico and the intendants of Guadalajara and Valladolid (Michoacán) were in favor of freedom of the press. The first two feared that if it were not granted, the rebels would have been given another argument for the cause of the revolution. All three argued further that if abuses occurred the censorship board could punish the delinquents. None of them apparently realized that the law permitted all political opinions to be published, and that even if a publication was found objectionable, no authority could proceed against a writer until a final verdict came from the supreme censorship board, resident at that time in Cádiz. Under the provisions of the decree, any writer could enjoy a considerable length of time during which his writings would be in circulation even though they might later be declared illegal and ordered collected.[5]

The delaying tactics of Viceroy Venegas in not executing the law were noted by the delegates from New Spain, who began to press the Cortes to compel its promulgation. The most outspoken opponent to the viceregal inaction was Deputy Miguel Ramos Arizpe, representing the provinces of Coahuila, Nuevo León, Tamaulipas, and Texas. On June 11, 1811, he forcefully called the attention of the Cortes to the fact that the Law of Freedom of the Press had not been implemented in New Spain and demanded its immediate promulgation.[6]

Six months later, on January 16, 1812, he renewed his demands. He reminded the Cortes that the law had not been implemented in New Spain, and insisted that the people of Mexico be allowed to enjoy this

[4] "Representación de los oidores de México a las Cortes de España contra la Constitución de 1812," in Carlos María de Bustamante, *Cuadro histórico de la revolución mexicana iniciada el 1 septiembre de 1810 por el C. Miguel Hidalgo y Costilla, cura del pueblo de Dolores en el obispado de Michoacán*, II, 362–363; Alamán, *Historia de Méjico*, III, 276.

[5] Bustamante, *Cuadro histórico*, II, 364. The Cortes on March 10, 1811, ordered that two copies of each imprint published in the Spanish dominions be forwarded to it—one for its archives and another for its library. The Regency issued the order on March 27, 1811, and so informed the Cortes on April 1, 1811. Spain, Cortes, 1810–1813, *Diario de las Córtes*, IV, 166, 434. This order had nothing to do with censorship, as has sometimes been believed when referring to the list of copies of imprints sent to Spain by the viceroy of Mexico in compliance with the order. Cf. Jefferson Rea Spell, *The Life and Works of José Joaquín Fernández de Lizardi*, p. 15, and "Fernandez de Lizardi: A Bibliography," *HAHR*, VII (November, 1927), 491.

[6] Spain, Cortes, 1810–1813, *Diario de las Córtes*, VI, 279.

privilege as a counterbalance to the abuses of public officials. He proposed that the Regency send the Law of November 10 to Venegas for a second time, with instructions that, if it had not already been promulgated, it be published immediately. To support his argument, he stated that the Law was already in effect in all of Spain, South America, Guatemala, and Cuba, but not yet in Mexico. Freedom of the press, he continued, was a means of educating the people and providing a channel of communication to the government. Despite his plea, the Cortes hesitated and, instead of ordering Venegas to publish the law, compromised by asking the Regency to indicate if the law had been put into effect in New Spain.[7]

The Regency informed the Cortes on February 1, 1812, of a letter from Venegas, dated March 21, 1811, in which he offered to comply with the law, but did not indicate that he had done so. Ramos Arizpe urged again that the Viceroy be instructed, if he had not already done so, to execute the law immediately.

Mariano Mendiola of Querétaro supported Ramos Arizpe with the statement that all publications sent by the Viceroy to the Cortes bore a note "with permission," an indication of the absence of a free press. Jose María Gutiérrez de Terán from New Spain also complained that the Regency had been in receipt of the Viceroy's letter for over six or seven months and reminded the Cortes of the statute which deprived an official of his office if he failed to execute a law or decree of the Cortes within three days after receipt. He pleaded on behalf of the American deputies for justice, equality, and impartiality and for further strengthening of ties between the two hemispheres. He stated further that the main cause of the revolution in Mexico had been the lack of a general understanding which could only be obtained by a free press, and which even at this late date, if accomplished, would help bring about an end to the rebellion.

Ramos Arizpe concluded the day's discussion by denouncing as tyrannical the action of Venegas in not publishing the law. He noted that the people of Spain with a free press had not been fooled by Napoleon's agents who dispensed false information, whereas, the people of Mexico, lacking a free press, had been led to believe that the war in Spain was lost and that Mexico would suffer Spain's fate. Only through a free press could the Mexican people know what was being done for them by the Cortes, Ramos Arizpe said. By not grant-

[7] *Ibid.*, XI, 282.

ing freedom of the press to Mexico, the Cortes would be contributing to its enslavement.

Following this discussion the Cortes resolved that the Viceroy be instructed to execute the Law of Freedom of the Press immediately. This was to be done even if there were only four members of the provincial censorship board available. At the same time the Cortes instructed the Supreme Censorship Board to nominate another candidate to replace the deceased Guillermo Aguirre.[8]

The Supreme Censorship Board complied promptly by nominating Pedro de la Puente as the fifth member to the Mexico City board. The Cortes at first withheld its approval, on the basis that the law provided that no magistrate could be a member of the board, and asked that a new name be submitted.[9] However his nomination was finally approved by the Cortes on February 5, 1812. Furthermore, the action of the Cortes was carried out by the Regency, which on February 6 ordered Venegas to proclaim the Freedom of the Press Law in New Spain without delay.[10]

Pending observance of the Cortes' order to the Viceroy, Ramos Arizpe set about to get the Press Law revised. Never completely satisfied with the decree, since he considered it written in haste, on February 13, 1812, he began a campaign for its revision. First, he stated that although Article 4 prescribed punishment for authors of libelous, calumnious, or licentious material, the works labeled "subversive to the fundamental laws" were not sufficiently defined and were therefore subject to the arbitrary decisions of the censors. This situation eventually would have the effect of stifling freedom of the press, he said, for legitimate criticism under the existing law could be declared subversive if officials affected were corrupt, and soon the nation would again be led like the blind by them. Furthermore, Ramos Arizpe declared, a perpetual board of nine or five members, as indicated in Article 13, might serve only to restrict rather than stimulate opinions. He therefore proposed: 1) that "the fundamental laws of the monarchy" mentioned in Article 4 be specifically defined as the laws declaring the nation's sovereignty, the equality of rights, a moderate monarchy, the division of powers, and the unity of the Catholic Church; 2) that Article 13, granting the Supreme Censorship Board

---

[8] *Ibid.*, XI, 439–442.
[9] *Ibid.*, XI, 458.
[10] Alamán, *Historia de Méjico*, III, 268.

the right to nominate provincial board members, be revised to provide that the electors of the provincial deputation, at the time of selecting the deputation, be empowered also to appoint the members of the provincial censorship board; 3) that in the Americas, final jurisdiction be granted to the provincial censorship boards, with only notification of actions taken sent to the supreme board; and 4) that the Cortes appoint a special committee to propose further changes for legal protection of the freedom to think and print.[11]

Another deputy from Mexico City, José María Guridi y Alcocer, also suggested reforms. He proposed on March 15, 1812, that censors be nominated in the same manner as deputies and that their appointments be renewable from time to time, that they be qualified through education and profession and not be employed in any other government office. Since prolongation of time between hearings was injurious to authors, a specific time limit should be designated, he said. He urged the adoption of the system used by the judiciary in appealing cases to higher courts and recommended that since the justices who brought cases before the censorship boards had very little time to read all the printed publications, they should be replaced by officials responsible solely for this examination. He, like Ramos Arizpe, wanted abuses of freedom of the press more clearly defined and the corresponding punishment outlined.[12]

Since the Constitution was nearing completion, the Cortes took no action on the proposals by Ramos Arizpe and Guridi y Alcocer. Proclaimed officially in Spain on March 19, 1812, its Article 371 stated that all Spaniards under the restriction and responsibility set forth by the laws were free to write, print, and publish their political ideas without the necessity of licenses, revisions, or approval prior to publication.[13]

The Regency's order of February 6 to put the Freedom of the Press Law into effect in New Spain was received by the Viceroy along with the news of the completed Constitution. With the official promulgation of the Constitution in Mexico on September 30, 1812, Venegas could no longer find excuses to delay execution of the Free Press Law. The injection of this new liberty into Mexico was a momentous in-

---

[11] *Ibid.*, XII, 20–23. This speech is also found in *México en las Cortes de Cádiz: Documentos*, pp. 207–208.

[12] Alamán, *Historia de Méjico*, XII, 271–273.

[13] Spain, Constitution, *Constitución política de la monarquía española promulgada en Cádiz el 19 de marzo de 1812*, p. 46.

novation when contrasted with conditions previously prevailing in the colony. In America, as in Spain, the press had been subject to inspection by the civil and ecclesiastic authorities and nothing could be published without prior licenses from both. The examination searched for anything contrary to the laws, critical of the royal family, or contrary to the dogma of the Catholic Church. An additional restriction was that no book about the Indies could be published without prior approval of the Council of the Indies. Nor could books which dealt with the Indies be sent to the Americas, whether printed in Spain or in foreign countries, without the same permission of this Council. To see that no books dealing in profane subjects or works of imagination were taken to the New World, all books had to be registered before leaving Spain, and upon arrival were subject to a visit on the ships (*visita de navios*)[14] by the Inquisition authorities to ensure that prohibited volumes were not unloaded at the ports.

In contrast with these restrictions, the Law of Freedom of the Press seemed to grant unlimited freedom. The only defense against abuses of the law was the Mexico City provincial censorship board, whose five members were duly sworn into office on October 5.

The writers who tried out the new freedom of the press could hardly believe it. Carlos María de Bustamante, one of the first journalists to take advantage of the situation, began *El Juguetillo* by asking "¿Conqué podemos hablar?" ("So now we can speak?"). Although only six numbers of this serial were issued at this time, it was widely parodied and imitated by other publications, such as *El Juguetón* and *Juguetes contra el Juguetillo*.[15]

Another popular publication was *El Pensador mejicano*, which furnished its author, José Joaquín Fernández de Lizardi, with a pseudonym. During the free press period, nine issues, each on a different topic, were circulated. The first dealt with freedom of the press; in it Fernández de Lizardi echoed the arguments which had appeared

[14] See Henry Charles Lea, *Chapters from the Religious History of Spain Connected with the Inquisition*, pp. 20–50. However, there is evidence that through special readers' licenses, many "learned and discreet men" were given permission to read and retain books forbidden for general circulation; see José Torre Revello, *El libro, la imprenta y el periodismo en América durante la dominación española*, p. 107.

[15] *El Juguetón* No. 1 was announced in both the *Diario de México* and the *Gazeta de México* on November 17, 1812; No. 2 was announced only in the *Diario*, on November 28. The *Gazeta* entitled it, "El Juguetón papel flamante, que se presenta con visos de periódico. No. 1 escríbelo su autor: imprímelo el impresor, y lo publican los muchachos."

earlier in the reprint *El voto de la nación española.*[16] He expressed
pleasure in the new freedom but asked that it not bring blasphemy
against religion or libel against the government. In the ninth issue,
dated December 3, Fernández de Lizardi pretended to felicitate
Viceroy Venegas on his birthday by printing:

> But the forcefulness of truth!
> Today your Excellency will see yourself
> by means of my pen, a miserable mortal,
> a man like all and an atom comtemptible
> in the sight of the Almighty. Today your
> Excellency will see yourself as a man who,
> by reason of being one, is subject to
> deceit, to prejudice and to passions . . .[17]

This birthday greeting was taken by the Viceroy as an insult. He
was already aggravated because only creoles had been named parish
electors on November 29 in the first step taken toward the naming of
the municipal council for Mexico City, and he foresaw the likelihood
that that body would be composed of sympathizers with the American cause. Furthermore, on the evening of November 29, after the
parish election, people had run through the streets yelling, "Viva the
authors of *El Juguetillo* and *El Pensador mejicano,* because they tell
the unvarnished truth."[18]

Despite its auspicious beginning, freedom of the press in New
Spain lasted exactly two months. Announcements in the *Diario de
México* and *Gazeta de México* of the new publications appearing
during this time total only thirty-five new imprints; however, the list
is incomplete, as it omits, for example, *El Pensador mejicano.* The
Diario, as soon as restrictions were lifted, at once printed the entire
Law of Freedom of the Press, up to that time unpublished in Mexico.
Also, with no comment, the same newspaper reproduced in Spanish,

---

[16] *El Voto de la nación española,* first published in Seville in 1809, was republished in Mexico in 1810 by Manuel Antonio Valdés. See Thomas Fonso Walker,
"Pre-Revolutionary Pamphleteering in Mexico, 1808–1810" (unpublished Ph.D.
dissertation, University of Texas, 1951), pp. 232–236.

[17] José Joaquín Fernández de Lizardi, "Al excelentísimo Señor Francisco Xavier
Venegas, Virey, governador y capitán general de este N.E. en el día 3 de di-
ciembre de 1812. El Pensador Mexicano dedica afectuoso el siguiente periódico,"
El Pensador mejicano, No. 9.

[18] "Declaración de D. Manuel Palacio Lanzagorta sobre los movimientos popu-
lares de los días 29 y 30 de noviembre de 1812," Rafael de Alba, ed., *La Constitución de 1812 en la Nueva España,* II, 216–217.

between October 23 and November 7, the Constitution of the United States, including the Bill of Rights.[19] The *Diario* of November 14, 1812, contained the "Manifiesto del govierno de Buenos Aires," dated December 11, 1811, issued by the exulting revolutionary Argentine triumvirate.

The reaction of the Viceroy to these events was to consult with the Audiencia.[20] Backed by a plurality of sixteen out of seventeen votes, Venegas on December 5, suspended all laws relating to freedom of the press. Despite Article 371 of the Constitution, which prohibited prior censorship, the Viceroy ordered the provincial censorship board to examine henceforth every piece of writing intended for publication. In addition, Venegas reserved to himself the right to restore liberty of the press when the revolution had ceased.[21]

The periodicals of Mexico City to be precensored included the *Gazeta del gobierno de México*, subject to review by José María Fagoaga, and the *Amigo de la patria*, a pro-Spanish paper backed by Archdeacon Beristáin, which was assigned to both Pedro Fonte and Agustín Pomposo Fernández de San Salvador. The *Diario de México* reported to its readers that it had suspended publication from December 4 to 10 because neither Beristáin nor Ambrosio Saguarzuieta of the Audiencia would notify the editors who was to review the publication for illicit material. Only on December 8 was Pedro de la Puente assigned to the *Diario*. He passed it on the ninth and it reappeared the next day.[22]

Fearing arrest, Carlos María de Bustamante fled Mexico City and joined the rebels, where he used his pen and editorial ability in their cause. Fernández de Lizardi was jailed. In prison he wrote *El Pensador mejicano*, No. 10 (December 21, 1812) which was annotated "Passed for printing, Beristáin." In his own defense Fernández de Lizardi wrote that there had been other writers who during the free-press period had been much more outspoken against viceregal policies. He named Bustamante, Dr. Peredo, and Joseph Julio García de Torres, all of whom had vigorously opposed in writing an edict issued

[19] Nettie Lee Benson, "Washington, Symbol of the United States in Mexico, 1800–1823," *Library Chronicle of The University of Texas*, II, No. 4.

[20] Alamán, *Historia de Méjico*, III, 276. Alamán points out that this was an illegal move, since the Audiencia under the Constitution became a purely judicial body.

[21] "Bando publicado el 5 del corriente," *Gazeta del gobierno de México*, December 8, 1812, XXVI, 1292–1293.

[22] *Diario de México*, XVII, 659–661.

by Venegas on June 25 which declared that the rebel clergy, as well
as editors of gazettes and publishers of incendiary papers, would be
tried by a military court and shot.[23]
    The Mexican insurgents reacted to the suspension of the free press
through their organ the *Correo americano del sur,* which urged the
people to arm themselves. It reasoned that the laws that had just been
sworn to were now violated, particularly the laws which pretended to
pacify America, for if the Constitution were observed, it would calm
the greater part of the revolt. Reflecting on the viceregal action in
suspending the constitutional guarantees, José María Morelos wrote
Ignacio Rayón in January of 1813: "We see the legality of their conduct: they called elections in Mexico to lay their hands on the electors; they granted permission to print in order to apprehend the
authors."[24]
    Félix Calleja replaced Venegas as viceroy of New Spain on March
4, 1813, and, with the exception of Article 371, began implementing
the Constitution. To the citizens of Mexico he explained that the well-
being of the nation obliged him to keep the freedom of the press suspended because its promulgation would contribute to the continuance
of the revolution.[25]
    News of the suspension of the short-lived freedom of the press in
New Spain was related to the Cortes on May 17, 1813, by the Secretary of Ecclesiastical Affairs and Justice. This official had been notified by the Regency of a communication from an attorney of the
Audiencia of Mexico, who reported that the viceroy had suspended
freedom of the press. Ramos Arizpe, angered by the news, demanded
that the Regency take appropriate action "to show the world, and
especially the Spaniards that its zeal and energy for the compliance
of the Constitution and laws was impartial and not confined to the
area within the walls of Cádiz."[26] The Regency had taken firm measures on matters of much less importance, he continued, and he

    [23] José Joaquín Fernández de Lizardi in a letter to Viceroy Venegas, dated
January 17, 1813, in *Documentos históricos mexicanos,* ed. Genaro García, VI,
470.
    [24] Alamán, *Historia de Méjico,* III, 297.
    [25] "Fragmento del manifiesto de Virrey Calleja a los inhabitantes de Nueva
España, publicada en 22 de junio de 1814," in Alba, *La Constitución de 1812,* II,
246–247.
    [26] Spain, Cortes, 1810–1813. *Diario de las sesiones de las Cortes generales y
extraordinarias* (hereinafter cited as *Diario de las sesiones de Cortes*), VII, 5316–
5318.

awaited a report informing the Cortes what actions had been taken regarding this serious violation.

After more than six weeks of regential inactivity following his outburst, Ramos Arizpe, on July 11, 1813, again asked for a report on the suspension of the law. He pointed out that representatives from America had been patient in the hope that the Regency would take some action but said it was now mandatory that a report be made to the Cortes. His demand that such a regential report be submitted immediately was signed by twenty-eight other deputies, eight of whom were from Mexico: José María Couto, Andrés Sabariego, José Miguel Gordoa, Joaquín Maniau, José Cayetano de Foncerrada, Mariano Mendiola, Octavio Obregón, and Francisco Fernández Munilla. Put to a vote, the proposal was approved by the Cortes.[27]

The Secretary of Ecclesiastical Affairs and Justice replied to the Cortes on July 24, 1813, that the Regency, through the Secretary of War, had been notified by the Viceroy of New Spain in a letter dated December 14, 1812, of the reasons for the suspension of freedom of the press in Mexico. These reasons were not quoted. On the same date an attorney of the Mexican Audiencia, Juan Ramón Ores, had written the Regency that he had not supported the suspension of the law but instead had proposed that the viceroy establish in Mexico a supreme censorship board like that resident in Cádiz. Accompanying Ores' communication was a copy of the decree suspending freedom of the press, along with subsequent orders by the viceroy directing the provincial board to review all materials prior to publication.

The Regency, having learned from the two communications that one of the most essential articles of the Constitution had been violated by the viceroy, ordered on the same day that he lift the suspension and expressed surprise at his so acting without having sent the government a complete report of his reasons. At the same time the Regency ordered the Council of State to render its opinion on the matter. The Council reported that there was not enough evidence available and recommended no revocation of the viceroy's action until more information was available. Two different opinions by members of the Council of State were expressed at that time. Councillor Antonio Ranz Romanillos held that freedom of the press should remain

---

[27] *Ibid.*, VII, 5684. Twenty-nine deputies' names are affixed to the petition, although Alamán, *Historia de Méjico*, III, 279, states there were thirty-one. Antonio Joaquín Pérez of Puebla did not sign.

suspended until the insurgents had laid down their arms and agreed to respect and obey the laws. On the other hand, Councillor Marqués de Piedra Blanca, an American, disagreed strongly with this view and stated that the Audiencia as well as the viceroy should be punished for their actions. The Regency had finally decided that since it had already ordered the suspension lifted, any further action could be postponed, for Venegas had been replaced by Félix Calleja, who had already promised that a full and complete report on the whole matter would be presented to the Cortes.

The Regency concluded its report to the Cortes by recommending that provincial censorship boards be established in all the principal cities in addition to those already in the provincial capitals. Sr. Mejía and Sr. Calatrava moved that the government be asked for both the report of the Council of State and the opinion of the Audiencia of Mexico and that all information be referred to the Committee on Freedom of the Press.[28]

Venegas had installed the provincial censorship board of Mexico City, as required by law, but he had apparently ignored it and its function. The Supreme Censorship Board reported to the Cortes on July 24, 1813, that it had received three communications from the Mexico City board, all criticizing Venegas. The first, dated October 15, 1812, commented on the noticeably unnecessary delay of Venegas in putting the law into effect in Mexico. The other two, both dated December 12 (seven days after Venegas' suspension of the law) and accompanied by supporting documents, would, the Board said, inform the Cortes of the "scandalous suspension" of the law by Venegas, in accord with the Audiencia, on the pretext of abuses of the law. The Supreme Censorship Board observed also that the accompanying documents showed that the abuses were very few and frivolous.[29] The Mexico City board reported that it had not been consulted by the viceroy on the matter of suspension nor had more than two cases been brought before it for censoring. One case concerned an epigram in the *Diario de México* which stated that many military men left home poor and returned rich and unscathed; the second was an issue of *El Pensador mejicano* which had not been forwarded through proper channels and therefore was not heard by the provincial body.[30]

[28] Spain, Cortes, 1810–1813. *Diario de las sesiones de las Cortes*, VIII, 5787–5788.
[29] *Ibid.*, pp. 5788–5789.
[30] Alamán, *Historia de Méjico*, III, 281–283.

The Supreme Censorship Board felt that legal measures should be taken, for, if freedom of the press were allowed to be destroyed in New Spain, ultimately its destruction would occur in old Spain. This full report was also sent to the Committee on Freedom of the Press.[31]

Before the end of 1813 the Audiencia of Mexico also presented its account to the Cortes of the suspension of some of the constitutional laws and freedom of the press. The abuses committed during the two months of the free press were enumerated at great length. The third issue of *El Pensador mejicano* had accused the viceroys of being absolute sovereigns, basing their princeship on the slavery of the Indians. The fifth *Pensador* had demanded that Mexico adopt another political system, since "there is no civilized nation which has had a worse government than ours, the very worst in America," and "despots and bad government invented the insurrection, not Father Hidalgo." The seventh issue proposed an armistice with the revolutionists in order to have time to determine the problems "underlying the rebellion and lay them before the Cortes."[32]

The *Diario de México,* according to the Audiencia, had from the very first disseminated ideas of sedition under the guise of anecdotes and equivocal expressions and had accused the Spanish troops of cowardice. The same paper declared that the rebels should be treated as peaceful citizens who thought what they were doing was right. It also contended that Bustamante, one of the editors of the *Diario,* was in touch with the president of the Revolutionary Junta, Ignacio Rayón. Furthermore, Bustamante, in his *Juguetillo* No. 4 and No. 6, and other authors, under the protection of the freedom of the press law, had indicated their disapproval of the actions of the viceregal government's Security Council.

In summary, the Audiencia listed the following among the abuses committed: defenders of the nation were told that the war was vile; indulgence was advocated for traitors, vindication was sought for Hidalgo, good government was accused of being tyrannical and despotic, lucrative employment was said to be denied Americans as they were prohibited from engaging in industrial development, ecclesias-

---

[31] Spain, Cortes, 1810–1813, *Diario de sesiones de las Cortes,* VIII, 5789. Signing for the Supreme Censorship Board were Pedro Chaves (bishop of Arequipa), president, José Miguel Ramírez, Martín González de Nava, Miguel Moreno, Manuel José Quintana, Manuel Llano, Vicente Sancho, Felipe Bauzá, Eugenio de Tapia, and Martín de Hugalde, secretary.

[32] "Representación de los oidores de México a las Cortes de España contra la *Constitución de 1812*," in Bustamante, *Cuadro histórico,* II, 343–423.

tics who aided the enemy were defended. The Audiencia also charged that it was an insult to call the Viceroy a despicable atom. It concluded that the ideas and expressions of the rebels were being openly copied.[33]

Despite the fact that the press in royalist New Spain was under preventative censorship, the Cortes continued its efforts to reform the law as it applied to Spain and its colonies. A bill entitled "Additions to the Law of Freedom of the Press" began its passage through the Cortes on April 28, 1813, and was passed on June 10, along with two other decrees on the same subject.

Decree 263 reflected the influence of several of the reforms suggested in February and March of 1812 by Ramos Arizpe and Guridi y Alcocer in that it provided that members of the censorship boards be renewed biennially, the larger number the first year and the smaller number the next. No one serving in civil or ecclesiastical office, such as a prelate, magistrate, judge, or deputy to the Cortes, could be appointed to the boards. Membership to the supreme and provincial boards was increased by three alternate members, to serve in the absence of the regular appointees. Any document which conspired directly to incite the public to sedition was to be labeled "seditious." All writings contrary to the Constitution should be referred to the Cortes by the boards.[34] Municipal councils annually were to appoint an official whose duty it was to denounce the objectionable material before the appropriate judge or magistrate. The judge, in turn should submit the imprints to the provincial censorship boards for judgment and verdict. If the plaintiff desired further appeal, the judge should return the papers to the provincial boards for a second hearing, after which the plaintiff could make one final appeal to the Supreme Censorship Board. If the accusation charged only personal libel, a second hearing was to be denied, and the case was then to be turned over to the proper authorities. All resources of the law were to be employed when the censored papers were subversive. Writings by regular or secular clergy were to be considered under the same provisions as other citizens. Lastly, any edict contrary to the Constitution or the laws of the king or the Regency should be brought directly before the superior political chief, in the colonies, and the Council of State, in Spain.[35]

[33] *Ibid.*, p. 381.
[34] Spain, Laws and Statutes, 1810–1822, *Decretos*, IV, 87–92.
[35] *Ibid.*

A second decree also dated June 10 entitled "Regulations of the censorship boards," provided that members of the nine-man Supreme Censorship Board should serve rotating terms as president for four months at a time. There was also an appointed secretary, an assistant secretary, and a doorman. Its budget was to be approved by the Cortes and paid from the General Treasury. The Board was to hold regular weekly sessions with special ones allowed. Decisions were to be by plurality of votes, and written votes were permitted when a member could not be present. Votes were to be recorded in the censorship book and copies of the censored books were to be placed in a library. The Board should report directly to the Cortes in all matters relating to freedom of the press.

Provincial boards of five members were nominated by the supreme board and approved by the Cortes. Each provincial board should select its own secretary and doorman. The meetings were to be held in a public building and proceedings to follow the rules laid down for the Supreme Board. The local provincial deputation was to provide maintenance, but no member of any board could receive compensation or emolument.[36]

In the nature of a copyright law, a third decree, promulgated simultaneously by the Cortes, granted an author the right to print his works during his lifetime as many times as he pleased. His heirs were given the right to his works for ten years after his death. A corporate author was limited to the right to publication for forty years from the time of first printing.[37]

These decrees were effective immediately, and a new supreme censorship board was installed in Spain on June 27, 1813. One of its first functions was the nomination of new members to the provincial board of México, serving currently, contrary to the law, as a pre-censorship board, and the creation of a new provincial board for Mérida in Yucatán. Nominated for Mexico City were José Mariá Alcalá and the Marqués de Castañiza, ecclesiastics; José María Fagoaga, the Marqués de Guardiola, and Tomás Salgado, lay members; and Pedro González, Francisco Manuel Sánchez de Tagle, and Agustín Villanueva, alternates. These nominees were approved by the Cortes on July 11, 1813,[38] and on July 25, 1813, it approved a provincial censorship board for Yucatán consisting of José María Calzadillo, Vicente

[36] *Ibid.*, IV, 93–97 (Decree No. 264).
[37] *Ibid.*, IV, 98–99 (Decree No. 265).
[38] Spain, Cortes, 1810–1813, *Diario de las sesiones de las Córtes*, VII, 5684.

Veláquez, Pablo Moreno, Lorenzo Zavala, Pedro Alméida, and alternates Manuel Jiménez, José Matías Quintana, and Jaime Tinto.[39]

Although the sixty days of freedom in New Spain ended in December, 1812, a flow of uncensored material had continued to arrive from the mother country as long as the constitutional regime lasted. The fact that there was press freedom in Spain itself allowed the dissemination in Mexico of news from the free press. Through the circulation of periodicals, pamphlets, and books printed in Spain and abroad, especially in London and Philadelphia, the Mexican public became aware of the revolts and political changes taking place in other Spanish colonies. From September, 1810 to May, 1814, the *Diario de las discusiones y actas de las Cortes* was the most effective organ in supplying to New Spain unrestricted information on the liberal ideas voiced in the Cortes itself.

The royalist cause was gradually gaining ground in Spain, however, and on April 12, 1814, four of the delegates from Mexico joined in signing a manifesto to restore absolute monarchy. These delegates were later called *"persas."* According to an old custom, five days following the death of a king were spent in anarchy in order that the succeeding regime should be received gratefully to restore order. The *"persas"* who signed the manifesto claimed that having spent four years of anarchy under the Cortes, they were ready and anxious to return to the former system of government. They averred that the press under the Constitution had been reduced to insulting good vassals, diverting the energies of the magistrates, and making odious remarks against innocent persons and that seditious and revolutionary papers, including writings unfavorable to ministers of the Church had been distributed to all parts of the country. Signing this manifesto from Mexico were Antonio Joaquín Pérez of Puebla, Ángel Alonso y Pantiga of Yucatan, José Cayetano de Foncerreda of Valladolid, and Salvador Sanmartín of New Spain.[40]

Ferdinand VII assumed full powers on May 4, 1814. His first action was to abolish the Cortes, which, he stated, had usurped his power

[39] *Ibid.*, p. 5791.

[40] "Representación y manifiesto que algunos de los diputados a las Córtes ordinarias firmaron en los mayores apuros de su apresión en Madrid, para que la magestad del sr. D. Fernando el 7 a la entrada en España de vuelta de su cautividad, se penetrase del estado de la nación, del deseo de sus provincias, y del remedio que creían oportuno; todo fué representado a S.M. en Valencia por uno de dichos diputados, y se imprimió en cumplimento de real órden," reprinted in *El Redactor mexicano, periódico aventurero*, December 5, 1814, No. 20, p. 169.

and forced the Constitution on the people. He charged that deputies to the Cortes had abused freedom of the press by making royal power seem odious, by using the words "king" and "despot" synonymously. Anyone who contradicted the deputies had been persecuted, and the deputies had thereby been allowed to further spread revolutionary and seditious ideas. The King assured the people that liberty and security would be restored and that all would be able to communicate through the press those ideas and thoughts which were within the "limits of reason." Henceforth religion and government were to be respected.[41]

Pérez, of Puebla, was rewarded for his infidelity to the Constitution with a bishop's mitre. Ramos Arizpe, Gutiérrez de Terán, Maniau, and other liberal deputies were either jailed or escaped into self-imposed exile.

The Law of the Press of 1805 was reinstated. Judge of the Press, Nicolás María Sierra, and the censors took over the precensoring of all material to be published. The king, under Article 17, prohibited in Spain all except two newspapers. He said that this limitation was necessary because in Spain freedom of the press was easily abused.[42]

In Mexico the rules for precensoring were strictly enforced. Fernández de Lizardi, turned novelist in order to hoodwink the censors, was allowed permission to publish only three of his four volumes of *El periquillo sarniento* (1816). Books concerning constitutional law were banned by an edict of 1816.[43]

Following the liberal Riego revolt in Spain early in 1820, the Cortes was called back into session on June 26; and one of its first acts was to order the reinstatement of the Supreme Censorship Board that had been installed on June 27, 1813, and dissolved on May 4, 1814. After reassembling, the Board elected Felipe Bauzá president and an American from Veracruz, Pablo de la Llave, vice-president, and promptly asked the Cortes to fill the vacancies which had occurred during the six-year interval of inactivity. These had occurred as follows: the Bishop of Arequipa, Don Pedro Chaves de la Rosa, and

[41] "Célebre manifiesto de 4 de mayo en Valencia," in Jose María Gamboa, *Leyes constitucionales de México durante el siglo XIX*, pp. 35–44.
[42] Angel González Palencia, *Estudio histórico sobre la censura gubernativa en España, 1800–1833*, I, XVI.
[43] "Bando del Virrey Apodaca con el Real Decreto de 22 de mayo de 1816 que ordena se recojan las publicaciones de propaganda de los principios constitucionales, prohibe su lectura y enseñanza, y manda se castigue los contraventores de dicha prohibición," in Alba, *La Constitución de 1812*, II, 162–163.

José Robello were deceased; José Miguel Ramírez from Oaxaca, Miguel Moreno, and Manuel Llano had been sent overseas; Martín González de Navas, Eugenio de Tapia, and Vicente Sancho had been elected deputies to the Cortes and were ineligible to serve; Juan Acevedo was preparing to leave for an embassy post in Paris; Manuel José Quintana was no longer eligible under Article 1 of the June 10, 1813, law, since he had already served two years; and Felipe Bauzá asked to be excused. This left only Pablo de la Llave, the former Mexican deputy to the Cortes, eligible and available to serve. However, at the proposal of Deputy Navas, the Cortes authorized the last four men to constitute the board until further appointments could be made.[44] These vacancies were filled on September 12, 1820, by the appointment of four new members. With the departure of Acevedo, the number serving on the board amounted to seven instead of the required nine, but authorization for this change had been granted by the Cortes, in view of pending changes in the law.[45]

Deputy Eugenio de Tapia, a former member of the Supreme Censorship Board, informed the Cortes on July 17, 1820, that a new law on freedom of the press was needed. He proposed that municipal councils appoint and be responsible for a legal attorney (*fiscal*) who would read all printed materials and bring any objectionable matter before the provincial board. He pointed out, as had Ramos Arizpe and Guridi y Alcocer before him, that the law was vague about the meaning of the terms "subversive," "seditious," "calumnious," or "injurious," and that by leaving interpretation to a justice harsh sentences could be imposed or a comparable offender let off with a light sentence. He continued that when the legislators had granted freedom to express "political opinions" in 1813, they had not intended to leave out freedom to publish scientific and literary works. By the former law bishops had precensorship of religious works, including the Sacred Scriptures, theology, morals, mysticism, and ascetism, but not ecclesiastical discipline. As a result of this discussion, the Cortes appointed a committee on freedom of the press.[46]

The committee went to work immediately to replace the 1813 law. A new bill had its first reading in the Cortes on September 15, 1820,

[44] Spain, Cortes, 1820, *Diario de las sesiones de Cortes*, I, 254.

[45] *Ibid.*, II, 894.

[46] *Ibid.*, I, 179–180. The Cortes replaced Peñafiel with García Page, on March 14, 1821. *Ibid.*, I, 472.

was approved on October 22, and promulgated by Ferdinand VII on November 5, 1820. It gave every Spaniard the right to publish his work without prior censorship. Excluded from the law, however, were works counter to the doctrines of religion or the Constitution. These were to be called "subversive," and were punishable in three degrees. First-degree offenses included publications advocating disobedience of the laws; second-degree offenses were satires or invectives provoking disobedience; and third were offenses to morals and decency. Infractions carried jail sentences of six, four, and two years respectively. Writings against personal honor and reputation were labeled "inflamatory libels" (Arts. 2–17).

Cases of "subversion" could be denounced by any Spaniard. All other cases were initiated by a legal attorney (*fiscal*), municipal syndic (*síndico del ayuntamiento*), political chief (*jefe politico*), or constitutional mayor (*alcalde constitucional*). The legal attorney was to be appointed annually by the provincial deputation, and was eligible for reappointment. All printers were required to send the legal attorney a copy of all works or papers printed in his province, or pay a fine of five ducados (Arts. 32–35). The procedure for trials began with the constitutional mayor of the capital of the province, who would call together all the lay judges (*jueces de hecho*). These lay judges, the number of whom was to be three times that of the membership of the municipal councils, were to be selected by an absolute plurality of the constitutional municipal council of the capital of the province fifteen days after its installation. A lay judge had to be a resident of the capital, a good citizen of twenty-five years of age; not eligible were civil servants or ecclesiastics, political chiefs, intendents, commanders of the army, secretaries, and councillors of state (Arts. 36–42). After a publication was denounced, nine lay judges, chosen by lot, would sit as a grand jury and decide by a two-thirds majority whether there was cause for trial (Arts. 43–48). If there was cause, another twelve lay judges, again chosen by lot, would sit as a trial jury, giving its verdict to the judge of the primary court of claims, who would execute the sentence (Arts. 49–74). To further ensure freedom of the press, Article 78 stated that the Cortes should appoint biennially, at the beginning of its sessions, a board for the protection of freedom of the press (*junta de protección de libertad de imprenta*), resident in Madrid, composed of seven members whose first order of business should be the nomination of members for three subordinate boards in Mexico City, Lima, and Manila. Qualifications for membership consisted of being an educated citizen of twenty-five years of age.

The board was given five specific duties: to report to the Cortes any doubts or unusual situations within it jurisdiction, to notify the Cortes of complaints by authors and editors, to present annual reports on the state of the freedom of the press, to examine the reports of pending or completed cases submitted to it quarterly by the judges of primary courts, and to see that names of offenders and their sentences were published in the government gazette. Until such time as a board could be appointed for the following year the Supreme Censorship Board was to carry out the duties of the board for the protection of freedom of the press.[47]

During the passage of the bill, Ramos Arizpe, who had resumed his seat when the new Cortes was called, remarked that there were many kinds of punishment for those who abused the freedom of the press, but none for the person who falsely accused an innocent person. During the debate on Article 37 Ramos Arizpe also asked that the word "absolute" be inserted to ensure that lay judges would be elected by "absolute plurality" of the municipal council. This would counterbalance the legal attorneys who were to be selected by the provincial deputation.[48] Deputy Montoya's proposal to have boards for the protection of freedom of the press in the capital of every captaincy general and not to limit them to the existing three in America was not admitted to discussion.[49]

The Supreme Censorship Board served in its dual capacity until May 7, 1821, when a separate board for the protection of freedom of the press was nominated. Manuel Quintana, elected president, Felipe Bauzá, Manuel Carrillo, José Luiz Munarriz, Antonio Gutiérrez, Manuel Antonio Velasco, and Gregorio Sáinz de Villavieja were sworn into office. The rules for the board's internal administration were presented to the Cortes for approval on June 8, 1821, at which time they were sent to the committee on freedom of the press. These were returned approved on June 18, and were passed by the Cortes.[50]

[47] "Reglamento acerca de la libertad de imprenta de 22 de octubre de 1820," Spain, Cortes, 1810–1813, *Decretos*, VI, 234–244 (Decreto 55).

[48] Spain, Cortes, 1820, *Diario de las Cortes*, III, 1433; 1486–1487.

[49] *Ibid.*, p. 1492.

[50] Spain, Cortes, 1821. *Diario de las sesiones de Cortes*, III, 2337.

The internal regulation of the boards for the protection of freedom of the press prescribed a membership of seven members who received no salary, and a secretary, a scribe, and a doorman who would be compensated. The boards were to meet at a place designated by the Cortes, holding weekly sessions for regular business; special sessions were allowed. Decisions were by plurality of members; each was required to vote; and the votes were to be recorded. The overseas boards of Mexico and Lima were to consist of seven members, but because of the smaller population, the Manila board was to be composed of five. These boards were to meet in the same building as did the provincial deputation and the expenses of the board were to be met by the provincial deputation.[51]

The Constitution of 1812 was reproclaimed in Mexico City with the viceroy, Audiencia, and other authorities taking the oath of office on June 17, 1820. With Article 371 on freedom of the press back in force, Viceroy Juan Ruíz de Apodaca urgently recommended writers to use the granted liberty with moderation while at the same time enlightening the government and promoting the national welfare.[52]

The appointees named by the Cortes on July 11, 1813 for the Mexican provincial censorship board were reassembled and sworn in on June 21, 1820. However, only the three alternates, Pedro González, Francisco Manuel de Tagle, and Agustín Villanueva were present: José María Alcalá was in Madrid, the Marqués de Castañiza was serving as the Bishop of Durango, the Marqués de Guardiola, although in Mexico, asked to be excused for economic reasons, and José María Fagoaga and Tomás Salgado were incumbents of other offices and therefore ineligible.[53]

On August 9, 1820, the Cortes approved the nominations to the provincial censorship boards for Mexico City and Guadalajara. To serve in Mexico City were Miguel Guiridi y Alcocer, deputy to the Cortes during 1810–1813, Manuel Goméz, José Mariano Zardenete, the Marqués de San Juan de Rayas, Pedro Acevedo, Andrés del Río, and alternates José Vicente Ortíz, the Marqués de Apartado, and Carlos María de Bustamante. Bustamante was never sworn into office as the provincial censorship board of Mexico City had judged his *Memoria*

---

[51] *Ibid.*, III, pp. 2336–2367.
[52] "Edict of June 19, 1820," in H. H. Bancroft, *History of Mexico*, XII, 699.
[53] "Renovación de los nuevos censores," in Alba, *La Constitución de 1812*, I, 126–127.

presentada al Exmo. Ayuntamiento constitucional de Mexico injurious to the authorities and "other decent people" and had had the publication collected.[54]

Appointed to the Guadalajara provincial censorship board were Miguel Ramírez, José María Tamayo, Salvador García Diego, Antonio Fuentes, Manuel Norgueras, and, as alternates, José María Vallarta, Manuel de la Fuente y Pacheco, and José María Ilizaliturri.[55]

Although the new Freedom of the Press Law had been passed in the Cortes in October of 1820, superseding the 1813 law, the Mexico City provincial censorship board continued to function under the earlier law for nearly a year more. Many of the cases referred to it for decision involved political writings, to determine whether or not they were subversive and if so, to what degree. An example was the publication *Verdadera explicación de la voz independencia*, which was brought in for hearing on October 22, 1820. The legal attorney alleged that the publication was derogatory to the superior political chief of Guadalajara. The Mexico City censorship board decreed that although the paper did point out the advantages of the republican form of government, it did not violate any of the fundamental laws, and therefore could not be classed as seditious.[56]

On April 18, 1821, a publication entitled *Acta celebrada en Iguala. El primero de marzo juramento al día siguiente prestó el sr. Iturbide con la oficialidad y tropa a su mano*[57] received the provincial board's attention. The author, who signed himself "M. M." reasoned that sooner or later, with or without war, independence for New Spain would come about and, therefore, the public should be aware of the happenings at Iguala during the preceding February. Viceroy Ruíz de Apodaca stated that "M. M.'s" publication was seditious since it advocated independence, and the justice of the peace recommended that all copies be collected. The censorship board met on April 19 and endorsed the verdict. Another case brought before the provincial board, but apparently only for its information, was a de-

[54] "Minuta reservada del Virrey, con informes acerca del Marqués de Rayas y de D. Carlos Bustamente," *ibid.*

[55] Spain, Cortes, 1820, *Diario de las Cortes*, I, 442.

[56] Letter from the legal attorney (not named) of the Mexican provincial censorship board to the Supreme Censorship Board, dated October 23, 1820, in México, Archivo general de la Nación, Ramo de historia, Vol. 398 (microfilm).

[57] "M. M.," *Acta celebrada en Iguala. El primero de marzo juramento al día siguiente prestó el sr. Iturbide con la oficialidad y tropa a su mano.*

cree by the viceroy against street vendors selling seditious circulars. He forbade persons of either sex to peddle these offensive publications to the public, inasmuch as most of them were, he said, anticonstitutional, contrary to the truth, against the government and authorities, and insulting to the *peninsulares*. He decreed therefore, that henceforth all papers should be sold at the printer's shop or at regular stores.[58]

When Iturbide and his victorious "trigarantine" army entered Mexico City in September, 1821, to set up an independent Mexican government, the Provisional Sovereign Governing Junta did not abolish the system established by the Cortes for freedom of the press but supported it by ordering on October 9, 1821, that the law of the Cortes of November 5, 1820, be promulgated, printed, and circulated in Mexico.[59]

Two weeks later the new decree was somewhat modified by the Mexican Regency. Many writers had felt free to discuss the Plan of Iguala, with opinions differing from those of the government. To arrest this dangerous influence, the Regency, by decree of October 22, 1821, issued an edict pronouncing authors attacking the Plan of Iguala guilty of treason against the state. The edict contended that freedom of the press was a channel which allowed writers to circulate papers full of "antipolitic, subversive, criminal, and embittered expressions," diverting public opinion from the Three Guarantees and the principles of the Plan of Iguala which were ratified by the Treaty of Córdoba. Any author who directly or indirectly attacked one of the Guarantees of Union, Religion, or Independence would be considered an enemy of the nation and would be punished accordingly. The appropriate officials were asked to redouble their efforts in seeking out those works which, by insulting citizens and disturb-

[58] "Sobre prohibición que los muchachos pregonen los papeles públicos," signed by the Conde de Venadito, March 9, 1821, in México, Archivo general de la nación, Ramo de Historia, vol. 398 (microfilm). Handwriting of another person on the document states, "This did not have any effect."

[59] "Previene se publique en forma el último reglamento de libertad de imprenta," Decreto X de 9 de octubre de 1821, in Mexico, Laws, statutes, etc., *Colección de decretos y órdenes que ha expedido la soberana junta provisional gubernativa del imperio mexicano desde su instalación en 28 de setiembre de 1820 hasta 24 de febrero de 1821*, p. 20.

Alamán, *Historia de Méjico*, states that the decree went into effect on June 23, 1821, but the author of this paper has not been able to verify this statement.

ing the social order, brought dishonor on the right of freedom of Press.[60]

However the attacks on the ideas and principles of the Plan of Iguala continued. The long-standing conflict between the Spanish-born citizens of Mexico and the native-born creoles appeared in the open on December 11, 1821, when Francisco Lagranda, native of Spain, accused Iturbide of not supporting the Guarantee of Union. In a publication entitled *Consejo prudente sobre una de las garantías,* Lagranda advised Spaniards to leave Mexico in order to save their lives. He stated that when the poor creoles and the downtrodden Indians became powerful, they would overrun the Spaniards, and not even Iturbide would be able to hold them in check.[61] As a result of this publication, the Spaniards in Mexico City were thrown into panic, and, fearing for their lives, rushed to get passports in order to leave for Spain.

The Provisional Sovereign Governing Junta met in emergency session the next day and ordered the legal attorney to take steps immediately to have the *Consejo prudente sobre una de las garantías,* as well as any other works in similar vein, censored. The Junta further ordered the holding up of the weekly mail the next day, and denounced Lagranda's work as subversive and scandalous. The Junta reassured the People of New Spain that all articles of the Plan of Iguala and Treaty of Córdoba were being fulfilled. It promised to take measures to correct the abuses of freedom of the press.[62]

Lagranda was arrested, tried by the lay judges, and sentenced to six years in prison for subversion in the first degree. However, the actual time he spent in prison was only a few months, for with the opening of the First Congress in Mexico on February 22, 1822, a general amnesty and pardon was decreed for all persons imprisoned, judged or persecuted for their political opinions, whether by word or by writing.[63]

The Provisional Sovereign Governing Junta, after its experience

[60] Edict issued by the Regency on October 22, 1821, and signed by Iturbide and members of the Regency.

[61] Francisco Lagranda, *Consejo prudente sobre una de las garantías.*

[62] "Providencias que en él se dictan con motivo del folleto titulado, Consejo prudente sobre una de las tres Garantias," Decreto XXI de 12 de diciembre de 1821, in México, Laws, Statutes, etc. *Colección de los decretos y órdenes del soberano Congreso, Mexicano desde su instalación en 24 de febrero de 1822, hasta 30 de octubre de 1823.*

[63] Alamán, *Historia de Méjico,* V, 477–478.

with Francisco Lagranda on December 12, issued the next day a reform to the Cortes' 1820 Law of Freedom of the Press. The new law
reiterated in Article 1 the fundamental precepts of the Mexican empire: 1) suppression of all churches but the Roman Catholic Church,
2) independence from Spain, 3) equal rights for citizens born on
either side of the ocean, 4) a hereditary constitutional monarchy according to the Plan of Iguala, 5) a representative government, 6)
separation of government powers into executive, legislative, and
judicial. The Spanish law of 1820 was changed to read that any writer
attacking *directly* any of the above precepts would be tried for subversion and would be imprisoned for six, four, or two years, according to the degree of subversion. Any writer attacking the precepts
indirectly would serve half the time of those sentenced for subversion.

The new law increased the number of constitutional mayors (alcaldes) to six for Mexico City, and added another legal attorney
(*fiscal*) to the required one in each capital where there were more
than two printing presses. The procedure for handling cases began
with the legal attorney's bringing the objectionable material before
the constitutional mayor, who selected by lot nine lay judges (*jueces
de hecho*) to sit as a grand jury. If there were cause for trial, the constitutional mayor would select by lot another twelve lay judges to sit
as a trial jury. There were fines for nonperformance of duty on
the part of the government officials. All fines which were originally
(i.e. in the Cortes' 1820 law) levied in ducats (*ducados*) would now
be changed to pesos. Any difficulty in processing the case would be
referred to the Board for the Protection of the Freedom of the Press.[64]

The Mexican deputies may not have contributed much to the beginning struggle for more freedom for the press as they participated
in the Spanish Cortes in September, 1810, but some soon identified
themselves as its most ardent supporters, not only for its proclamation
and expansion in Spain but also in Mexico. If it had not been for the
unceasing work of Ramos Arizpe, Guridí y Alcocer, Montoya, Gutiérrez de Terán, Pablo de la Llave, and others it is doubtful that freedom of the press would have been extended to Mexico. This freedom,
once there, played its part well, so well in fact that the laws as worked
out by the Cortes with the constant participation of the Mexican

---

[64] "Reglamento de libertad de imprenta de 13 de diciembre de 1821," in *ibid.*,
I, 113–119. In the *Gaceta imperial de México* of December 22, 1821, the law was
given the more appropriate title of "Reglamento adicional para la libertad de
imprenta."

deputies became a part of the Spanish law that was not only recognized by independent Mexico but incorporated into its system of law. The labor of the Mexican deputies for freedom of the press for New Spain not only gave that country a well-enunciated law when independence came in 1821 but also provided the framework for carrying out the law. By late 1821 Mexicans had seen service on the boards and the courts provided by the law. The freedom granted had been tasted and relished by both publishers and public and was not a right which either would relinquish easily. The work of the Mexicans in the Cortes had made a strong impact on the future of their native land.

5. Effect of the Cortes, 1810–1822, on Church Reform in Spain and Mexico

James M. Breedlove

The union between "altar and throne" has rarely been as intimate as it was in Spain and its American empire at the beginning of the nineteenth century. As a result, the relationship between church and state has been a major issue in the political and social history of all the former Spanish colonies of Latin America, especially in Mexico, where it is a crucial problem to the present day. It was certainly an important issue in the reform-minded Spanish Cortes which met from 1810 to 1814 and 1820 to 1822. This paper will consider some of the more important ecclesiastical provisions, both statutory and constitutional, proposed in and enacted by the Cortes, in an effort to understand the position of the Mexican delegates to that body in regard to the church-state relationship and the state's role in reforming the Church (specifically the Catholic Church). The Mexican delegates were not particularly vocal when these various provisions were discussed in the Cortes, although often their very silence seemed to express their approval of Church reform. However, several members from Mexico expressed themselves often enough that some positive conclusions as to their attitudes may be drawn.

It would be redundant to detail the condition of the Church and clergy in New Spain in 1810. Pertinent information is readily available in the well-known primary sources of Alexander Humboldt and Manuel Abad y Queipo and is adequately summarized by several modern writers, among them Lillian Fisher[1] and Karl Schmitt.[2] That

---

[1] Lillian Estelle Fisher, *The Background of the Revolution for Mexican Independence.*

[2] Karl M. Schmitt, "The Clergy and the Independence of New Spain," *HAHR,* XXXIV, No. 3 (August, 1954), 289–312.

the Church in New Spain at the time of the Cortes was in considerable need of financial, administrative, and spiritual reform was, to many members of the Mexican delegation, beyond dispute.

The first measures introduced in the Cortes which would affect the Church were not in the nature of permanent reforms but were temporary financial expedients designed to aid the nation in its prosecution of the war with Napoleon. On December 1, 1810, the Cortes decreed that all benefices falling vacant from that date would not be filled for a certain length of time so that their income might be applied to the needs of the state. The decree specifically included the overseas dominions.[3] The extension of this decree to America was evidently disputed, because on April 10, 1811, the ecclesiastical committee of the Cortes recommended that America be exempted from its provisions because the prebends there were few and unless they were filled many churches would have to close for lack of priests. In addition, the committee recommended that Americans be given consideration equal to that of Spaniards in the provision of American benefices.[4] The proposal to exempt America from the December 1 decree was not opposed by any of the American delegation and was approved by the Cortes.[5] In a short debate the second recommendation was supported by a prominent Spanish member, Joaquín Lorenzo Villanueva, who went so far as to advocate adoption of a proposal by one of the Peruvian delegates which would have provided that, instead of mere equality, Americans be given actual preference in the filling of benefices in their countries. This proposal was opposed by Spaniards Jaime Creus and Vicente Pasqual, who maintained that Americans, who were so anxious to be equal to Spaniards, should not expect more than equality.[6]

When the debate was resumed on April 13, José Beye Cisneros, a delegate from New Spain, said that since Spain had poured out its blood for America and had sustained it for more than three centuries at least one-half of the benefices should be reserved for Spaniards. Juan José Güereña, of Durango, went even further in the opposite

[3] "Decreto XVI de 1 de diciembre de 1810," in Spain, Cortes, 1810–1813, *Colección de los decretos de las Cortes*, I, 32–33 (hereinafter referred to as *Decretos*).

[4] Spain, Cortes, 1810–1813, *Diario de las discusiones y actas de las Cortes*, V, 52 (hereinafter referred to as *Diario de las Cortes*).

[5] *Ibid.*, p. 57.

[6] *Ibid.*, pp. 51–53.

direction, proposing that, since the Spanish and American churches were one, benefices in both lands should be filled without distinction by either Americans or Spaniards.[7] Villanueva demurred at this and pointed out that, in regard to Güereña's proposal, America could hardly spare any of its few priests to fill posts in the Peninsula. Mariano Mendiola, of Querétaro, agreed with his Spanish colleague, advising the Cortes that Güereña's position was not in accord with justice, public convenience, or the laws of the land. The provision of benefices, according to Mendiola, had the benefit of the faithful as its object; therefore, those who knew the area, the languages, and the customs should be appointed to fill benefices in a given region.[8] The Cortes voted to suspend resolution of Güereña's proposition,[9] and evidently it was not taken up again, as there are no more references made to it in the *Diario*. The debate shows that the Mexican delegation was split on the issue, with Güereña and Beye Cisneros supporting the right of Spaniards to receive American benefices and Mendiola upholding American regional interests.

On April 16, the appropriate decree was issued exempting America from the suspension of benefices. In view of the disturbed conditions in the colonies at the time, it is interesting to note that the decree says that suspension would, among other things, do away with the temporal income of the zealous parish priests who sustained the love of religion, country, and king in the overseas dominions.[10] It would appear that the Cortes had motives other than that of justice.

However Mendiola may have felt about leniency in the provision of benefices in America, he certainly felt that the overseas dominions should aid the mother country in its war with France. He proposed, on January 19, 1811, that the portion of tithes in America which were ordinarily paid to priests for the administration of the sacraments should be turned over for the time being to the Cortes to be applied against war expenses. According to him, the amount involved was not very large and he believed that the Cortes should command that the expenses of the administration of the sacraments should be borne by the individual churches.[11] After a short debate the matter was

[7] *Ibid.*, pp. 55–56.
[8] *Ibid.*, p. 57.
[9] *Ibid.*
[10] "Decreto LVII de 16 de abril de 1811," in Spain, Cortes, 1810–1813, *Decretos*, I, 129–130.
[11] Spain, Cortes, 1810–1813, *Diario de las Cortes*, III, 35.

referred to the Finance Committee and evidently, since it is not mentioned later in the *Diario*, was never reported back to the Cortes.[12]

In another effort to finance the war, the Cortes in 1810 had decreed that all ornamental gold and silver owned by individuals and by churches would be taken over by the government to aid the Treasury. Only those ornaments absolutely necessary for use in Church services were to be exempted. There had been considerable difficulty in enforcing this law in Spain, and on March 1, 1811, the Cortes appointed a committee to aid in its execution.[13] On April 6, the Treasury Committee asked the Cortes if the forced loan should be extended to America and if a smaller quota of American-owned ornaments should be required.[14] Debate on this question began on April 8. During its courst Antonio J. Joaquín Pérez, an ecclesiastic and deputy from Puebla, supported extension to America but asked that exactions be made first of private persons and then of the Church. He also asked that parish and Indian churches be exempted because the removal of ornaments from them would scandalize the faithful.[15] One of Pérez' colleagues, José Guridi y Alcocer, of Tlaxcala, opposed extension altogether on the ground that the insurrectionists in New Spain would make political capital out of a forced loan. He also agreed with the argument of the Pueblan deputy that removal of Church ornaments would scandalize the superstitious and ignorant parishioners of the country.[16] José Simeón Uría, of Guadalajara, and José Cayetano de Foncerrada, of Michoacán, joined Guridi y Alcocer in opposing extension of the law to America. Mexican delegate Mendiola did not state his position clearly, asking that the decision be postponed until the Ecclesiastical Committee should define the terms of the loan more exactly. The only delegate from New Spain who supported extension without qualification was Octaviano Obregón, of Guanajuato, who said that it was in the interest of the Church in America that the French be driven out of Spain and that the rich churches of New Spain could well afford to make the loan. The proposition was passed on April 9 with the Pérez amendment exempting the Indian and parish churches.[17] The decree, however, was never published in America.[18]

The American alternate deputies in the Cortes presented to that

[12] *Ibid.*, pp. 35–37.   [16] *Ibid.*, pp. 23–24.
[13] *Ibid.*, IV, 54–64.   [17] *Ibid.*, pp. 19–38.
[14] *Ibid.*, V, 6.   [18] Lucas Alamán, *Historia de Méjico*, III, 57.
[15] *Ibid.*, p. 23.

body, on December 16, 1810, eleven proposals concerning the colonies. The last of these asked that the Jesuits be readmitted to America to promote learning and to further the work of the Indian missions.[19] This proposal was dropped, no one speaking in its favor.[20] Alamán wrote, "This . . . could find little favor in a congress in which most of the ecclesiastics were Jansenists and in which the rest of the deputies were men imbued with the principles of eighteenth century French philosophy."[21] A valid interpretation of the rejection of this proposal and of Alamán's comment upon it might be that the great majority of the deputies, including those from New Spain, were regalists who believed in state control of the Church, a belief strongly rooted in Spanish tradition and in the practice of the *patronato real.* The Jesuits were notoriously ultramontane, which is why Charles III had felt it necessary to expel them in 1767. It is hardly surprising that the Cortes should drop the matter with such dispatch.

On several occasions Mexicans spoke on Church matters in New Spain; two of the discussions threw light on their attitudes toward reform, a third dealt with the relationship of Church and state, and one was concerned with the role of the Church in education. These matters will be discussed in the above order before consideration is given to the ecclesiastical provisions of the Constitution of 1812.

José Eduardo Cárdenas, the deputy from Tabasco, in a report to the Cortes on his province, said that the state of the Church there was deplorable due to the distance of the area from the episcopal see in Mérida de Yucatán. He pointed out that Yucatecans were favored in the provision of Tabascan chaplaincies and benefices; in fact, he wrote, no Tabascan had ever been given a benefice connected with the cathedral in Mérida. Cárdenas accused the priests who came to his province from Yucatán of impoverishing their parishioners and said that ecclesiastical discipline was almost nonexistent.[22] He wrote: ". . . we shouldn't worry whether or not the bishops are rich but if the sheep are well cared for."[23] The militant curate concluded that the Church in America, with its canons, cathedral chapters, and magnificent churches, bore little resemblance to the religion founded by

---

[19] Spain, Cortes, 1810–1813, *Diaro de las Cortes,* III, 305.
[20] *Ibid.*
[21] Alamán, *Historia de Méjico,* III, 49.
[22] José Eduardo Cárdenas, *Memoria a favor de la provincia de Tabasco, en la Nueva España,* pp. 20–24.
[23] *Ibid.,* p. 78.

Christ.[24] Such a man seemed certainly disposed to drastic reform of the Church.

In a similar report to the Cortes, Pedro Bautista Pino, of Nuevo México, discussed the ecclesiastical government of Nuevo México, which was in the diocese of Durango. The Church there was administered by Franciscans, except for one parish which had secular priests. In 1812, according to Pino, no bishop had visited the area in more than fifty years. Ecclesiastical discipline and the spiritual life of the laity had consequently suffered greatly from this neglect. Pino asked the Cortes to give Nuevo México its own bishop.[25] Pino, like Cárdenas, was not a man disposed to the status quo.

Acting upon Pino's request, the Cortes decreed the erection of a diocese in Nuevo México. This action involved the delimitation of boundaries with the old diocese of Durango. The Overseas Committee recommended, on April 30, 1813, that the Secretary of Ecclesiastical Affairs and Justice issue the royal *cédulas* consequent to the decree to the political chief of Nuevo México and to the bishop of Durango, "so that with his [the bishop's] consent and intervention" the boundary commission could proceed with its work.[26] A debate ensued in which Miguel Ramos Arizpe, of Coahuila, revealed his position on an important aspect of the relationship between Church and state. Ramos Arizpe objected to the use of the word "consent" (*anuencia*) because he believed that the consent of the bishop was not necessary in the boundary decision; he cited one of the Laws of the Indies which said that such matters were to be decided by government officials, not by the bishops.[27] His view was that the matter under discussion was a temporal one and not within the jurisdiction of the Church. The Cortes evidently disagreed, for the offensive word was kept in the decree. The Mexican delegate then tried, unsuccessfully, to enforce his point by offering an amendment which read: "If the bishop does not consent to the boundaries, the vice-patron [in this case, the political chief] . . . will enforce it."[28] Ramos Arizpe's stand in this matter was a thoroughly regalist one in respect to the rights of the sovereign vis-à-vis those of the Church.

[24] *Ibid.*, p. 80.

[25] Pedro Bautista Pino, *Noticias históricas y estadísticas de la antigua provincia del Nuevo México*, pp. 31–33.

[26] Spain, Cortes, 1810–1813, *Diario de las Cortes*, XVIII, 469–470.

[27] *Ibid.*, p. 470.

[28] *Ibid.*, p. 474.

Another Mexican delegate, José Beye Cisneros, was concerned with the role of the Church in education in New Spain. His proposal in this regard was not admitted to the floor of the Cortes for debate but it is important because it illustrates his attitude so clearly. On March 15, 1812, he proposed that the monasteries and convents in Mexico City be required to establish free schools for both boys and girls and to provide one or two of their members to teach Christian doctrine, the obligations of Spaniards, reading, and writing. The convents were wealthy, he pointed out, and many of them had been founded for educational purposes but had not fulfilled them. Since the free schools in the city were not sufficient for the population, the Mexican delegate recommended that no license be given for the foundation of convents and monasteries without imposing upon them the obligation of maintaining free schools.[29]

The Cortes had arrogated to itself, however, as its main business, the writing of a Constitution for the government of the Spanish empire. This task was completed in March, 1812, and the document was promulgated on March 19.[30] Five articles, or sections of articles, related directly to the Church, one of which, Article 249, will be discussed as an example of the debates which took place concerning the constitutional position of the Church and ecclesiastics.

Article 12 stated that the religion of Spain was and would be the one, true, catholic, Roman, and apostolic religion and that the nation would protect it with wise and just laws and prohibit the exercise of any other religion.[31] This was certainly not a radical or even liberal provision as there was no allowance whatsoever for the slightest public deviation from the Roman Catholic religion. *El Español*, the liberal Spanish newspaper published in London, commented very harshly on this article, saying, "Article 12 of the Constitution is a cloud which darkens the light of liberty that is dawning in Spain."[32]

Article 171 regulated the operation of the Patronato Real. The significant innovation here was that the *patronato* was put under broader jurisdiction than had been the case previously. Powers of the king were outlined. Section 6 stated that the king would fill all bisphoprics

---

[29] Spain, Cortes, 1810–1813, *México en las Cortes de Cádiz: Documentos*, pp. 199–201.

[30] *Ibid., Diario de las Cortes*, XII, 317–320.

[31] Spain, Constitution, *Constitución política de la monarquía española, promulgada en Cádiz á 19 de marzo de 1812*.

[32] *El Español*, May 30, 1812.

and benefices of the royal prerogative, following the recommendations of the Council of State.[33] Section 15 said that the king would concede the publication of, or retain, conciliar decrees and pontifical bulls with the consent of the Cortes; the Council of State was empowered to judge the king's decisions in certain cases, but those decrees or bulls containing matters in possible conflict with Spanish law were to be decided by the Supreme Court.[34] The jurisdiction of the *pase regio* was thus considerably broadened by this section.

Article 249 concerned the ecclesiastical *fuero,* stating that ecclesiastics would continue to enjoy the *fuero* of their estate in the terms which the laws provided or might provide in the future. This article gave rise to lengthy debate in the Cortes, which will be discussed shortly. The *fuero* was limited in Article 261, section 8, which provided that the Supreme Court would have final jurisdiction over ecclesiastical court decisions. No new power or authority was granted the state over the Church by any of these articles. They were all well grounded in Spanish tradition and precedent; rather it was the concept of the state itself which had been changed. Jurisdiction over the Church, which under the enlightened despotism of the Bourbons resided in the king alone, was broadened and granted to other branches of the government. Another important development was that these powers and jurisdictions were given constitutional sanction. One modern, pro-Church writer in Mexico, saying that the above articles, especially Article 249, clearly subordinated the clergy to civil authority, seems to believe that this subordination was something new in Spain, and condemns the Cortes because of it.[35] His condemnation, if based on the novelty of the constitutional provisions, is unwarranted.

When Article 249, dealing with the ecclesiastical *fuero,* had come before the Cortes for consideration on November 16, 1811, one of the Spanish delegates, José María Calatrava, objected to it on the grounds that it did not limit the power of the Church courts specifically to spiritual and disciplinary matters. He pointed out that the preceding article, 248, provided that no *fuero* would be recognized in civil or criminal cases and that the article following 249 limited the military *fuero* to matters concerning military discipline only. Calatrava showed his regalist views in his observation that the Church enjoyed

[33] Spain, Constitution, p. 23.
[34] *Ibid.,* p. 24.
[35] Jesús García Gutiérrez, *Acción anticatólica en México,* p. 26.

its *fuero* not by divine right but by grace of the king. He asked the Cortes not to approve the article in the form presented, and wanted to suppress it altogether.[36] He was evidently unaware that the *fuero* had been partially abolished in criminal cases and considerably diminished in civil cases in the eighteenth century.[37] Also, he seemed to ignore that Article 249 recognized the right of the Cortes to modify the *fuero.*

The only delegate from New Spain to speak in the debate was Juan José Güereña. He supported the article, pointing out that it was founded in Spanish tradition and in that of the Church. Güereña's belief, as opposed to that of Calatrava, was that Church reform should be brought about not so much by the state as through Church councils. He stated that even if the force of tradition should be disregarded in this matter, it would still benefit the nation to preserve the *fuero* of the clergy, which worked in the nation's interest. The Mexican concluded by observing that as matters stood then, both the Church and the state had a hand in ecclesiastical discipline and that the constitutional committee maturely and prudently recognized that no constitutional innovation should be made in the *fuero.*[38] After further debate the article was approved as proposed on November 17, 1811.[39]

After the work on the Constitution was completed, the Cortes continued its sessions until September, 1813. In this period several serious proposals for Church reform were made. Among them were provisions for convent reform and for the sale of Church property. The Mexican delegation did not take an active part in the debates concerning these measures. No Mexican recorded a vote in opposition to any of the reform measures, so it can be assumed that generally the Mexican delegates were in favor of reform. Their silence is not surprising since they usually participated only in those questions which specifically concerned America.

On February 18, 1813, the Cortes decreed that no convent which had been abandoned or destroyed as a result of the French invasion might be re-established unless it had at least twelve professed mem-

---

[36] Spain, Cortes, 1810–1813, *Diario de sesiones de las Cortes generales y extraordinarias,* III, 2267–2268 (hereinafter referred to as *Diario de sesiones de las Cortes*).

[37] Manuel Abad Queipo, *Colección de los escritos más importantes que en diferentes épocas dirigió al gobierno Don Manuel Abad Queipo,* pp. 1–95.

[38] Spain, Cortes, 1810–1813, *Diario de sesiones de las Cortes,* III, 2269–2270.

[39] *Ibid.,* p. 2277.

bers. Furthermore, in towns where there had been several convents of the same order, only one of that order might be re-established.[40] This decree set an important precedent for more radical reforms in the Cortes of 1820–1821.

On September 8, 1813, the Cortes voted to use part of the benefices of convents to help pay the public debt. They were to be turned over to the *Junta Nacional de Crédito Público*.[41] Some deputies recorded their opposition to this measure but none of the Mexican delegation was among them.[42]

One other important matter relative to Church reform which was considered by the Cortes in 1813 should be mentioned. It concerned the old dispute of bishops in America over the religious in their dioceses. As a result of a protest of the Bishop of Guayana, the Committee on Overseas Affairs on September 4, 1813, recommended and the Cortes approved proposals resolving the difficulty in favor of the prelates. The approved provisions stated that all reductions and curacies of missionary orders which had been established for at least ten years were to be turned over to the diocesan authorities. The transferred curacies were to be filled canonically by the bishops according to the *patronato real*. Finally, the prelates were given the right to fill parish vacancies with qualified members of the orders.[43]

These laws passed in 1813 would have considerably diminished the power and wealth of the religious orders both in Spain and America. However, there is no evidence that they were put into effect in New Spain. Undoubtedly there was little time to do so, for the next year Ferdinand VII restored autocratic rule to the Spanish empire. It would appear that the majority of the Mexican delegation to the Cortes was in favor of the reform measures and the assertion of state authority over the Church.

The Constitution of Cádiz reached Mexico in September, 1812. There seems to have been no hesitation on the part of New Spain's clergy, either high or low, in taking the oath to uphold the document. The viceregal court and high clergy of Mexico City swore their adherence to the new law on September 30. A Mass was celebrated in the cathedral by Archdeacon Beristáin, who preached a sermon ex-

---

[40] "Decreto CCXXII de 18 de febrero de 1813," in Spain, Cortes, 1810–1813, *Decretos*, III, 212–213.
[41] Spain, Cortes, 1810–1813, *Diario de sesiones de las Cortes*, VIII, 6168.
[42] *Ibid.*
[43] *Ibid.*, pp. 6121–6122.

horting the faithful to support the Constitution. After the Mass a Te Deum was sung. In the next few days the oath was administered in all the parishes, convents, and monasteries of the city.[44] Alamán says that the kings had never been sworn to with such solemnity, especially by all the corporations.[45]

One writer says that the bishops of Puebla, Vallodolid de Michoacán, Mérida de Yucatán, Monterrey, and the cathedral chapter of México opposed the Constitution's liberalism, particularly because of disturbed conditions in New Spain at the time.[46] Alamán is cited as the source for this observation. However, the Mexican historian was referring only to the provisions and decrees granting liberty of press. He does not say the bishops opposed the Constitution as such.[47]

One group of the lower clergy supported the Constitution enthusiastically and wanted it to be fully enforced. This was the Asociación sanjuanista of Mérida de Yucatán, which had been formed as a purely religious society some time before the installation of the Cortes of Cádiz. In spite of, or because of, the religious spirit of its members, they were not at all in sympathy with the domination by and the enrichment of the upper clergy of the area.[48] During the year of 1812 the Asociación became increasingly interested in political affairs. The members followed newspaper accounts of proceedings in the Cortes and ardently discussed the reforms proposed in that body. The sanjuanistas accepted liberal reform principles without vacillation and were enthusiastic supporters of the Constitution, endeavoring to spread support for it throughout Yucatán. In 1814, with the return of Ferdinand VII to the throne, the Asociación was disbanded and several of its members arrested.[49]

Ferdinand VII, who had recently returned to his throne, issued a decree in May, 1814, annulling everything which had taken place during his absence. The Cortes was dissolved and many of its more liberal members were imprisoned, among whom were Miguel Ramos Arizpe, Joaquín Maniau, and José María Gutiérrez de Terán of New Spain. Pérez was president of the Cortes at the time of its dissolution

[44] *Diario de México*, October 17, 1812.
[45] Alamán, *Historia de Méjico*, III, 280.
[46] Schmitt, "The Clergy and the Independence of New Spain," *HAHR*, p. 295.
[47] Alamán, *Historia de Méjico*, III, 284.
[48] Eligio Ancona, *Historia de Yucatán desde la época más remota hasta nuestros días*, III, 21.
[49] *Ibid.*, pp. 19–81.

and complied with royal orders most willingly.[50] The news reached Mexico in the summer and evidently met with no protest from the upper clergy; indeed, it has been observed that they were much relieved by the turn of events.[51] Ferdinand's autocratic rule lasted six years and even the insurrection begun by Father Hidalgo in New Spain calmed down somewhat during that period.

The attempted return to the status quo was ended on January 1, 1820. The Riego revolt which began on that day swept Spain, the Constitution of 1812 was restored, and the Cortes reconvened in June. New Spain learned of the revolt in April and on June 1 the archbishop and cathedral chapter of the capital once again swore their allegiance to the Constitution, the religious communities following their example during the next week.[52] Part of the clergy in the archdiocese of México, however, were evidently openly condemning the new regime, for Archbishop Fonte found it necessary to issue an edict on July 18 in which he defended the Constitution.[53] He advised his clergy that they must teach obedience to legitimate civil authority as long as it did not command them to offend God, which, according to Fonte, the Constitution of 1812 did not. He forbade the discussion of political matters from the pulpit. Fonte observed in the edict that freedom of the press and abolition of the Inquisition seemed to be the major objections of the clergy to the constitutional system. In regard to the latter he wrote: ". . . the conservation and triumph of our holy religion does not depend on the support which the . . . Inquisition may have been able to give it."[54] As to freedom of the press, he recommended that it be used in upholding religious truth.[55]

The Cortes which reconvened in Madrid in June, 1820, was a more radical body than its Cádiz predecessor. The Mexican delegation was much larger than in the earlier Cortes. It included such men as José Miguel Gordoa, Lucas Alamán, Pablo de la Llave, Miguel Ramos Arizpe, and Lorenzo de Zavala, some of whom had been in the Cortes before and all of whom were active in the political affairs of independent Mexico. Ramos Arizpe and another of the Mexican delegates,

[50] Alamán, *Historia de Méjico*, IV, 139–141.
[51] Schmitt, "The Clergy and the Independence of New Spain," *HAHR*, p. 290.
[52] Alamán, *Historia de Méjico*, V, 1718.
[53] Fortino H. Vera (comp.), *Colección de documentos eclesiásticos de México*, II, 341–347.
[54] *Ibid.*, p. 344.
[55] *Ibid.*, p. 343.

José María Couto, served on the Ecclesiastical Committee of the Cortes during the 1820 sessions.[56] This Committee was not so much concerned with statutory reform of the Church as with investigating and legislating on specific questions; e.g., army chaplain's salaries, the publication of papal bulls, and excessive charges by the clergy for religious services.[57] As members of the Committee, however, Ramos Arizpe and Couto were in close touch with many aspects of the Church's position in relation to the state.

A series of anticlerical laws was initiated almost immediately—legislation of a far more radical nature than any passed between 1810 and 1814. One of the first matters to be considered was the expulsion of the Jesuits, the order having been re-established by the king in 1816. The Finance and Legislative Committees, on August 11, 1820, presented to the Cortes a very detailed exposition of the manner by which the order had been re-established, stating that it had not fulfilled legal requirements and formalities and that therefore the re-establishment was null and void. They recommended that those Jesuits who had since returned to Spain and those recently professed be secularized and that their benefices be turned over to the public treasury.[58] The proposal was approved on August 14, no Mexican delegates having taken part in the debates;[59] but neither did any Mexican support the Order strongly enough to offer a personal vote in favor of its retention. On the same day the Cortes decided that the possessions and the treasures acquired by the Jesuits should be turned over to the Treasury to be sold.[60] The proper decree was issued on August 17.[61]

The Legislative Committee, on September 9, recommended that ecclesiastics be deprived of their *fuero* and be subjected to civil jurisdiction in cases involving crimes legally punishable by death or bodily injury; included in the proposal were even those crimes for which such penalties were no longer enforced.[62] After considerable discussion this proposal was approved on September 25 and the resulting

---

[56] Spain, Cortes, 1820–1821, *Diario de las sesiones de Cortes*, I, 20, and II, 907.
[57] *Ibid.*, II, 1465–1467, and III, 1653, 1817–1819.
[58] Spain, Cortes, 1820–1821, *Diario de las Cortes*, II, 293–299.
[59] *Ibid.*, III, 8–32.
[60] *Ibid.*
[61] "Decreto XII de 17 de agosto de 1820," in Spain, Cortes, 1820–1821, *Decretos*, VI, 43–44.
[62] Spain, Cortes, 1820–1821, *Diario de las Cortes*, V, 132–140.

decree was issued the next day.[63] No Mexican delegate took part in the debates relative to the *desafuero*. However, it is important to note that Ramos Arizpe and Couto were the only Mexicans to publicly record their vote, and then only against the provisions which included crimes *no longer punishable, in practice, by death or bodily punishment* (emphasis mine).[64]

Prior to this time the incomplete work of the Cortes of Cádiz concerning reform of the regular religious orders was taken up. On July 23 Vicente Sancho of Valencia made a lengthy and detailed proposal for such reform.[65] His recommendations were sent on August 9 to a special committee composed of nine Spaniards,[66] which presented the results of its deliberations to the Cortes on September 9. Its recommendations were generally similar to those of Sancho. Its twenty-six articles provided for the suppression of all monastaries of the monastic (as distinguished from the mendicant) orders, as well as the convents and colleges of the four military orders, with the benefices connected with any of these restored to their original jurisdiction, both episcopal and royal, for appointment. Exact pension rates were set for the regulars of the suppressed convents until they could be secularized or could obtain civil or ecclesiastical positions to sustain themselves. Only in special cases could monasteries of fewer than twenty-four ordained members continue to exist and each township could have no more than one convent of a given order within its boundaries. In no case could new members be ordained or novices accepted. Convents of nuns were also suppressed and monks and nuns alike were urged to secularize, with special provisions made to protect them and sustain them should they do so.

All the regular clergy was to be subject to the bishops and each convent or monastery continuing in existence was to elect its own official from its own local membership and was not to be subject to any regular prelate outside its monastery or convent. The income from all possessions and real estate of the suppressed monasteries, convents, and colleges was to be applied to the public credit and any income of those continuing in existence until their membership secularized or

---

[63] "Decreto XXXVI de 26 septiembre de 1820," in Spain, Cortes, 1820–1821, *Decretos*, VI, 141–142.

[64] Spain, Cortes, 1820–1821, *Diario de las sesiones de Cortes*, II, 1237.

[65] Spain, Cortes, 1820–1821, *Diario de las Cortes*, I, 298–300.

[66] *Ibid.*, III, 232–233.

died, above that needed to sustain it decently, was also to go to the public treasury. The government was to use the buildings for the public good; the political chiefs were to take charge of all pictures, books, and library materials which should be placed in libraries, museums, academies, and other establishments for public education; and the respective bishops were to dispose of the sacred vessels, jewels, ornaments, images, altars, organs, choir books, and other utensils to provide for the poorer parish churches. Finally, the bishops were to temporarily supply, until the new division of parishes was made, the churches made vacant by the law but thought necessary for the salvation of souls.[67]

Bishop Castrillo, a member of the committee, said that the three principal points on which the recommendations were based were: subjection of the regular clergy to the respective bishops and elimination of all monastic prelates except those elected by the members of the local convents for their respective houses; reduction of the number of convents; and application to the public credit of the wealth of those suppressed. He said that the subjection of the regular clergy to the bishops was a necessary step to preserve the unity and rule of ecclesiastical discipline and that reduction of the number of monasteries was necessary for the common good of the nation. He pointed out that according to the census of 1797 there were in Spain 61,327 religious living in 2,051 monasteries and convents, and that even if the number were smaller in 1820, it would still be very large in proportion to the population of the nation. He recalled further that in the past, kings like Ferdinand VI and Charles III had recognized the need of reducing the monasteries and convents and inverting their wealth into the royal treasury, and that the Cortes of Vallodolid in 1523, of Toledo in 1525, of Segovia in 1532, of Madrid in 1534, and another of Vallodolid of 1537, and others had asked the king for reduction of the monasteries. The committee felt therefore, he continued, that for the good of the nation it was necessary to reduce the convents to a number in proportion to the needs of the people and that the country needed the wealth which was to be gained by the reduction.[68]

Discussion began on the bill in a special night session on September 21, 1820. As a whole there was very little opposition manifested to it

[67] *Ibid.*, V, 115–121.
[68] *Ibid.*, VI, No. 10 (September 21, 1820), 2–5.

by either Spaniards or Americans. Several Mexicans did offer modifications; some of which were accepted. Article 1 as first approved read:

All monasteries of monastic orders[69] shall be suppressed, as well as those of the regular canons and clergy of the order of St. Benedict, the Cloistral Congregation of Tarraconense and Caesar Augustus, St. Augustine, and the Premonstratensians, and the convents and colleges of the military orders of Santiago, Calatrava, Alcántara and Montesa and those of San Juan de Jerusalem, San Juan de Dios, and the Bethlehemites.

It was passed on a roll-call vote of 107 to 31 on September 22, with the whole Mexican delegation present (Couto, Fagoaga, Cortazar, Michelena, Ramos Arizpe, Montoya, and La Llave) voting for it.[70] On the following day, Fagoaga offered an amendment to the effect that an additional phrase be added at the end: "and those of all other hospitalers." He admitted that when these orders were founded in the distant past they were needed because there were few or no hospitals; now, he said, they were no longer needed and should be abolished. His amendment was approved.[71]

Both Michelena and Ramos Arizpe were concerned with the articles on pensions. Michelena's request that pension rates for Americans be adjusted to American monetary values was accepted.[72] His recommendation was accepted that Article 19 be returned to committee to consider what proportion of the dowries of nuns entering convents in America should be restored to them if they became secularized,[73] but the final decree did not indicate that the committee made any change as a result of this recommendation.

Ramos Arizpe asked that monks under fifty years of age who were permanently ill be given the same pension provided for all those over fifty[74] and that the supplementary salary be granted those who were secularized just as soon as their status was changed.[75] This recommendation was written into the law but the pension proposal was not.

[69] The monastic orders referred to here were the Benedictine, Bernardine, Hieronymite, Carthusian, and Basilian orders (*ibid.*, V, 124–125). Apparently the mendicant orders were not to be included in this part of the bill.

[70] *Ibid.*, VI, No. 11 (September 22, 1820), 39–41.

[71] *Ibid.*, VI, No. 12 (September 23, 1820), 16–17.

[72] *Ibid.*, VI, No. 12 (September 23, 1820), 27.

[73] *Ibid.*, VII, No. 1 (September 25, 1820), 29.

[74] Spain, Cortes, 1820–1821, *Diario de las sesiones de Cortes*, II, 1305–1306.

[75] Spain, Cortes, 1820–1821, *Diario de las Cortes*, VI, No. 13 (September 23, 1820), 23.

Ramos Arizpe entered the debates once again to give his support to Article 8, which was intended to subject the regular clergy to episcopal jurisdiction. He believed that this would result in better organization and more effective evangelization in missionary areas, especially in America.[76] No delegate representing New Spain voiced any opposition to the measures regulating the orders and it can be reasonably assumed that they supported all of the other articles. By October 1, the committee's bill had been approved, with only minor changes, and the decree enacting it into law was issued on that date.[77]

Perhaps it is well to point out here that while the first articles dealt with specific orders, calling for their suppression and eventual liquidation (by prohibiting ordination of new members, acceptance of novices, and establishment of new houses), other provisions, from Article 8 on, applied to all the regular orders, including the mendicants, such as Franciscans, Dominicans, etc., and would, if continued in force, contribute to the liquidation of the mendicant orders by prohibiting them too from establishing new houses, ordaining new members, or accepting novices. This law surely turned many to Iturbide's revolutionary cause in 1821.

During the same month of September, while the debates and voting on the *desafuero* and regular monastic orders were going on, another important restriction on the Church was proposed to the Cortes. The Legislative Committee presented a bill, on September 3, abolishing entailments on real estate, including both lay and clerical properties. Articles 1, 6, 9, and 10 of the proposal were particularly applicable to the Church. Article 1 suppressed all property entailments; Article 6 prohibited future restrictions on the free exchange of real estate; Article 9 (which became Article 15 of the final decree) prohibited churches, monasteries, convents, hospitals, hospices, private teaching institutions, confraternities, brotherhoods, and all other establishments, whether clerical or lay, from acquiring entailed real estate by donation, will, purchase, debt, or any other method. Article 10 (which became Article 16 of the final decree) forbade the same institutions to impose or acquire rents from real estate, to use such property as security for borrowing money, or to acquire property by means of foreclosure on loans.[78] Couto, Fagoaga, Michelena, Cortazar, Cañedo,

---

[76] *Ibid.*, VI, No. 13 (September 23, 1820), 20–21.
[77] "Decreto XLII de 1 de octubre de 1820" in Spain, Cortes, 1820–1821, *Decretos*, VI, 155–159.
[78] Spain, Cortes, 1820–1821, *Diario de las sesiones de Cortes*, I, 801.

and La Llave were among those who officially recorded their approval of Article 1 in the *Diario* on September 14.[79] Ramos Arizpe was
not recorded for or against the article. He may not have been present
on the fourteenth.

Articles 6, 9, and 10 were discussed and approved on September 16.
No Mexicans participated in the debate on these articles nor did they
record any votes in opposition in the *Diario*.[80] The final decree was
approved on September 27 under the title "Suppression of all kinds of
entailments."[81]

It has been stated that the decrees, concerning the Jesuits, the *desafuero*, and monastic reform, were published in Mexico in January,
1821, and that they were a direct cause of the high clergy's support of
independence.[82] Compared with the reforms of the 1810–1814 Cortes
these measures were much more radical and the continued rule of the
Cortes appeared to be much more likely than in the earlier period.
Only one of them is to be found in the January issues of the *Gaceta* of
the Mexican government—the decree expelling the Jesuits was published there on January 25, 1821.[83] Yet the others were undoubtedly
known in the country, for the Bishop of Guadalajara published a
pastoral letter against them,[84] and they were mentioned by the Archdeacon of the cathedral of Valladolid de Michoacán, Manuel de la
Bárcena, in his *Manifiesto al mundo . . .,* which was an exhortation in
favor of Mexican independence.[85] Bárcena argued that he had sworn
to uphold the Constitution and laws of Spain, but not to support the
rule of tyrants, by whom he evidently meant the Cortes. He wrote that
the extinction of monasteries and the *desafuero* of the clergy had
scandalized the people and were the impelling causes of the movement for independence. On the whole, Bárcena was willing to accept
a Spanish king but protested the rule of the Cortes.[86] His beliefs were
evidently shared by many of the members of the upper clergy in New

[79] *Ibid.,* II, 1010–1012.
[80] *Ibid.,* pp. 1052–1057.
[81] Spain, Cortes, 1820–1821, *Diario de las Cortes,* VII, No. 4 (September 27,
1820), 11; and "Decreto XXXVIII de 27 de septiembre de 1820," in Spain,
Cortes, 1820–1821, *Decretos,* VI, 145–149.
[82] Schmitt, "The Clergy and the Independence of New Spain," *HAHR,* p. 308.
[83] *Gaceta del gobierno de México,* January 25, 1821.
[84] Alamán, *Historia de Méjico,* V, 39–40.
[85] Manuel de la Bárcena, *Manifiesto al mundo la justicia y la necesidad de la
independencia de la Nueva España.*
[86] *Ibid.*

Spain who supported the Plan of Iguala proclaimed by Iturbide in February, 1821.

The measures passed by the Cortes regulating the Church had very little immediate effect upon that institution in New Spain; the return of Ferdinand VII prevented their execution in 1814, and in 1820 and 1821 their immediate result seems to have been the furtherance of the movement for independence. The Mexican deputies in the Cortes did not take a very active part in the formation of this legislation although by their very silence they appear to have been favorably disposed toward it. Such men as Pino and Cárdenas advocated definite reforms in their provinces. Beye Cisneros wanted the Church to assume greater responsibilities in the field of education. Ramos Arizpe strongly asserted the rights of the state over the Church in certain areas, supported legislation which would subject the regular clergy to the authority of the bishops, and supported the law regulating monasteries. Güereña spoke in favor of the ecclesiastical *fuero* but at the same time said that the discipline of the clergy was a justified concern of the state. Guridi y Alcocer, Foncerrada, and Uría opposed the forced loan on Church ornaments, while Obregón and Pérez supported it; Mendiola's position on this issue remains unclear. Couto, Fagoaga, Michelena, Cortazar, Montoya, and La Llave publicly recorded their support of the law regulating monastic orders and the suppression of entailments. Both Ramos Arizpe and Couto served on the Ecclesiastical Committee in 1820 and dealt with specific questions of Church-state relations. On the whole, then, opinion within the delegation was diverse; yet not one of the Mexicans appears to have actively opposed Church reform.

While the ecclesiastical legislation of the Spanish Cortes was not permanently executed in New Spain, it set important precedents which were later followed by Mexican governments. Many of the men mentioned in this paper and several other Mexican deputies to the Cortes of 1810–1814 and of 1820–1821 were active and influential in Mexico's independent government. Mariano Michelena was a substitute member of the triumvirate which served as the executive during the Constitutional Congress from 1822 to 1824.[87] Also members of this Congress were José Miguel Gordoa, Lucas Alamán, Lorenzo de Zavala, José Miguel Guridi y Alcocer, Ignacio Mora, Luciano Castorena, and José Hernández Chico, all of whom were members of the

[87] Hubert Howe Bancroft, *History of Mexico*, V, 8.

Cortes at various times.[88] Ramos Arizpe was the president of the Constitutional Committee in that Congress. It is therefore not surprising that the ecclesiastical provisions of the Mexican Constitution are strikingly similar to those of the Constitution of 1812, or that, in fact, some are exactly the same.[89]

However, on August 7, 1823, the Mexican Congress abrogated part of the law of September 27, 1820, which suppressed entailed estates. Those provisions dealing with the Church's *manos muertas* were annulled. Article 14 of the 1823 law states that ecclesiastical chaplaincies, charitable institutions, and entailed estates of the Church are no longer subject to the 1820 law," leaving in force the old laws concerning acquisition of real estate and its amortization."[90]

The reforms enacted under the liberal government of Valentín Gómez Farías in 1833 and 1834 bear resemblance to those of the Cortes. Gómez Farías had himself been elected to the 1822–1823 Cortes but, since Mexican independence had become an accomplished fact,[91] he never went to Spain. It is not unlikely, however, that he was well acquainted with the work of that body. Ramos Arizpe was Minister of Justice and Ecclesiastical Affairs from December 29, 1832, to September, 1833. He was succeeded by Andrés Quintana Roo, who, like Gómez Farías, had been elected to the 1822–1823 Cortes but had never taken his seat; he remained in the Ministry until July, 1834.[92] In 1833 Lorenzo de Zavala presented a project to the Congress which recommended the suppression of monasteries and the sale of clerical property, the proceeds of which would be turned over to the state.[93] This was similar to the recommendations which were presented to the Cortes in September, 1820, as discussed earlier

[88] *Ibid.*, pp. 10–11. See also Chapter I, *supra.*

[89] Cf. Articles 3, 50, Section 12; Article 100, Sections 13 and 21; Article 116, Section 9; Article 137, Section 3; and Article 154 of "Constitución federal de los Estados Unidos Mexicanos, sancionada por el Congreso general constituyente, el 4 de octubre de 1824," in Mexico, Constitution, *Colección de constituciones de los Estados Unidos Mexicanos*, I, pp. 35, 51, 72–73, 77, 83, 88.

[90] Mexico, Laws, statutes, etc. *Legislación mexicana o colección completa de las disposiciones legislativas expedidas desde la independencia de la república,* I, 664.

[91] *Gaceta del gobierno México,* May 31, 1821.

[92] Genaro García "Secretarios de Estado del Gobierno Mexicano" (unpublished manuscript in Latin American Collection, University of Texas Library, Austin).

[93] José María Luis Mora, *Obras sueltas,* I, cxliii.

in this essay. Although Zavala had not yet arrived to take his seat on the latter date, he was probably aware of the proposals.

The law secularizing[94] the missions of California, enacted by the Gómez Farías government, subjecting the missions to the jurisdiction of the bishops, although much more far reaching in other respects, was quite similar to the decree of the Cortes of September 4, 1813, and to the later law of October 1, 1820,[95] both previously discussed here. The decision in 1833 to turn the property of the Convent of San Camilo, whose members had been expelled from Mexico, over to the state for its use had a precedent in the Cortes' decision of September, 1813, to use part of convent benefices to help pay the public debt.[96] The law of 1834 which ceded the property of the Jesuits was precedented by the similar action of the Cortes in August, 1820.[97] In regard to entailed ecclesiastical real estate, Gómez Farías, while vice-president during the war with the United States in 1847, issued a decree allowing the sale or mortgage of *manos muertas*, the proceeds of which were to go to the Treasury for the prosecution of the war.[98] Certainly a precedent for this action, even though it was prompted by a national emergency, can be found in the law on entailments of September 27, 1820.

The laws and constitutional provisions dealing with the Church in independent Mexico had well-defined precedents in the deliberation and decisions of the Spanish Cortes. It was in the Cortes that questions concerning the position of the Church in nineteenth-century society were first faced by many of the most influential men of the early republic. In a very real sense, then, the Cortes was an essential preliminary to the proposal and enactment of Mexican law on ecclesiastical matters.

[94] "Secularizing" at this particular time meant that the missions were removed from the jurisdiction of the monastic orders, which had formerly had exclusive control over them, and were put under the control of the bishops, who were to fill the mission positions with secular clergy.

[95] Ricardo Delgado Román (comp.), *Valentín Gómez Farías, Ideario reformista*, pp. 71–74.

[96] *Ibid.*, pp. 71, 76–80.

[97] *Ibid.*, pp. 83–84.

[98] *Ibid.*, pp. 103–105.

6. The Army of New Spain and the Mexican Delegation to the Spanish Cortes

Neill Macaulay

Mexico became independent only after the army of New Spain had been thoroughly subverted. During the unsettled 1808–1810 period there was significant dissention within the viceregal forces as certain creole officers toyed with the idea of independence. But late in 1810 the army responded to strong leadership as creoles and Spaniards closed ranks and presented a solid front to those who sought to end Spanish rule in Mexico. From 1810 to 1820 the viceroy's army was the major obstacle standing in the way of revolutionary victory. During these years Miguel Hidalgo, José María Morelos, Vicente Guerrero, and the other insurgent chieftains were unable to overcome this obstacle by direct military action. But in 1821 Mexican independence was assured when the major part of the viceroy's army deserted their commander-in-chief and followed Colonel Agustín de Iturbide into an alliance with the revolutionists.

The royalist troops in Mexico revolted after the liberal government of Spain made clear its intention to deprive the army and the militia of many of their privileges. Every standard history of the period gives an account of the disaffection of the military, but little attention has been paid to the role of the Mexican delegation to the Spanish Cortes in bringing about this disaffection. Several Mexican delegates to the Cortes in 1820 conspicuously supported the drastic laws of military reform that provoked the mutiny of the army of New Spain. Support of these enactments was only one of many actions taken by certain Mexican delegates which seem to have been aimed at undermining the Spanish army in Mexico. In the Cortes of 1810–1814 the Mexican delegates, Miguel Guridi y Alcocer and Miguel Ramos Arizpe, were outspoken in their advocacy of measures which would have severely hampered the army in its operations against the Mexican rebels and weakened the authority and prestige of its commander-in-chief, the viceroy. After the dissolution of the Cortes in 1814, ex-delegate Antonio Joaquín Pérez joined in a campaign against Viceroy Félix María Calleja which resulted in Calleja's recall and his replacement by Juan Ruíz de Apodaca, a commander who lacked his predecessor's forcefulness and his popularity with the troops. After the restoration of constitutional government in Spain in 1820, the Mexican delegates Ramos Arizpe and Mariano Michelena helped draw up legislation that would have deprived the army of New Spain of its privileged legal position.

By their actions these delegates were furthering the cause of Mexican independence. Whether they were consciously working all along for independence cannot be said with certainty. What is certain is that all four of the delegates mentioned—Guridi y Alcocer, Ramos Arizpe, Pérez, and Michelena—welcomed independence when it came, and all achieved prominence in the government of newly independent Mexico. Other Mexican delegates to the Spanish Cortes served the cause of independence, wittingly or unwittingly, but these four stand out. Guridi y Alcocer was a parish priest, fifty-eight years old in 1821, an eloquent orator and a passionate liberal; Ramos Arizpe was forty-six, a liberal priest, articulate and ambitious, who had just emerged from six years' confinement in Spain; Pérez was a bishop, conservative but opportunistic, fifty-eight years old in 1821; Michelena was an army officer, only thirty-two, but a man who had been involved in revolutionary activity in both Mexico and Spain and had spent several years in the king's prisons.[1] The work done by these men in undermining the Spanish army helped make Iturbide's Plan of Iguala feasible in 1821.

At the beginning of the nineteenth century the armed forces directly under the command of the viceroy and captain general of the kingdom of New Spain numbered about 30,000 officers and men.

[1] Biographical material on Pérez and Guridi y Alcocer may be found in Francisco Pimentel, *Historia crítica de la poesía en México*, Vol. V: *Obras completas de don Francisco Pimentel*, 414, 455. There is a biographical sketch of Michelena in Alejandro Villaseñor y Villaseñor, *Biografías de los héroes y caudillos de la independencia*, Vol. III: *Obras del Lic. Alejandro Villaseñor y Villaseñor*, I, 16–19. Ramos Arizpe gives an account of his life up to 1822 in a pamphlet he published anonymously, *Idea general sobre la conducta política de D. Miguel Ramos de Arizpe, natural de la provincia de Coahuila, como diputado que ha sido por esta provincia en las Cortes generales y extraordinarias, y en las ordinarias de la Monarquía española desde el año de 1810 hasta el de 1820.*

These included 6,150 regular troops, 11,330 provincial militia, 1,059 urban militia, 7,103 coastal militia, 4,320 frontier militia and an undetermined number of replacement militia. This force did not include troops stationed in the Interior Provinces which were not generally available to the captain general and were not considered part of the army of New Spain proper.[2] The colonial army was increased in 1806 when a British attack on New Spain was feared.[3] In 1808 Baron Alexander von Humboldt noted that there were some 9,000 regular troops in the colony and about 22,000 militiamen, excluding the forces in the Interior Provinces and in Yucatán. About half of this total force was mounted, Humboldt observed. He also noted that the militia was far inferior to the regular contingent in armament and discipline. "In the Spanish colonies," Humboldt wrote, "there is no military spirit, only the vanity of a small number of families whose chiefs aspire to the titles of colonel and brigadier."[4]

But it was not vanity alone that made Mexicans seek commissions in the royal army and militia. The colonial officer had a distinct advantage over his nonmilitary compatriots in matters of criminal and civil law. By the Spanish Military Ordinance of 1768 all regular army officers enjoyed the complete *fuero militar*—that is, most criminal and civil cases brought against them had to be tried in military courts; a royal decree of 1793 required that only certain cases involving inheritances be tried in ordinary courts.[5] By 1795 all militia officers in New Spain, whether on active duty or not, had been granted the complete *fuero*.[6] Cases against these part-time officers, who regularly engaged in commerce and other civilian activities, had to be taken to military courts, where the defendants almost invariably received preferential treatment.[7] Enlisted regulars and enlisted militiamen on active duty also enjoyed the complete *fuero*. Even when they were not on active duty, enlisted militiamen enjoyed it in criminal cases. This privilege was regularly abused and militiamen often seemed immune from pun-

[2] Lyle N. McAlister, *The "Fuero Militar" in New Spain, 1764–1800*, pp. 93–99.
[3] Julio Zárate, *La guerra de independencia*, Vol. III of *México a través de los siglos*, ed. Vicente Riva Palacio, p. 37.
[4] Alexander von Humboldt, *Ensayo político sobre Nueva España*, IV, 189–194. See also María del Carmen Velásquez, *El estado de guerra en Nueva España, 1760–1808*.
[5] McAlister, *"Fuero Militar,"* pp. 7, 77, 78.
[6] *Ibid.*, pp. 87–88.
[7] *Ibid.*, pp. 31–39.

ishment for offenses committed against civilians.[8] In 1797 a royal order declared that the extension of military jurisdiction to cases involving mining and mercantile law was contrary to the laws of Castile. Military and civil officials in Mexico City could not agree on the meaning of the royal order, and the military persisted in claiming jurisdiction in all cases formerly covered by their *fuero*. The controversy extended into the Mexican War for Independence, as the troops of the king continued to enjoy their privileged position before the law.[9]

In September, 1808, a revolutionary era dawned in Mexico with the overthrow of the commander of the army of New Spain, Viceroy José de Iturrigaray. A number of army officers supported the coup against Iturrigaray, who, they feared, was planning to share the government of the colony with creole advocates of reform.[10] Among the supporters of the new government of Pedro Garibay was the Spaniard Félix María Calleja, who was rewarded with the command of the Tenth Brigade of mixed regulars and militia at San Luís Potosí.[11] Other military men, mainly creoles, had favored the programs of Iturrigaray and were unwilling to accept the new government. Late in 1808 Lieutenant Mariano Michelena and a group of young creole officers joined with native clergymen in Valladolid de Michoacán in a conspiracy to seize the colonial government and, apparently, declare Mexico independent of Spain.[12] According to Carlos María Bustamente, the Valladolid plot was betrayed by Lieutenant Agustín de Iturbide.[13] Michelena was arrested and, in 1810, imprisoned at Ulúa fortress; three years later he was released from Ulúa on condition that he go to Spain and join the forces fighting the French there.[14]

Fear of an army uprising led Garibay and his successor, Archbishop Francisco Javier Lizana y Beaumont, to reduce concentrations larger than one regiment and scatter the troops in small units throughout

[8] *Ibid.*, pp. 55–58.
[9] *Ibid.*, pp. 88–89.
[10] Lucas Alamán, *Historia de Méjico*, I, 236–249.
[11] Zárate, *Guerra de independencia*, p. 147.
[12] José Mariano de Michelena, "Relación formada por el señor Michelena de lo ocurido en Valladolid (Morelia) en 1809, y preparativos para la revolución de 1810," in J. E. Hernández y Dávalos, *Colección de documentos para la historia de la guerra de independencia de México*, II, 5–7.
[13] Carlos María Bustamante, Copia de la memoria de Iturbide con comentarios, University of Texas Library, Latin American Collection, HD 17–8.4255.
[14] Villaseñor, *Biografías*, pp. 17–18.

the colony.[15] Early in 1810 the bishop-elect of Michoacán—Manuel Abad y Queipo, a Spaniard—sent a letter to the Regency then ruling unoccupied Spain, warning that the defenses of the colony had been seriously weakened under the existing colonial government, and urging that a viceroy of proven military ability be sent to govern New Spain.[16] A new viceroy, Lieutenant General Francisco Javier Venegas, arrived in Mexico City on September 14, 1810, and assumed command of the government and armed forces of New Spain.[17]

Meanwhile the Spanish Regency had decreed that all provinces of the Spanish empire elect delegates to the national congress—the Cortes—which was to be convened in Spain.[18] Thus for the first time the people of Mexico were to be given representation in the government that ruled over them. The elections for Mexican delegates to the Cortes were held in the summer of 1810, at a time when the viceroyalty was presided over by the weak and vacillating Archbishop Lizana y Beaumont. It was a period of agitation and instability, both in Mexico and in Spain, and, according to Abad y Queipo, no time for innovations in government.[19] Revolutionary conspirators took advantage of the situation, and a serious insurrection broke out on September 16, 1810, when Father Miguel Hidalgo issued his Cry of Dolores. The insurgent priest's avowed objectives were to overthrow the viceroy and establish a popular government to rule Mexico in the name of Ferdinand VII, the deposed Spanish king, then a prisoner in France.[20]

Viceroy Venegas was only two days in office when the rebellion broke out. His army was scattered and demoralized as a result of its mismanagement by his predecessors; some creole officers and their troops were participating in the rebellion and others were considering going over to the insurgents. Most of Hidalgo's followers, however, had no military background, but the huge popular force he concentrated under his command was imbued with a revolutionary enthusiasm that made up for its lack of arms and discipline. Venegas

[15] Alamán, *Historia de Méjico*, I, 282–283.
[16] Spain, Cortes, 1810–1813, *Diario de las discusiones y actas de las Cortes*, IV, 192 (hereinafter cited as *Diario de las Cortes*).
[17] *Gaceta del gobierno de México*, September 14, 1810, p. 745.
[18] *Ibid.*, May 16, 1810, p. 413.
[19] Manuel Abad y Queipo, *Representación a S. M. el 20 de junio de 1815 por el obispo electo de Michoacán el Exmo. Dn. Manuel Abad y Queipo, sobre la situación política de nuestras Americas*, University of Texas Library, Latin American Collection, G-360.
[20] Alamán, *Historia de Méjico*, I, 378–379.

was in a race against time: unless he could quickly reorganize and reinvigorate his army, it seemed certain that Hidalgo's hordes would overrun the colony. The rebel movement soon lost momentum, however, partly as a result of Hidalgo's vacillations. By November, 1810, the energetic Brigadier Calleja had gathered under his command a well-armed force of several thousand mounted troops and put them at the service of the viceroy. Calleja's brigade was battle-tested at Aculco, where it effectively checked Hidalgo's advance on November 7, 1810. Although many of his officers had considered defecting to the rebels prior to this action, Calleja's inspirational leadership at Aculco held the brigade together and ended the danger of mutiny among his troops.[21]

Hidalgo's defeat at Aculco and the bloody excesses of his Indian and mestizo followers caused him to lose favor among the creoles of New Spain. The Hidalgo threat to the viceregal government, however, was not ended until Calleja's brigade decisively defeated the insurgents at Calderón Bridge in Nueva Galicia on January 7, 1811, after which the revolutionary army disintegrated. In March, 1811, the rebel priest fell into the hands of royalist troops and in July he was executed.[22]

As the army of New Spain pressed its campaign against the insurgents, its commander-in-chief came under bitter criticism from Hidalgo's sympathizers in Mexico and in Europe. The Spanish-controlled *Consulado de México*, fearing that these attacks would result in Venegas' recall, submitted a memorial dated February 19, 1811, urging the Cortes not to remove him.[23] But the criticism continued, with the editor of *El Español* in London accusing the Viceroy of savagery and inhumanity and of "trying to make himself a Napoleon at the expense of civilians and Indians."[24] *El Español* was read by many members of the Spanish Cortes, but, according to Lucas Alamán, liked by few.[25] Several Mexican delegates may have shared *El Español's* sympathy for Hidalgo's revolution, but only one, José Beye Cisneros, seemed willing to admit it.[26]

When Hidalgo was defeated, the municipal council of Mexico City petitioned the Cortes that Venegas be awarded the Grand Cross of

[21] H. G. Ward, *Mexico*, I, 128–129.
[22] Zárate, *Guerra de Independencia*, pp. 85–226.
[23] Spain, Cortes, 1810–1813, *Diario de las Cortes*, III, 387.
[24] *El Español* (London), April 30, 1811, pp. 86–87.
[25] Alamán, *Historia de Méjico*, III, 26.
[26] *Ibid.*, p. 61.

Charles III. The Viceroy certainly did not deserve all the credit for defeating Hidalgo but, as the royalists of Mexico City realized, he was the symbol of Spanish rule in the colony and the cause of Spain would suffer unless the Spanish government expressed strong and unequivocal support of its beleaguered representative in Mexico. Whatever their feelings might have been toward the Viceroy, none of the Mexican delegates could publicly object to awarding him the Grand Cross. However, the Mexican delegates Mariano Mendiola, Joaquín Maniau, and Guridi y Alcocer saw to it that all praise did not go to Venegas. By the resolution that was adopted, the Viceroy had to share the laurels of victory with the army of New Spain.[27] The churchman Abad y Queipo later charged that revolutionary sympathizers were trying to degrade Venegas in preparation to having him replaced as viceroy by Calleja—a man they felt could be more easily converted to the cause of independence.[28]

At the same time they were praising the army of New Spain, Mexican delegates were helping prepare a draft constitution for the Spanish monarchy that would have deprived the army of its privileged legal position. Pérez and Mendiola were on the committee drawing up the proposed constitution.[29] Article 247 of the draft stated that "in all common affairs, civil and criminal, there will be but one body of laws for all classes of people."[30] By Article 249 military jurisdiction was to be limited to cases in which an infraction of discipline was involved. Introduction of these articles touched off a lengthy debate on November 11, 1811, in which several delegates questioned the wisdom and justice of taking privileges away from the soldiers who were then engaged in a desperate struggle for the survival of the Spanish nation. The Mexican delegation, however, remained silent on the question. The Cortes postponed action on it by amending Article 249 (Article 250 of the Constitution as it was adopted in 1812) to allow the *fuero militar* to remain unchanged until the Cortes could establish a new set of army regulations.[31] It was not until June 12, 1812, that the Cortes again took up the matter of bringing the armed forces under "laws and rules in conformity with the circumstances."[32] A board of fifteen military experts, not members of the

[27] Spain, Cortes, 1810–1813, *Diario de las Cortes*, V, 240–243.
[28] Abad y Queipo, *Representación a S. M.*
[29] Alamán, *Historia de Méjico*, III, 70.
[30] Spain, Cortes, 1810–1813, *Diario de las Cortes*, X, 112.
[31] *Ibid.*, X, 138–150.
[32] *Ibid.*, XIII, 252, 274–282.

Cortes, was subsequently appointed to draw up a new military constitution to replace the old Ordinance of 1768. The board of officers was supposedly hard at work on the project by October 31, but by June 30 of the next year they still had not produced a draft of the new regulations.[33]

If the Mexican delegation was silent on this subject, some of its members were outspoken on other matters of military reform. Ramos Arizpe spoke out repeatedly in favor of the elimination of the army from civil government. He wanted the political chief of each province to be free from military control and responsible to a popularly elected civilian government.[34] Furthermore, he supported Article 365 of the Constitution, which made it illegal for the militia of a province to be employed outside that province without authorization from the Cortes.[35] Had such a requirement been in force in New Spain in 1810, Hidalgo would have overrun the colony. As it happened, the rebellion was crushed in the province of Nueva Galicia by a viceregal force made up largely of militia from the province of San Luís Potosí. Had Viceroy Venegas been compelled to await permission from the Cortes to employ these militiamen outside their province, his cause would have been lost.

Guridi y Alcocer was another outspoken advocate of complete control of the military by the Cortes.[36] He was also an implacable foe of military government in the overseas provinces. When the Cortes was informed, on February 11, 1811, that the captain general of Puerto Rico had suspended all civil rights in order to deal with a revolutionary situation, Guridi y Alcocer eloquently expressed his indignation. He urged that prompt measures be taken to end military rule in Puerto Rico, and also to prevent its recurrence in any of the other provinces.[37] When a second serious revolutionary situation developed in New Spain late in 1811, Viceroy Venegas' denial of civil liberties became an issue in the Spanish Cortes. In a speech on January 16, 1812, Ramos Arizpe found it incomprehensible that Venegas would deny freedom of the press to the "most loyal inhabitants" of

[33] *Ibid.*, XIV, 43–48, 194.
[34] *Ibid.*, XI, 239–240; Miguel Ramos Arizpe, *Memoria que el Doctor D. Miguel Ramos de Arizpe, Cura de Borbón, y Diputado en las presentes Cortes generales y extraordinarias de España por la provincia de Coahuila*, pp. 31–34.
[35] Spain, Cortes, 1810–1813, *Diario de las Cortes*, XI, 300.
[36] See his speech of October 10, 1811, on the king's right to declare war. Spain, Cortes, 1810–1812, *Diario de las Cortes*, IX, 194–195.
[37] *Ibid.*, III, 355.

New Spain.[38] While Ramos Arizpe spoke, a rebel army under José María Morelos was extending its control over a vast area south of Mexico City, and three battalions of royal troops were being landed at Veracruz to help put down the insurrection.[39]

Ramos Arizpe and his liberal colleagues in the Cortes could not have been ignorant of the critical military situation in New Spain, yet they continued to press for political reforms that diminished the viceroy's ability to deal effectively with the rebels. On October 5, 1812, Venegas promulgated the liberal Constitution of 1812 in New Spain, much against his will, and thereby sanctioned freedom of the press and exchanged the exalted title of "Viceroy" for that of "Superior Political Chief"—though he retained the title "Captain General" and command of the army. In accordance with the Constitution, arrangements were made to hold parish elections in the provinces of New Spain to choose electors who, in turn, would select each province's delegates to the Spanish Cortes and the members of its Provincial Deputation. The parish elections in Mexico City were scheduled for Sunday, November 29, 1812.[40]

These elections were held at a time when armed rebels controlled much of the countryside around Mexico City and a secret revolutionary society, the Guadalupes, were active inside the capital.[41] The revolutionary underground was well organized for the event and prepared ballots listing their favorites, to be passed out to illiterates and deposited by them at the polls.[42] As election day approached, the newspapers *El Jugetillo* and *El Pensador Mejicano* appealed to anti-Spanish passions with a series of attacks on Venegas' administration.[43] The elections were undoubtedly fair and the results reflected the will of the people of Mexico City. The electorate, however, was not content to express its will only at the polling places. On the afternoon of November 29 crowds of voters gathered in the streets shout-

---

[38] *Ibid.*, XI, 282.

[39] Zárate, *Guerra de Independencia*, pp. 278–280.

[40] Nettie Lee Benson, "The Contested Mexican Election of 1812," *HAHR*, XXVI (August, 1946), 336–337.

[41] Wilbur J. Timmons, "Los Guadalupes: A Secret Society in the Mexican Revolution for Independence," *HAHR*, XXX (November, 1950), 453–479.

[42] *Ibid.*, pp. 464–465; Benson, "The Contested Mexican Election of 1812," p. 348.

[43] Jefferson Rea Spell, *The Life and Works of José Joaquín Fernández de Lizardi*, pp. 17–18.

ing "Long live the creoles!" and "Death to the Gachupines!"[44] Cheers were heard for the editors of *El Pensador mejicano* and *El Jugetillo,* "because they tell the unvarnished truth."[45] The commotion continued throughout the night and into the next day when it was learned that not a single Spaniard had been elected. Mexican mobs shouted "Now it is we who command! Long live the electors! Long live Father Morelos! Long live the insurgents and death to *todos los carajos gachupines!*"[46] The Guadalupes were jubilant and wrote to Morelos that the elections were "the first step toward the establishment of Mexican liberty."[47]

Defeat of the Spanish party in the elections was a terrific blow to the prestige of the Captain General. The creole press was emboldened, and on December 3 *El Pensador mejicano* published a scurrilous attack on Venegas.[48] The next day the Viceroy reacted by jailing the editor of the newspaper and on December 5 he suspended freedom of the press in New Spain, and did not further implement the electoral process in the province of Mexico.[49] These measures were, of course, contrary to the letter and spirit of the government then in power in Spain. But as the head of a government under revolutionary attack and as the commander-in-chief of an army engaged in military operations against armed insurgents, Venegas was justified in taking this action. Nevertheless he acted too late; his effectiveness as leader of the antirevolutionary cause had already been destroyed.

He was replaced on March 4, 1813, by General Calleja, a Spaniard who had resided in the colony for many years and who knew the ways of the Mexicans.[50] Any hopes the insurgents had of converting Calleja to the cause of independence were dashed soon after he took office. "If you were not my friends," he announced to a pair of Guadalupes who came to negotiate with him, "I would have you shot."[51] The

---

[44] Affidavit of José Palacios Lanzagorta, in Rafael Alba, ed. *La constitución de 1812 en la Nueva España,* p. 247.

[45] Affidavit of Manuel Palacios Lanzagorta, *Ibid.,* pp. 216–217.

[46] Affidavit of Julián Roldán, *ibid.,* pp. 248–250.

[47] The Guadalupes to Morelos, December 7, 1812, Correspondencia de los Guadalupanos, University of Texas Library, Latin American Collection, G-346.

[48] *El Pensador mejicano* (Mexico City), December 3, 1812.

[49] Alamán, *Historia de Méjico,* III, 294–295.

[50] Zárate, *Guerra de Independencia,* p. 372.

[51] Anastacio Zerecero, *Memorias para la historia de las revoluciones en México,* pp. 252–254.

new captain general proceeded with the suspended elections, confident that he could handle developments as they arose. Nevertheless he failed in his efforts to bring pressure on the electors of Mexico City to make them select members of the Spanish party. The Guadalupes wrote to Morelos after the electors met, informing him that all their candidates had been elected—including Guridi y Alcocer, who had returned from the Cortes as vicar general of the Archbishopric of Mexico and was now elected to the Provincial Deputation.[52] The Cortes delegates elected from Mexico City, Calleja believed, were all revolutionists, so he denied them funds for transportation to Spain. Two, Manuel Cortazar and José María Alcalá, eventually sailed anyway. When he learned of their departure, the wily Captain General sent a letter to the Ministry of Justice declaring them subversives.[53] Other Cortes delegates expressed to the Guadalupes a preference for serving in the revolutionary Congress at Chilpancingo rather than in the "illegitimate assembly at Cádiz."[54]

Although Calleja recognized the Constitution, he continued to deny the colonists their constitutional right of freedom of the press. The section guaranteeing this right, the Captain General claimed, was "the only article that the welfare of the country has required me to maintain suspended."[55] In the Cortes, Ramos Arizpe roundly denounced the suppression of constitutional guarantees in New Spain. Blandly ignoring the revolution that was raging in his homeland, he insisted on May 18, 1813, that freedom of the press was as applicable in New Spain as it was in the Spanish city of Cádiz.[56] He and thirty other American deputies, on July 11, 1813, addressed a memorial to the Regency, protesting the lack of constitutional liberties in New Spain.[57] The Regency replied on July 24 with the opinion that the policy of the Captain General of New Spain should continue until

[52] The Guadalupes to Morelos, April 9 and August 13, 1813, University of Texas Library, Latin American Collection.
[53] Félix María Calleja, "Informe del exmo. Sr. Virrey D. Félix Calleja sobre el estado de la N.E. dirigido al Ministerio de Gracia y Justicia en 18 de Agosto de 1814," University of Texas Library, Latin American Collection, JGI-XXVI-2.
[54] The Guadalupes to Morelos, November 3, 1813, *ibid.*
[55] Félix María Calleja, "Manifesto del Virrey Calleja a los habitantes de Nueva España publicado el 22 de junio de 1812," extract in Alba, *La constitución de 1812 en Nueva España*, p. 246.
[56] Spain, Cortes, 1810–1813, *Diario de las sesiones de las Cortes generales y extraordinarias*, VII, 5318 (hereinafter cited as *Diario de las sesiones de las Cortes*).
[57] *Ibid.*, VIII, 5684–5685.

circumstances changed.[58] The matter was passed to a Cortes committee, which subsequently recommended that a military regime be authorized in New Spain for as long as the revolution lasted. This recommendation, according to Lucas Alamán, was welcomed by the Regency, and Calleja was given a free hand in dealing with the rebels.[59]

Within a year and a half the Captain General had smashed the Guadalupe ring and his army had administered a series of staggering defeats to the rebels.[60] According to Calleja's admirer Alamán, an average of twenty-five Mexicans faced firing squads daily in the early months of 1814.[61] Nevertheless Calleja later complained to the Minister of Justice that the constitutional system hindered his pacification of the colony. The rebels in New Spain, he asserted, maintained constant communication with their representatives in the Cortes, who informed them of steps being taken by the government to combat the insurrection.[62]

The Cortes adjourned on September 14, 1813, after an idealistic closing address by the president of the Cortes, José Miguel Gordoa, a Mexican. He urged the delegates to return to their provinces and instruct the rebels in civic virtue.[63] The Cortes reconvened on March 1, 1814, but this session was short-lived. Napoleon had been defeated and King Ferdinand returned to Spain amidst much rejoicing. Sentiment for a return to absolute monarchy was rising. Mexican Delegate Pérez presented the King a petition signed by him and sixty-eight other delegates, including three Mexicans, urging the monarch to dissolve the Cortes and resume absolute rule.[64] This was done on May 9, 1814, and the King rewarded Pérez by making him Bishop of Puebla; Ramos Arizpe and several other Mexicans who opposed the restoration of absolutism were jailed.[65]

In New Spain Calleja hailed the end of constitutionalism and urged his soldiers to honor the king above all else. "Your service puts you

[58] *Ibid.*, pp. 5787–5788.
[59] Alamán, *Historia de Méjico*, III, 300.
[60] Timmons, "Los Guadalupes," p. 479.
[61] Alamán, *Historia de Méjico*, IV, 123.
[62] Félix María Calleja, "Informe . . . al Ministerio de Gracia y Justicia.
[63] Spain, Cortes, 1810–1813, *Diario de las sesiones de las Cortes*, VIII, 6226.
[64] "Importante representación de 69 diputados a las Cortes ordinarias, presentada a Fernando VII a su regreso a España, 12 de Abril de 1814," in Hernández y Dávalos, *Colección de documentos*, V, 377–412.
[65] Alamán, *Historia de Méjico*, IV, 141.

among the first of his subjects," the Viceroy declared. "For your service you enjoy the high *fueros* that are due the defenders of the fatherland and of the sovereign." These *fueros*, Calleja announced, "were to have been taken away under the illusory liberal system."[66] The monarch, then, was the source of the army's privileges; any diminution of the king's authority would threaten the vested interests of the armed forces. Calleja's proclamation identified the constitutional system as the natural enemy of the military establishment. This lesson was not lost on the army of New Spain.

By the end of 1815 Calleja's troops had crushed Morelos' revolutionary movement and the insurgent chieftain had been executed. But Calleja's victories earned him little gratitude from the Spanish court. The vain and foolish King resented the Viceroy for having been appointed by the Regency and not by him. The meddlesome Abad y Queipo informed His Majesty that Calleja had been the favorite of Mexican liberals in 1812 and claimed he lacked the will and the military competence to pacify the colony.[67] The new Bishop of Puebla, ex-Cortes deputy Antonio Joaquín Pérez, also joined in the campaign against Calleja. Soon after returning to New Spain, the Bishop wrote Calleja that he was shocked to learn what had been going on during his absence. Pérez charged in his letter of April 14, 1816, that the Viceroy's army had despoiled the country and spilled innocent blood; in the towns his troops liberated, innocent people were murdered and robbed on the pretense that they were rebel sympathizers; excessive and arbitrary forced contributions were collected throughout the colony; small farmers, storekeepers, and other property owners were reduced to misery for suspected complicity with the insurgents; the king's revenues from the silver mines and church funds were seized by Calleja's troops without proper authorization.[68]

Calleja replied on June 12, 1816, answering Pérez' letter point by point. He did not deny that excesses were committed, but pointed out that there would always be abuses as long as human nature re-

[66] Félix María Calleja, "Proclama del Exmo. Sr. Virey de esta Nueva España D. Félix María Calleja a sus bizarras tropas," in *Gaceta del gobierno de México*, September 6, 1814, p. 1011.

[67] Abad y Queipo, *Representación a S. M.*

[68] Pérez to Calleja, April 14, 1816, in "Controversia entre el obispo de Puebla y el virrey Calleja," *Boletín del Archivo General de la Nación*, IV (September, 1933), 657–664.

mained as it was; the army was fighting savage revolutionists who had declared war to the death against the Spanish throne; the vacillations of the Spanish constitutional government—in which Pérez was so prominent—encouraged the rebels and spurred them on to greater ferocity; Calleja had no choice but to take it upon himself to adopt strong measures in dealing with the enemy; these measures brought success and reduced the revolutionary armies to "wandering bands of desperadoes hiding out in the hills and in the unhealthy regions"; Calleja needed funds to finance his operations and he raised them by the best means available; the contributors should consider their money well-spent; whenever possible he had given an accounting of these funds; when abuses were brought to his attention he took prompt steps to punish the guilty parties.[69] Calleja's defense was ineffective, and on September 20, 1816, he was replaced by Juan Ruíz de Apodaca.[70]

Carlos María Bustamente, Calleja's enemy, agreed with his admirer, Alamán, that the royalist commander had great military talent. He was loved by his troops and mixed freely with them, yet he always retained the respect due a general and was a firm disciplinarian. He confided in his regional commanders and delegated to them broad authority to take the actions their particular circumstances required. His positive but flexible leadership produced a highly efficient army of over forty thousand disciplined troops.[71] As long as this force retained its effectiveness and remained faithful to the king, there was no hope of a revolutionary victory in Mexico.

Viceroy Apodaca lacked Calleja's single-minded ruthlessness and was less suited to deal with the exigencies of revolutionary Mexico.[72] Nevertheless, he inherited from his predecessor the military means to deal with the insurgents and, except for lingering guerrilla activity and one rebel expedition from the United States that was quickly defeated, the country was at peace during the first three years of his administration. Apodaca offered amnesty to all rebels who would peacefully lay down their arms. Many, seeing their military situation

---

[69] Calleja to Pérez, June 12, 1816, *ibid.*, pp. 664–684.

[70] *Gaceta del gobierno de México*, September 24, 1816, pp. 931–932.

[71] Zárate, *Guerra de Independencia*, pp. 520–521; Carlos María Bustamante, *Campañas del general D. Félix María Calleja, commandante en gefe del ejército llamado del centro.*

[72] Alamán, *Historia de Méjico*, IV, 481–482; Zárate, *Guerra de Independencia*, p. 527.

hopeless, took advantage of the offer and withdrew from the struggle to await a more favorable time for revolution.[73]

The opportunity came in 1820. Early that year there was a revolution in Spain led by liberal army officers, among whom was the Mexican Michelena. The King was forced to reinstate the Constitution of 1812 and reconvene the Cortes. Ramos Arizpe was released from a monastery in Valencia where he had been confined since 1815 and— along with Michelena and five other Mexicans then in Spain—he was named stand-in delegate to the Cortes until a regular Mexican delegation could be elected and sent to Spain. Viceroy Apodaca reinstated the Constitution in New Spain on May 27, 1820, and ordered the holding of elections.[74]

Many military men in New Spain were clearly unhappy with the restoration of constitutionalism. Spanish General José Dávila reportedly remarked to a group of liberal merchants at Veracruz, "Gentlemen, you have made me proclaim and swear to the Constitution; now expect independence, for that is going to be the result of all this."[75] Not long afterwards creole Colonel José Cristóbal Villaseñor began conspiring with a group that included Juan Francisco Azcárate, a lawyer and former supporter of Iturrigaray, to declare Mexico independent. But Colonel Villaseñor died on January 21, 1821,[76] and it remained for another creole officer to lead the colony to independence. Colonel Agustín de Iturbide deplored the "lack of moderation in the supporters of the new system, the indecision of the authorities and the conduct of the government of Madrid and of the Cortes."[77] It was the Cortes that struck directly at the vested interests of the military.

On August 4, 1820, the Cortes ordered published and distributed a projected law that would make all militiamen serving on active duty in Spain subject to civil jurisdiction for all offenses except those purely military.[78] This proposal was enacted into law on August 23. That same day the Mexican delegation—less only one member, Juan

[73] William Forrest Sprague, *Vicente Guerrero, Mexican Liberator: A Study in Patriotism*, pp. 29–39.

[74] Alamán, *Historia de Méjico*, V, 6–30.

[75] *Ibid.*, p. 16.

[76] *Ibid.*, pp. 37, 76.

[77] Agustín de Iturbide, *Carrera militar y política de don Agustín de Iturbide*, pp. 9–10.

[78] Spain, Cortes, 1820, *Diario de las sesiones de Cortes*, I, 379–380.

de Dios Cañedo—proposed that the law be extended to all the overseas provinces except Cuba. This proposal was not adopted, but Michelena, Ramos Arizpe, and seven other American delegates were named to a committee to draw up a bill for the regulation of the overseas militia.[79] The proposed law submitted by the Michelena committee and subsequently adopted by the Cortes on September 29, 1820, deprived the colonial militia of its privilege of trial by courtsmartial for nonmilitary offenses.[80]

News of this attack on the *fuero militar* reached Mexico in October, 1820.[81] As early as July 4 the army of New Spain had learned that work had resumed on a new military constitution.[82] Now ex-Viceroy Calleja's assertion that the liberal system was the natural enemy of the armed forces apparently was being borne out. But the army was not the only institution under attack in the Cortes: by the end of October Mexican clergymen had learned that bills were being considered to restrict the privileges of the Church. Early in November a group of clergymen and army officers, headed by Iturbide, began conspiring to declare Mexico independent of Spain [83] and, presumably, to set up a regime that would protect their vested interests.

Chances for the plot's success increased as the Cortes continued to enact reforms. First the Church *fuero* was abolished.[84] A week later, on October 25, 1820, a projected constitutional law for the regular army in Spain was put before the Cortes. Article 116 declared that the legal privileges of the armed forces constituted an onerous incongruity in the existing political order. Succeeding articles denied military jurisdiction in all civil cases and in all criminal cases except those of a strictly military nature.[85] The projected law was ordered published and distributed throughout the empire[86] and in 1821 it was

---

[79] *Ibid.*, pp. 627–628.
[80] *Ibid.*, II, 1300–1301.
[81] *Gaceta del gobierno de México*, October 28, 1820, p. 1108.
[82] *Ibid.*, July 4, 1820, p. 649.
[83] Alamán, *Historia de Méjico*, V, 25–30, 45.
[84] Karl M. Schmitt, "The Clergy and the Independence of New Spain, *HAHR*, XXXIV (August, 1954), 306–307.
[85] Spain, Cortes, 1820, *Diario de las sesiones*, III, 1896–1904. This proposed law was drawn up in less than three months by a special commission of the Cortes that took up the work of the military commission that was occupied with the project from 1812 to 1814. *Ibid.*, I, 397.
[86] *Ibid.*, III, 2033.

reprinted in Mexico.[87] The law was enacted on May 7, 1821, and the army in Spain lost its *fuero*.[88] Michelena then proposed that a committee be created to draw up a similar law that would apply to the army in the overseas provinces and, on June 10, 1821, his proposal was adopted.[89] "The Cortes," Iturbide later declared, "seemed determined to lose these possessions, according to the decrees it issued and the speeches that some deputies made."[90]

Among the churchmen associated with Iturbide's conspiracy during the winter of 1820–1821 was Bishop Pérez of Puebla, who had reason to fear the Cortes because of his collaboration with the king in the dissolution of that body in 1814.[91] Among the military men who joined the plot that winter were Spanish Brigadier Pedro Celestino Negrete, a commander of regular troops in New Galicia,[92] and creole Lieutenant Colonel Manuel Gómez Pedraza, a militia officer who had been elected to the Cortes in 1820.[93] On February 24, 1821, three weeks after Gómez Pedraza sailed from Veracruz to take his seat in the Cortes, Iturbide proclaimed his Plan of Iguala.[94] The plan provided for an independent Mexican monarchy, preferably ruled by a member of the Spanish royal family. Article 17 declared that the army of the new kingdom would be governed by the Spanish Ordinance of 1768, which recognized military jurisdiction in civil and criminal matters involving soldiers and militiamen.[95] When Iturbide proclaimed his plan he had the support of most of the major insurgent guerrilla leaders. Within three months he won most of the army of New Spain over to his cause.[96]

---

[87] *Proyecto de ley constitutiva del ejército, presentado a las Cortes por las comisiones unidas de organización de fuerza armada y de milicias.*

[88] Spain, Cortes, 1821, *Diario de las sesiones de Cortes*, II, 1454–1455.

[89] *Ibid.*, III, 2155.

[90] Iturbide, *Carrera militar y política*, p. 10.

[91] Alamán, *Historia de Méjico*, V, 67.

[92] Manuel Rivera Cambas, *Los gobernantes de México: galería de biografías y retratos de los Vireyes, Emperadores, Presidentes y otros gobernantes que ha tenido México desde Don Hernando Cortes hasta el C. Benito Juárez*, II, 99.

[93] Manuel Gómez Pedraza, *Manifiesto que Manuel Gómez Pedraza, ciudadano de la República de Méjico, dedica a su compatriotas; o sea una reseña de su vida pública*, pp. 6–11; Rivera Cambas, *Los gobernantes de México*, II, 164.

[94] Nettie Lee Benson, "Iturbide y los planes de independencia," *Historia Mexicana*, II (January–March, 1953), 440–444.

[95] "Plan de Iguala de 24 de febrero de 1821," in Felipe Terra Ramírez, *Leyes fundamentales de México, 1808–1957*, pp. 114–115.

[96] Alamán, *Historia de Méjico*, V, 132–239.

Meanwhile, in the Cortes, Ramos Arizpe and Michelena seemed to be doing all they could to further the cause of Mexican independence. They were joined by the rest of the Mexican delegation in petitioning the Minister of War on January 22, 1821, to recall Viceroy Apodaca and most of the other Spanish generals in America who had had any success in fighting the insurgents. The Mexicans proposed that Apodaca be replaced by Ramos Arizpe's old friend, General Juan O'Donojú, a man of liberal inclination.[97]

By July, 1821, the army of New Spain was thoroughly subverted. Viceroy Apodaca was hopelessly incapable of handling the situation. A group of Spanish officers, aware of the need for stronger leadership, forced Apodaca to resign in favor of General Francisco Novella. The officers who backed Novella, Alamán strongly implies, were Freemasons and shared the liberal ideas of their comrades who had overthrown absolutism in Spain the previous year. Whatever Novella's ideology, the new army commander was no more successful than his predecessor in preventing the disintegration of the viceregal forces. Royalist troops continued to desert to the enemy and on August 2, 1821, the city of Puebla fell to Iturbide's revolutionary forces.[98]

Meanwhile, Ramos Arizpe's friend O'Donojú arrived in Veracruz on July 30 as the new superior political chief and captain general of New Spain. He was soon in contact with Iturbide and on August 24, 1821, he signed the Treaty of Córdoba, recognizing Mexico as "a sovereign and independent nation."[99] When General Novella learned of the O'Donojú-Iturbide pact he gave up the struggle and accepted an armistice on September 8. Iturbide's army formally took possession of Mexico City on September 28 and set up a provisional government consisting of a five-man Regency headed by Iturbide and including O'Donojú, and a thirty-six man Governing Board presided over by Bishop Pérez. Another former Cortes delegate, Guridi y Alcocer, became president of the Governing Board on October 13, after Pérez filled a vacancy in the Regency caused by the death of O'Donojú. [100]

Mexican independence was now assured. Cortes delegates would

---

[97] [Miguel Ramos Arizpe, *et al.*], *Papel que la diputación mejicana dirige al excmo. señor Secretario de Estado y del Despacho de la Guerra.*

[98] Alamán, *Historia de Méjico*, V, 244–256.

[99] "Tratado de Cordoba de 24 de Agosto de 1821," in Terra Ramírez, *Leyes fundamentales de México*, p. 116.

[100] Alamán, *Historia de Méjico*, V, 292–298.

continue to debate the matter, and they would refuse to ratify the Treaty of Córdoba,[101] but the Spanish government now had no means to enforce its will in Mexico. The once mighty army of New Spain had been destroyed—not by revolutionary forces on the field of battle but, to a marked degree, by revolutionary sympathizers in the halls of the Spanish Cortes.

[101] Spain, Cortes, 1821–1822, *Diario de las sesiones de Cortes*, III, 2297–2309.

7. The Role of the Mexican Deputies in the Proposal and Enactment of Measures of Economic Reform Applicable to Mexico

John H. Hann

Although New Spain was included in Charles III's system of free trade within the empire only in 1789, the impact of the king's general economic reforms had been felt there earlier, bringing a notable increase in the area's economic activity. Spain's wars with England during the last years of the century and much of the first decade of the nineteenth century occasioned a relaxation of the Spanish control of the trade of Mexico. For two brief periods (1797–1799 and 1805–1809) the king temporarily removed the prohibition against trade by New Spain with foreign nations. And since Spain was less able to enforce its restrictions, the contraband trade flourished. By 1810 even some of the minor Mexican ports, such as Tampico, Tuxpan, and Guazacoalcos, were receiving European goods directly from other Spanish American ports, and the coastal trade between such ports in Mexican produce was beginning to assume some importance.[1] All of these factors contributed to an increase in the prosperity of at least some sectors of the Mexican economy.

---

[1] Juan Vicente de Revillagigedo, *El Virrey de Nueva España, conde de Revillagigedo, informa en el expediente sobre averiguar si hay decadencia en el comercio de aquellos reinos* (Vol. IV, pp. 6–7, in *Colección de documentos para la historia del comercio exterior de México*). Eusebio Ventura Beleña, *Informe reservado del oidor de la Audiencia de México, Don Eusebio Ventura Beleña, al excelentísimo señor Virrey de Nueva España, conde de Revillagigedo, sobre el actual estado del comercio del mismo reino, ibid.*; Robert Sidney Smith, "Shipping in the Port of Vera Cruz, 1790–1821," *HAHR*, XXIII (February, 1943), 13–14; José María Quiros, "Balanza del comercio marítimo de Vera-Cruz correspondiente al año de 1811, formada por el consulado en cumplimiento de las órdenes del rey," in Miguel Lerdo de Tejada, *Comercio esterior de México*, Appendix 24, note 10.

On the other hand, the disruption of normal trade patterns, which resulted from the wars, was a source of economic difficulties. It caused occasional severe shortages of imported articles. The growth of the contraband trade as a source of imports weakened the export market for Mexican products, as the smugglers generally had to be paid in money and bullion rather than in goods. Moreover, many galling restrictions on the development of trade, industry, and agriculture remained in force. The most pernicious and pervasive effects of these restraints came from the monopolistic control of trade exercised by the merchants of Mexico City, Veracruz, and Cádiz, through whose hands passed virtually all imports and exports.

Thus it is not surprising that economic reform should be one of the subjects in which a majority of the Mexican deputies took an interest. Among the deputies to the Cortes of 1810–1814 who showed a marked interest in one or more aspects of economic reform were Mariano Mendiola, José Miguel Gordoa y Barrios, Joaquín Maniau, Pedro Bautista Pino, José Simeón Uría, José Cayetano Foncerrada, and the seven alternate deputies. José Miguel Guridi y Alcocer and José Miguel Ramos Arispe were the most voluble and outspoken of all the Mexican deputies on this subject, as they were on so many others. José Ignacio Beye Cisneros, Miguel González Lastiri, and Antonio Joaquín Pérez were the Mexican deputies to this Cortes who seem to have manifested the least interest in economic reform. In the 1820 sessions Ramos Arispe and José Mariano Michelena were the two Mexicans active in introducing or supporting measures in this field. The rest of the Mexican deputies to that session, however, apparently supported the economic reforms for New Spain. In the 1821–1822 sessions Lucas Alamán joined Ramos Arispe and Michelena as an active advocate of those measures.

The first expression of the Mexican deputies' interest in economic reform appears in a paper, drawn up by the American alternate deputies and presented to the Cortes on December 16, 1810. They presented eleven reform proposals and professed that the Cortes' adoption of them would, by eliminating the principal grievances of the Americans, contribute substantially to the termination of the insurrections in the colonies. Six of the eleven proposals dealt with economic problems and three of the six involved trade reform (see Appendix A).

Those six measures sought the removal of restrictions on the development of agriculture, industry, and crafts; on the development of domestic and foreign trade; and on the development of mining. Since all the significant economic reforms for New Spain on which the Mexican deputies expressed themselves were related to the three broad fields of economic activity embraced by these six propositions, the three categories of agriculture-industry, trade, and mining, which they suggest, provide a convenient outline for the study of the Mexican deputies' role in the proposal and enactment of economic reforms which would affect their land.

The first of the economic provisions contained in the document of December 16, 1810, requested that the natives and inhabitants of America be allowed to plant whatever crops the climate and their skills made feasible. It also asked for freedom to establish industries and to exercise trades in the Americas.[2] This proposal, taken up by the Cortes in the public session of February 9, 1811, was approved apparently without opposition.[3]

Despite the lack of discussion when the measure was approved, there are sources of information on the attitude of various Mexican deputies toward the changes in policy which the proposition contained and grounds for presuming that the seven alternate deputies for Mexico as well as Guridi y Alcocer, who were among those who signed the original document of December 16, 1810, were supporters of the reforms which it advanced. Joaquín Pérez of Puebla, who also signed the document, did, however, vote against at least one of the revisions of policy which it embodied.[4]

Guridi y Alcocer's active support of the reform is indicated by his words to the Cortes on January 9, 1811. On that occasion he attributed the unrest then current in the Americas to dissatisfaction with the misery that had resulted from Spain's restrictions on the agriculture, industry, and commerce of the Americas. As examples he cited the government's prohibition of the cultivation of certain plants such as the olive and the grape, the government's frustration of Mexico's de-

---

[2] Spain, Cortes, 1810–1813, *Proposiciones que hacen al Congreso nacional los diputados de América y Asia*, p. 1 (hereinafter referred to as *Proposiciones*).
[3] Spain, Cortes, 1810–1813, *Diario de los discusiones y actas de las Cortes*, III, 299 (hereinafter referred to as *Diario de las Cortes*).
[4] Spain, Cortes, 1810–1813, *Representación de la diputación americana a las Cortes de España en 1° de agosto de 1811*, p. 16; Spain, Cortes, 1810–1813, *Actas de las sesiones secretas de las Cortes generales y extraordinarias de la nación española que se instalaron en la isla de León el día 21 septiembre de 1810 y cerraron sus sesiones in Cádiz el 14 de igual mes de 1813*, pp. 378–379 (hereinafter referred to as *Actas de las sesiones secretas.*)

sire to manufacture paper, and the government's nullification of Mexico's potential to trade her flour with the Windward Islands and her textiles with Peru.[5]

A year later one of the points in a bitter controversy between Guridi y Alcocer and Juan López Cancelada, editor of *El Telégrafo americano* and spokesman for the monopolist merchants of Cádiz, involved that same proposal. Guridi y Alcocer, admitting that a royal *cédula* of 1802 had sanctioned the planting of grapes and olives, pointed out that the *cédula* contained a proviso that the grapes and olives were not to be used to make wine, brandy, raisins, or oil. He admitted further that this proviso had been violated, but declared that the potentialities of the wine-making and oil-pressing industries had remained largely unrealized due to the fear that vines and trees might be destroyed if the industry became important enough to attract the attention of a viceroy inclined to insist on observance of the restrictive law.[6]

Guridi y Alcocer concluded his remarks in the Cortes with the observation that the only way in which Spain could preserve her colonies would be by permitting them to plant any crops their lands would produce, to manufacture whatever they could, and to sell their products to whoever would buy them. This request for equality of economic rights with the inhabitants of the mother country was one that would be repeated again and again in sessions of the Cortes, until Mexico declared its independence.[7]

Ramos Arispe not only gave firm support to measures for removing the restraints on the development of agriculture and industry in Mexico but also advocated positive government action to encourage their development. In his report to the Cortes of November 7, 1811, detailing conditions in the Eastern Interior Provinces, he deplored the government restrictions that had stunted the growth of the wine industry of Parras, the neglect that had permitted the spoliation of Texas' resources in game, mustangs, and cattle to the benefit of predatory foreigners, and the government indifference that had led to decay rather than progress in the industry and agriculture of the area.[8]

---

[5] Spain, Cortes, 1810–1813, *Diario de las Cortes*, II, 318–319.

[6] José Miguel Guridi y Alcocer, "Contestación de Don José Miguel Guridi y Alcocer a lo que contra él y los decretos de las Cortes se ha vertido en los números 13 y 14 del *Telégrafo americano*," *El Censor estraordinario*, pp. 2–8, 35–37.

[7] Spain, Cortes, 1810–1813, *Diario de las Cortes*, II, 319.

[8] Miguel Ramos de Arispe, *Report that Dr. Miguel Ramos de Arispe Presents*

His eloquent appeal for the liberation and encouragement of industry and agriculture was not just special pleading for his own Eastern Interior Provinces. He enthusiastically supported the exposition made by Pedro Bautista Pino to show the actual poverty and potential riches of the Western Interior Provinces and Nuevo México. In his speeches before the Cortes, Ramos Arispe stressed the need for the opening and developing of ports at Guaymas and on the Bay of San Bernardo (the Matagorda Bay area), if the riches of those provinces were to be realized, arguing that the constitutional and legal guarantees of the sacred right of property, as well as the proclamation of the untrammeled use of land and development of industry, were meaningless if the settlers in such remote regions were not allowed to import necessities and to export their surpluses in a manner that was economically feasible. On this occasion, when he submitted a resolution to the Cortes calling for the opening of the port of Guaymas for general domestic trade with a ten-year exemption from all import and export duties, he acted in the same spirit as he had when he proposed the opening of the ports of Brazo de Santiago, Soto la Marina, etc., and urged official encouragement of fairs in selected points of the Interior Provinces in order to make the opening of those ports effective.[9]

In a similar tone Pedro Bautista Pino, in his published report and in his speeches to the Cortes, appealed for government action to foster the development of agriculture and industry in place of the existing policy of hindrance of their progress. Detailing the potential riches of Sonora, Sinaloa, and Nuevo México, as represented by their resources in skins, furs, wool, cattle, ores, wine, lumber, etc., he asserted that the development of those riches depended most of all on the government's opening of accessible ports and encouragement of fairs. Such a policy, he maintained, would reduce by two-thirds the overland transportation costs on goods entering and leaving those provinces.[10]

---

to the August Congress on the Natural, Political, and Civil Condition of the Provinces of Coahuila, Nuevo León, Nuevo Santander, and Texas of the Four Eastern Interior Provinces of the Kingdom of Mexico.

[9] Spain, Cortes, 1810–1813, *Diario de las Cortes*, XVIII, 419–421; Ramos Arispe, *Report*, pp. 40–44.

[10] Pedro Bautista Pino, *Noticias históricas y estadísticas de la antigua provincia de Nuevo Méjico*, pp. 19–21; Spain, Cortes, 1810–1813, *Diario de las Cortes*, XVI, 161–163; XVII, 50; XVIII, 395–397, 419–422.

Among the other Mexican deputies who expressed opinions on the subject were José Cayetano Foncerrada, Mariano Mendiola, and Juan José Güereña. Foncerrada stressed the need for opening new ports in the north on the east and west coasts, for direct trade with Europe and Asia, as the means for assuring the growth and prosperity of those areas. On September 10, 1811, Mendiola reminded the Cortes that it had not yet published the act granting freedom for agriculture and industry, even though seven months had passed since the measure had been approved. Güereña, in a long speech to the Cortes on economic matters delivered on June 9, 1812, referred approvingly to the Cortes' action of the previous year, removing the restrictions on agriculture and industry. To reap the full benefit of the new freedom, he suggested the formation of economic societies by the provincial deputations under the powers given them by Article 335 of the Constitution which enjoined them to foster agriculture, industry, and trade.[11]

The statement by the American deputies, read to the Cortes on August 1, 1811, constituted a further testimony to the continued support accorded by the majority of the Mexican representatives to this measure to remove the restraints on agriculture and industry. They commended the Cortes for its action in removing those restrictions. The English editor, who published the document in London, commented that the measure may have been mentioned with the specific intent of reminding the Cortes that the act had not been published. It is worthy of note that this document was signed by thirteen Mexican deputies, two of whom, Beye de Cisneros and González Lastiri, had little to say on economic matters.[12]

The second of the economic measures among the eleven American propositions taken up by the Cortes requested that all government monopolies in America be suppressed and that direct taxes be substituted to supply the revenue lost thereby. The only one of real importance as a source of income was that involving the sale of tobacco.

Although no Mexican deputy participated in the discussion immediately focussed on this issue, a number of them expressed opinions

11 [José Cayetano Foncerrada], *Comercio libre vindicado de la nota de ruinoso a la España y a las Américas*, pp. 3–6, 12–26; Spain, Cortes, 1810–1813, *Actas de las sesiones secretas*, p. 408; Spain, Cortes, 1810–1813, *Diario de las Cortes*, XIII, 412–415.
12 Spain, Cortes, 1810–1813, *Representación*, pp. 14, 16, 18.

on the subject on other occasions. On September 15, 1811, Ramos Arispe, defending a proposal submitted by José Simeon Uría to allow the planting of tobacco in the region of Tepic and San Blas, argued that the freedom to plant tobacco anywhere was included in the general grant of freedom to agriculture conceded on February 9, 1811. Mendiola joined Ramos Arispe in support of the request made by Uría. And Pino, in his *Noticias*, strongly advocated the abolition of the government's exclusive right to the handling of tobacco.[13]

After a long delay the decrees for the suppression of both the tobacco and salt monopolies together with the minor ones on leather, alum, lead, and tin were approved by the Cortes. A direct tax was to be substituted for the lost tobacco revenue, with the cessation of the official control over tobacco in the various provinces dependent on the establishment of a direct tax and on prepayment of one-third of the revenue that would be lost.[14]

Since the decree was not implemented in New Spain, the question arose anew in the Cortes of 1820 and 1821. The Cortes of 1820 voted to suspend the application of the decree of September 13, 1813, which had ordered the suppression of the monopolies. When a special regulation liberalizing government policy toward the planting and sale of tobacco in Cuba was approved by the Cortes in 1821, Francisco Arroyo, a Mexican deputy, tried in vain to have the regulation extended to New Spain.[15]

In response to an April 2, 1811, request by the Regency that steps be taken to encourage industry and shipping in various west coast ports of New Spain, the Naval and Trade Committee presented ten articles designed to remove restrictions on pearl, otter, and whale hunting; to eliminate participation by government officials in those enterprises; and to stimulate investment in those activities through the grant of tax concessions. The Cortes adopted eight of the ten resolutions. Although the Mexican deputies made no comment on the

[13] *Ibid.*, *Diario de las Cortes*, V, 337–338; VII, 208–209; VIII, 316–323; Pino, *Noticias*, p. 64.

[14] Mexico, Secretariat of Foreign Relations, *La constitución de 1812 en la Nueva España* (Vol. V, pp. 137–139 of Publicaciones del Archivo general de la nación); *Diario de México*, XVII, No. 2585 (October 29, 1812), p. 505.

[15] Spain, Cortes, 1820, *Diario de las sesiones de las Cortes, Legislatura de 1820*, I, 27 (hereinafter referred to as *Legislatura de 1820*); Spain, Cortes, 1821, *Diario de las sesiones de Cortes. Legislatura de 1821*, III, 2447 (hereinafter referred to as *Legislatura de 1821*).

matter at that time, the measures were spoken of approvingly by Güereña on June 9, 1812, and by the thirteen Mexican deputies who signed the *Representation* of August 1, 1811.[16]

One of the most important questions related to agriculture debated in the Cortes by various Mexican deputies was that of the distribution of lands that were in the public domain. The discussion began on March 12, 1811, when the Overseas Committee submitted a number of proposals based on a communication from the viceroy of New Spain informing them that he had executed the previous Regency's decree exempting the Indians of New Spain from the personal tax and that he had extended it to the mulattoes and others of mixed blood, as the decree had enjoined. Since this act also provided for the apportionment of lands and water to the Indians, the question arose whether the Regency had meant to include those of mixed blood in the same benefaction. The viceroy asserted that interpretation of the decree in this fashion would require the expropriation of lands already held by Spaniards and Indians. Consequently the Overseas Committee suggested that those of mixed blood should be excluded from the apportionment of lands and waters. At this point José Simeon Uría objected that there were sufficient unappropriated lands in Mexico to permit giving land to all. Guridi y Alcocer, affirming that he had no objection to the allotment of unassigned lands to those of mixed blood, declared that in no case should public lands considered to belong to the Indians be included in the lands to be apportioned. Mendiola then suggested an addition to the proposal that would clearly exclude *ejidal* lands from those which might be assigned to Mexicans of mixed blood. The Cortes approved the measure in the form containing Mendiola's clarifying addition.[17]

A similar appeal for the distribution of land to those of mixed blood was made by Nuevo México's delegate, Pino, in the course of the debate on the resolutions which he had introduced late in 1812, requesting that the inhabitants of New Spain be required to dwell in villages in which land was to be provided for all. He argued that such a provision would do much to put an end to the rebellion, affirming that those who had joined Hidalgo would not have done so had they been landowners with something to lose by their act of rebellion.[18]

    [16] Spain, Cortes, 1810–1813, *Diario de las Cortes*, IV, 448–450; V, 68–69; XIII, 415; Spain, Cortes, 1810–1813, *Representación*, p. 14–16.
    [17] Spain, Cortes, 1810–1813, *Diario de las Cortes*, IV, 192–197.
    [18] *Ibid.*, XVI, 161–162; XVIII, 395.

Ramos Arispe was, perhaps, the Mexican deputy most interested in the question of land distribution, looking on it as the ideal means for increasing the wealth and size of the population of the northern provinces in order to protect them from incursions from the United States. In his *Report* he had touched on the subject. In the discussions on the constitutional articles establishing the powers of the provincial deputations for the political-economic government of the areas subject to them, he fought tenaciously for a grant of wide authority to the provincial deputations in the question of land distribution, so that they might take effective action as they saw the need for it without having to appeal to Spain for prior approval. He objected strongly to the content of Section 18 of Article 335 of the Constitution. (see Appendix B to this paper), which empowered the government to force those who lived far from the towns to settle in the environs of the towns, and unsuccessfully introduced an article of his own to replace it.[19]

In the Cortes of 1821 the question of land distribution again arose as a vital issue when an extensive bill was introduced to encourage settlement of the empty areas of northern New Spain by nationals and foreigners and to regulate the distribution of land. That Ramos Arispe was influential in the drawing-up of this bill appears to be indicated by the role he played in explaining the meaning of its provisions and in answering the objections raised to various of its sections. Many of the other Mexican deputies also took part in the discussion of one or another of the articles, objecting to their content or adding to or qualifying their scope. Among them were José María Puchet, Juan Bautista Valdés, Tomás Murphy, Francisco Fagoaga, Lucas Alamán, Pablo de La-Llave, Félix Quio Tehuanhuey, and José María Quirós y Millán. The most significant of the comments were those of Puchet, Valdés, and Quio Tehuanhuey, which urged caution in allowing citizens of the United States to settle in areas such as Texas which bordered on the United States, and those of Tomás Murphy, which complained about the uniformity in the size of the land grants and objected to the articles which exempted the settlers from all taxes for fifteen years and allowed their settlements to ignore all monopolies. After some revision the bill was passed on June 28, 1821, and Ramos

---

[19] Ramos Arispe, *Report*, p. 40; Spain, Cortes, 1810–1813, *Diario de sesiones de las Córtes generales e extraordinarias, 1810–1813*, VIII–IX, 5381–5394, 5400–5401, 5427–5428, 5457–5460, 5516.

Arispe was made president of the commission named to present it to the king for signature.[20]

Additional proposals related to agriculture which attracted the attention of several Mexican deputies were a suggested ten-year exemption of tithes and taxes on the planters of coffee, cacao, and hemp in New Spain, and a bill for the foundation of agricultural schools and experimental stations throughout Spain and its overseas provinces. Ramos Arispe and Francisco Molinos del Campo spoke in defense of the exemptions and Pablo de La-Llave asked that four agricultural schools and experimental stations be established in New Spain rather than the one that was contemplated in the bill, arguing that Mexico's diversity of hot and cold and wet and dry climates demanded more than one school.[21]

Without doubt the most significant economic reforms presented to the Cortes were those concerned with free trade. Three of the six economic proposals advanced by the American alternate deputies in December of 1810 dealt with that subject. The first requested for the Americas the right to sell any goods which they produced to whoever would buy them, as well as the right to import goods freely, either in Spanish or foreign bottoms, and, as a consequence of the foregoing, the opening of all Spanish American ports. The second asked for complete free trade within the Spanish empire. The third petitioned that the Spanish American ports be allowed to trade with the Philippine Islands and the rest of the ports of Asia (see Appendix A). Since the Spanish government contemplated using the offer of trade concessions as a bargaining point for a substantial loan from England, the Cortes decided that fundamental measures dealing with trade policy should be discussed only in secret session. The American alternate deputies, and others, objected in vain to this decision.[22]

Throughout much of the discussion on free trade, there was a fusion of the debates on the American proposals with the discussion of the guidelines for the trade concessions to England, which the Regency had asked the Cortes to lay down. Thus the suggestions for reform drawn up by the Trade Committee (see Appendix C) were meant to serve at one and the same time as an answer to the demands of the

[20] Spain, Cortes, 1821, *Legislatura de 1821*, III, 2081–2083, 2308–2309, 2345–2346, 2358–2359, 2434–2437, 2534, 2537, 2586, 2608–2609.

[21] *Ibid.*, 2113–2114, 2115.

[22] Spain, Cortes, 1810–1813, *Proposiciones*, p. 1; Joaquín Lorenzo Villanueva, *Mi viaje á las Córtes*, p. 120.

American deputies and as guidelines for the executive department in its negotiations with the British. Only when it became apparent that the majority opinion in the Cortes had swung into opposition to trade reform did the assembly separate the two issues. In their later stages the discussions on trade reform also became entangled at times with the debate of the English offer to mediate between Spain and her rebellious colonies.

The debates began on April 17, 1811, after a more than adequate delay to permit the committee concerned to collect documents and information, and extended over the next year and six months, with several long interruptions, during which the debates were recessed to allow the Cádiz merchants' guild to marshal its arguments against free trade in all its manifestations. The merchants guilds' campaigns seem to have been quite successful. Although several quite liberal trade acts were twice approved by the Cortes in preliminary and final draft forms (see Appendix C), the sessions were dissolved in 1814 without any of the approved trade reform acts having been published. The fate of the Regency's decree of May 17, 1810, authorizing free trade for New Spain as one of its reform measures, proved to be indicative of the sentiment of the elements in ultimate control of the situation in Spain. Under pressure from the Cádiz junta, the Regency had hastily withdrawn that decree, and then disowned it. In some fashion a Cortes that was liberal enough to approve generous trade reforms on two occasions was similarly prevailed upon to let the reform acts gather dust and even to show some animus against those same reforms within three months of their second approval of those acts.[23]

Despite the lengthy and often heated discussions that took place within and outside the Cortes over the trade proposals, the evidence indicating the attitude of the Mexican deputies is meagre. Unfortunately the reporters for the secret sessions generally confined themselves to observations that such and such a point had been discussed, without either naming the participants in the debate or indicating the tenor of their remarks. Indeed, if one relied on the account given by the recorder of the *Actas de las sesiones secretas* after December,

[23] Manuel de Albuerne, *Origen y estado de la causa formada sobre la real orden de 17 de mayo de 1810, que trata del comercio de América, passim;* Enrique del Valle Iberlucea, *Los diputados de Buenos Aires en las Cortes de Cádiz y el nuevo sistema de Gobierno económico de América,* pp. 120–123; Spain, Cortes, 1810–1813, *Actas de las sesiones secretas,* pp. 502–503.

1811, when the Cortes first manifested decided opposition to the whole program for the reform of the trade regulations, one would be led to believe that the subject had all but disappeared from the discussions in the assembly. Comparison with Villanueva's fragmentary remarks on the proceedings in the Cortes after this date reveals that the Cortes' reporter on at least one occasion entirely omitted mention of a spectacular objection by the American deputies to the direction being taken by the Cortes on the subject of trade reform. On the occasion in question, one learns from Villanueva's account that the American deputies walked out of the session en masse as a sign of protest. One can only conjecture that the Cortes' reporter's increased reticence after this date may have had an ulterior motivation. Whatever the reason, except for the several occasions when votes on important issues were recorded, one must rely almost entirely on reports addressed to the Cortes, and on allusions made to free trade in the midst of discussions on other matters, for information on the attitudes of the Mexican deputies on this subject.

Villanueva informs us that on April 10, 1811, some of the American deputies complained of the excessive delay in taking up this subject, asserting that the adoption of the free trade resolutions would contribute to the pacification of the rebels in the colonies. The representatives also insisted unsuccessfully that debate on the new commercial code be divorced from the discussion of the guidelines for the negotiations with England.[24]

On April 15, 1811, Joaquín Maniau, a deputy for Veracruz who had formerly been associated with that city's merchants guild, gave his opinion on the trade committee's recommendations (see Appendix C). Although the *Acts* of the secret sessions gave no indication concerning the nature of this opinion, Maniau's hostility toward at least some of those suggested reforms is revealed clearly by his behavior at a later date and by his August 19, 1811, report to the Ayuntamiento of Veracruz.

The committee's draft contained ten provisions for liberalizing trade regulations; they ranged from a grant of unrestricted trade within and outside the empire on Spanish and Spanish American vessels, to a measure giving free access to all Spanish American ports to the ships of all neutral and allied nations. When the latter radical measure came to a vote, Maniau was one of the two Mexican deputies

24 Villanueva, *Mi viaje á las Cortes*, p. 213.

who helped defeat the measure. When a later trade committee submitted the final drafts of the approved free trade measures on September 3, 1811, Maniau, objecting to the Cortes' publishing them
separately from the hopelessly blocked radical measure, secured the
return to committee of the four approved trade decrees.[25]

The Veracruz deputy objected vigorously to the concession of complete free trade embodied in Article 6 of the committee's recommendations (Appendix C), as well as to the grant contained in Article
2, under which, he charged, Havana merchants would monopolize
Mexican trade because of the privilege they already enjoyed of trad-
ing directly with the United States. In one statement he seems to have
expressed a willingness to countenance direct trade with neutral and
allied ports conducted by Spanish Americans in their own vessels,
under the conditions that such trade would not involve the export of
precious metals and that the same taxes would be paid as if the goods
had been transshipped via Spain. He devoted much more enthusiasm,
however, to a proposal which he himself formulated. It called for the
setting up of a number of free ports in the Peninsula at which the
English, the Spanish, and the Spanish Americans would carry on a
free trade in all goods except common cottons and printed cotton
goods. The goods transshipped from those free ports to America were
to be sent only under the Spanish flag and were to be consigned only
to Spaniards and Spanish Americans. The payment for such goods
could be made in specie on condition of paying the tax which should
be set on such an export of precious metals. His proposals were designed to safeguard Spanish and Spanish American merchants in the
New World from direct foreign competition.[26]

At the mid-April opening of discussions on the trade committee's
suggestions for reform, Guridi y Alcocer, Mendiola, and Uría were
also among those who spoke before the Cortes. Villanueva informs us
that Guridi y Alcocer supported the committee's recommendations.
His complete dedication to the cause of unrestricted free trade is also
abundantly evidenced in other sources. He was one of the few Mexican proprietary deputies who voted for the ill-fated ultra-liberal free
trade measure on August 13, 1811. Two days after the defeat of this
measure he submitted the following propositions which aptly reflect

[25] Spain, Cortes, 1810–1813, *Actas de las sesiones secretas*, pp. 254, 378–379,
401; Joaquín Maniau, "Puntos de vista," *La libertad del comercio en la Nueva
España en la segunda década del siglo XIX*, pp. 27–43.
[26] *Ibid.*, pp. 27–43.

the bitterness he felt over the defeat of that key portion of the free trade act:

1) If the Americas are not to be granted free trade with the allied and neutral nations, then the introduction into them of any foreign goods, even by Spanish vessels, should not be permitted.

2) Neither should the Americas be handed over to a foreign monopoly, by granting the trade with them to one nation alone, and much less, with the privilege of a set number of ships.[27]

Guridi y Alcocer also championed free trade in his reply to the bitter attacks on the program for free trade launched by Juan López Cancelada in his *El Telégrafo americano* and in his work entitled *Ruina de la Nueva España si se declara el comercio libre con los extrangeros.*[28]

Mariano Mendiola's position in the free trade controversy is not as clearly defined as is that of Guridi y Alcocer. Villanueva records that on April 18, 1811, Mendiola spoke against a measure that would permit the English to trade directly with the Spanish colonies. He was one of the Mexican deputies who did not vote in the August 13, 1811, referendum on the radical free trade act. He did, however, have some sympathy with the liberalization of the trade regulations. On May 28, 1811, he spoke at length in defense of the measure that would permit Spaniards in the Philippines an unrestricted right to bring Asiatic goods to both the Americas and the Peninsula. His support of moderate free trade reforms may also possibly be deduced from his castigation of the merchant guilds of Mexico City and Cádiz. On the day following the reading in the Cortes of the former's *Representación*, he gave it as his opinion that the mercantile elements were intrinsically in opposition to the national interest. A few days earlier he had submitted to the Cortes a resolution calling on that body to stimulate the zeal of the merchant guilds of the Peninsula to open funds in support of measures beneficial to the Americas with the same enthusiasm as that with which they gathered money to send troops to America.[29]

There are reasons to believe that Mendiola's position of qualified

---

[27] Spain, Cortes, 1810–1813, *Actas de las sesiones secretas*, p. 382.

[28] *Ibid.*, p. 379; Villanueva, *Mi viaje á las Cortes*, p. 218; Guridi y Alcocer, "Contestación," pp. 38–39.

[29] Villanueva, *Mi viaje á las Cortes*, pp. 218, 232; Spain, Cortes, 1810–1813, *Diario de las Cortes*, VII, 365; Spain, Cortes, 1810–1813, *Actas de las sesiones secretas*, p. 408.

or selective support for trade reforms was shared by several of his Mexican colleagues. The discussion of agricultural reforms in the first pages of this paper makes it clear that Ramos Arispe and Pino favored a liberalization of trade policy that would break the stranglehold maintained by the merchants of Veracruz, Mexico City, and Acapulco, by opening numerous small Mexican ports on both the east and west coasts to direct trade with Europe and Asia. The reading of Cárdenas' *Memoria* shows that he also opposed that monopoly of trade. Like Mendiola, these deputies did not participate in the August 13, 1811, vote on the radical free trade article.[30]

The vote on this issue merits close attention. Fortunately this measure, which would have permitted foreign ships to sail freely to Spanish American ports, was submitted to a roll-call vote. It was defeated by a margin of forty-four votes. The most striking feature of the vote is the absence of the names of eight of Mexico's proprietary deputies—Mendiola, Gordoa, Uría, Beye de Cisneros, González Lastiri, Cárdenas, Ramos Arispe, and Pino. The absence of so many delegates, in a vote on so important an issue, after it had been debated for a couple of days, does not seem to have been due to chance. It probably indicates that most, if not all, of Mexico's proprietary deputies who abstained from voting wanted a liberalization of trade policy, but were possibly dubious of the benefit to be derived by Mexico from allowing ships of foreign nations free entry into her ports. These delegates may well have been considering the threat to Mexico's weak and backward textile industry that would be represented by a flood of foreign-made cloth. The fact that several articles of the trade bill were specifically designed to foster development of the Spanish and Spanish American merchant marines may have been a further reason for doubt concerning the advisability of admitting foreign ships to their ports. Whatever the explanation may be, only two Mexican deputies, Pérez and Maniau, voted against the measure in comparison to the eight who abstained. The Mexican alternate delegates, Gutiérrez de Terán, Sabariego, Munilla, Couto, Maldonado, and San Martín, voted solidly for it. Obregón, who had been an alternate deputy before he became a proprietary deputy, was joined by only

<hr/>

[30] José Eduardo Cárdenas, *Memoria a favor de la provincia de Tabasco, en la Nueva España, presentada a S. M. las Cortes generales y extraordinarias*, pp. 81–84; Spain, Cortes, 1810–1813, *Actas de las sesiones secretas*, pp. 378–379.

three other Mexican proprietary deputies (Guridi y Alcocer, Foncerrada, and Güereña) in support of the article.[31]

Foncerrada's dedication to the cause of complete free trade is also evidenced from another source. He is the reputed author of a pamphlet entitled, *Comercio libre vindicado de la nota de ruinoso a la España y a las Américas,* in which he argues that both Spain and the New World will benefit from the abandonment of the former policy. The only other expression of opinion on the subject by Güereña apparently is his discourse to the Cortes on June 9, 1812, when he spoke glowingly of the potential of Mexico's trade with China.[32]

Unfortunately, the Cortes reporter made no record of the composition of the votes on the moderate trade reform articles, which were twice approved. However, the fact that the Cortes passed these articles suggests that they must have received firm support from the American deputies.

The last significant expressions of opinion on trade reform occurred late in 1811 and early in 1813. On December 17, 1811, a Spanish deputy, Morales Gallego, introduced a proposal to empower the Regency to procede with the loan negotiations, on the basis of offering England privileges to trade with Spanish America on a limited scale; that is, with limitations on the duration of the privilege, on the areas to which it would apply, on the number of ships to be involved annually, and on the goods that they might carry. His resolution also contained a proviso that the treaty entered into would not prejudice the pending discussions on a general trade code. The Cortes approved his proposition, but, significantly, struck out the proviso. On the following day a number of deputies requested that their opposition to this measure be recorded. Among them were eight Mexican deputies, namely, Mendiola, Gordoa, Ramos Arispe, Couto, Obregón, Guridi y Alcocer, Gutiérrez de Terán, and Maniau. Early in 1813 the overseas committee suggested that since the Manila Galleon had been abolished by one of the approved trade reform decrees (still unpublished), provision should be made for trade between the Philippines and South Sea ports. The committee proposed a restricted free trade, limited to a value double that allowed the Manila Galleon. The Cortes refused even to debate the question. It

---

[31] Spain, Cortes, 1810–1813, *Actas de las sesiones secretas,* pp. 378–379.

[32] Foncerrada, *Comercio libre,* pp. 3–28; Spain, Cortes, 1810–1813, *Diario de las Cortes,* XV, 415.

was on this occasion that the mass of the American deputies walked out of the session in protest.[33]

In mid–1812 trade reform received a fleeting mention in the Cortes. On July 3, the English minister in Cádiz asked that Mexico be included within the scope of the English mediation efforts as a condition *sine qua non* for the undertaking of those efforts. Guridi y Alcocer, who was on the Cortes' mediation committee, supported the idea of extending the English mediation to the conflict in Mexico, with the reservation, however, that the mediators should not be allowed to determine anything relative to the trade matters pending in the Cortes. Villanueva records that Ramos Arispe also supported this extension and that Pérez opposed it, the latter maintaining that the insurrectionists were simply bandits.[34]

The Cortes was dissolved without further action being taken on trade matters beyond the publishing of a decree officially suppressing the Manila Galleon. The traders of the Philippines were to be allowed to bring Asiatic goods to San Blas in their own ships. The Cortes decided, however, that the value of the goods which might be imported should remain the same as it had been under the privileges accorded the Galleon.[35]

In comparison with the obstacles placed in the way of the trade reform bills of this Cortes, the ease with which similar measures traveled through the 1820 Cortes is striking. The first assault, it is true, was rebuffed by the 1820 Cortes. But within a few weeks of that defeat, the same Cortes approved sweeping trade reforms that were introduced in the guise of new customs regulations. This was an ironic turn, for in the Cortes of 1810–1813 the demand for a uniform customs regulation was one of the obstacles used to block implementation of the approved trade reforms (see Appendix C).

The discussion on trade in 1820 began with an investigation into the allegedly scandalous special licenses which the government had been granting to favored individuals to import foreign goods in foreign ships under the same duty that these goods would have borne had they been imported in Spanish ships. The practice was a violation of the 1778 trade regulations. The finance committee submitted

[33] Spain, Cortes, 1810–1813, *Actas de las sesiones secretas*, pp. 502–503, 804; Villanueva, *Mi viaje á las Cortes*, pp. 492–493.
[34] Spain, Cortes, 1810–1813, *Actas de las sesiones secretas*, pp. 671–675; Villanueva, *Mi viaje á las Cortes*, pp. 379–380.
[35] Spain, Laws and Statutes, 1810–1822, *Colección de los decretos y órdenes que han expedido las Cortes generales y extraordinarias*, IV, 274–275.

a resolution asking, first, that the Cortes approve the government's action in suspending the remaining special trade licenses and the pending payments they involved, and, secondly, that the Cortes declare null and void all the transactions that had been conducted under these privileges since 1816. The Cortes approved both parts of the bill. Ramos Arispe and Fagoaga voted against the second part of the measure, while the five other Mexican deputies voted for the entire resolution. Ramos Arispe had insisted that the resolution be voted on by parts.[36]

After some discussion of the problems that had been alleged as justification for these special licenses, namely, the shortage of Spanish ships and the risk of attack associated with the use of Spanish ships, the finance committee, admitting the validity of these excuses, suggested that the permission to use foreign ships without paying higher duties be made general, at least until the ordinary session of the Cortes should convene in the following year. None of the Mexican deputies took part in the lengthy debates on this interim trade bill. The Cortes rejected the finance committee's proposal.[37]

The draft of a new customs code of thirty-four articles, introduced in the same Cortes on August 13, 1820, and clearly recognized by all to be nothing other than a set of trade regulations, had been approved by the end of September. Again the Mexican deputies, except for Ramos Arispe, did not take part in the discussions on the various articles of this bill. He suggested and obtained a number of minor modifications in the articles. He was particularly adverse to investigations of and restrictions on the movement of goods already within the frontiers of the country, favoring a rigorous vigilance on the frontiers and coasts to guard against the fraudulent entry of goods, but maintaining that all goods that had entered the country should be allowed to move freely without fear of an inquisition into the manner of their entry. He objected that the section of Article 26 (see Appendix D) that required that all ports to be opened for trade possess a maritime guild, would be prejudicial to America inasmuch as the ports of the Gulf of Mexico lacked maritime guilds because of their sparse population. After all the articles of this bill had been approved or returned to committee for amendment, Ramos Arispe produced one of the trade measures approved in the 1810–1813 Cortes—the

[36] Spain, Cortes, 1820, *Legislatura de 1820*, I, 274, 349, 352.
[37] *Ibid.*, pp. 306–318.

bill for developing the merchant marine, passed on August 11, 1811—
and asked that it be included in the customs regulations bill.[38]

This new customs regulation provided protective tariffs to safeguard and foster Spanish and colonial industry and agriculture, established equality of tariffs throughout the empire, permitted complete freedom of trade for Spanish vessels, subject only to the restrictions imposed by the tariff regulations, and allowed foreign ships to
trade with all open ports having first class depots (Appendix D, Article 6) on a reciprocity basis. Since Ramos Arispe was on the committee which drew up this bill, it may be assumed that he shares
some responsibility for its provisions. Although silence is not a proof
of assent, the fact that none of the other Mexican deputies either
commented on or suggested amendments to these articles may possibly indicate general accord with the reforms they contained.

The reforms are substantially the same as those which had been
approved in the 1810–1813 Cortes. They do go beyond the earlier
reforms, however, in permitting foreign ships a limited access to
some Spanish and Spanish American ports. That access was carefully circumscribed. The note of equality of treatment with the Peninsula, however, was emphasized in the 1820 reform. It is interesting to
speculate that the desire for just such a compromise may have influenced so many Mexican deputies on August 13, 1811, to abstain
from voting on the radical free trade article, for they did not wish
to go on record as opposed to free trade, yet feared the consequences
of unrestricted free trade.

At the end of the session of the Cortes of 1820, a bill, placing the
ports of Acapulco, San Blas, Campeche, and Veracruz among the
first-class depots, and the ports of Guaymas, Monterrey, Tampico,
and Bahía de San Bernardo (sic) among the second-class depots, and
declaring all these ports open for all licit commerce, was approved—
again without comment by the Mexican deputies. In the Cortes of
1821, however, Sánchez Resa, professing to speak for the deputies
of New Spain, asked that a new port be opened at Chacala in substi-
tution for San Blas, because the former site was more suitable. In
addition, alleging the need of an additional open port in the two
hundred leagues between the existing ports of Acapulco and San
Blas, he requested that Santiago be declared a second-class depot, in

[38] *Ibid.*, I, 490–491, 737–748; II, 1114, 1116; III, 2079–2080.

order to facilitate the development of the agriculture and industry of the provinces of Colima, Coahuayana, Amula, Ávalos, and part of Michoacán. Medina, stressing the ruinous state of the existing facilities at San Blas, seconded the measures introduced by Sánchez Resa.[39]

Ramos Arispe and Michelena were the authors of the only other expression of opinion on trade matters in the Cortes of 1820 and 1821. Ramos Arispe advocated the abolition of the Philippines Company's exclusive privilege to introduce goods from the Far East at Acapulco, charging that the privilege had been abused to the harm of Spain's industry, the Philippine Islands' agriculture, and Mexico's commerce. Michelena, in the discussion occasioned by the arrival in the Cortes of the news of Iturbide's revolt, spoke of the granting of free trade as one of the reforms that was strongly desired in New Spain, urging that its adoption in conjunction with some other measures would suffice to detach the liberal party there from its alliance with the conservatives in this rebellion.[40]

Mining was the third and last economic field in which the Mexican deputies manifested significant interest. One of the six economic measures in the American alternate deputies' document of December 16, 1810 (Appendix A), demanded the termination of the government's monopoly of mercury mining. The proposal proved superfluous. Due to the urgency of the need for mercury to work the silver mines of Mexico, which had been cut off from their normal source of supply by Napoleon's conquests, the Cortes adopted a similar resolution before the American measure came up for consideration.

This bill, removing the mercury mines in the Spanish dominions of America and Asia from the domain of the government monopoly, occasioned little debate. After it had been enacted, however, Obregón, deputy for Guanajuato, a silver mining area, hailed the Cortes' action as a proof of the legislature's interest in the welfare of the Americas, and several days later submitted to the Cortes three proposals designed to encourage the mining of silver. His bill, which suggested that rewards be given to those who discovered important sources of mercury and to those who invented mining processes that

    [39] Spain, Cortes, 1820, *Legislatura de 1820*, III, 1964; Spain, Cortes, 1821, *Legislatura de 1821*, II, 1336–1337.
    [40] Spain, Cortes, 1820, *Legislatura de 1820*, III, 1734; Spain, Cortes, 1821, *Legislatura de 1821*, III, 2045.

required less mercury, was approved by the Cortes on February 1, 1811.[41]

A number of other Mexican deputies to this Cortes showed an interest in remedying the problems that beset this industry so important to Mexico. On February 4, 1811, Guridi y Alcocer and Mendiola disparaged, as useless and harmful, several restrictive proposals introduced by a Spanish deputy, Quintana, to eliminate fraud in the handling of mercury. Gordoa recommended the establishment of additional mints in the areas in which silver was mined in order to relieve the miners of the expense, risks, and delays involved in sending their silver to Mexico City to be minted. On another occasion he urged that the tools and supplies used in mining be exempted from the taxes that made the exploitation of many marginal mines uneconomic. He also asked for a reduction in the price of mercury, and suggested that the royal fifth be reduced to a tenth. Maniau proposed that the mines in which operations had been affected by the activities of the insurrectionists be relieved of all taxes for a period of three years.[42]

The Mexican deputies to the Cortes of 1820 and 1821 showed a more extensive interest in providing remedies for the problems of the mining industry. In the 1820 legislature, Ramos Arispe and Michelena cosponsored a measure for the establishment of mints in Guadalajara and Zacatecas. Ramos Arispe, speaking in support of this act, declared that it was designed to give greater direction to the development of Zacatecas, San Luis Potosí, and Valladolid; it was felt that fostering the settlement and prosperity of the Californias would create a barrier to further penetration of Spanish territory by the United States. Ramos Arispe also spoke approvingly of the establishment of a mint in the town of Arispe.[43]

During the Legislature of 1821, the Cortes undertook a fundamental revision of the laws governing the contributions exacted from the miners, as well as of the rules for the administration and financing of the *cuerpo de minería*. Lucas Alamán submitted a bill containing twenty-nine articles designed to remedy the decadence of the industry by effecting these financial and administrative reforms. On introducing these proposals, he asserted that he had drawn them up

[41] Spain, Cortes, 1810–1813, *Diario de las Cortes*, III, 111, 126, 188–189.
[42] *Ibid.*, III, 237; X, 379–380; V, 193–199; XII, 214–215.
[43] Spain, Cortes, 1820, *Legislatura de 1820*, II, 1403, 1602; III, 2037, 2040.

with the assistance of Ramos Arispe, Cortazar, Michelena, Fagoaga, Pablo La-Llave, Couto, and Medina. The bill provided, in general, for the abolition of the royal fifth and various other exactions to which mining and minting were subject; the improvement of the supplying of materials essential to the industry, especially explosives and mercury; the reformation of the *cuerpo de minería* in the interest of simplicity and economy; and the provision of mining schools in Guanajuato and Zacatecas, with regulations to give preference to the graduates of such schools in the filling of vacancies in the mints (see Appendix E). Alamán, Ramos Arispe, and Andrés del Río played a leading role in the discussions on this bill. Other Mexican deputies who participated to a lesser degree were José María Puchet, Francisco Fagoaga, the Conde de Alcaráz, Ramírez, and Couto.[44]

Alamán, upon introducing this bill, deplored the Cortes' neglect of the reform of this branch of economic activity, the prosperity of which he considered to be the mainstay for the vigor of agriculture and trade in Mexico. He and del Río differed occasionally on the technical subject of the charges that would be necessary to cover the costs of the mints. Ramos Arispe and Ramírez defended the retention of articles in the bill that some objected to as merely reinforcing or calling attention to existing laws. Ramírez justified their retention by repeating a picturesque comment that he attributed to Solís in his *Historia de Méjico* to the effect that the kings of Spain possessed wide vision but short arms.[45]

In conclusion it must be said that a majority of the Mexican deputies to the Cortes of 1810–1813 demonstrated a significant interest in the promotion of a broad range of economic reforms for the improvement of the agriculture, industry, commerce, and mining of New Spain. Although the alternate deputies were responsible for the initial basic reform measures and provided a phalanx of voting support for them, they did not take an active part in the discussions. The proprietary deputies, with Ramos Arispe and Guridi y Alcocer in the forefront because of their wide interest and notable activity, furnished the data and the arguments in support of these reforms and introduced many particular bills to implement the broad reforms

---

[44] Spain, Cortes, 1821, *Legislatura de 1821*, II, 1408–1409; III, 2052–2055, 2105.

[45] *Ibid.*, III, 2055.

proposed by the alternate deputies. The Mexican deputies to the Cortes of 1820 expressed a similar interest in the promotion of economic reforms by sponsoring and voting for measures of this nature. Their activity, however, in the discussion of those issues was not noteworthy, except for that of Ramos Arispe.

Only a small proportion of the Mexican deputies to the Legislature of 1821 evinced an interest in furthering economic reforms in New Spain by introducing bills or taking part in the discussion on such measures as were introduced. Among those who did participate, Ramos Arispe and Lucas Alamán played the major role.

In the evaluation of the effectiveness of the economic reform activity of the Mexican deputies in all the sessions of the Cortes, one must conclude that, although their record, viewed superficially, is impressive, their achievement, studied more deeply, is not so solid. The approval of important reforms for the development of agriculture, industry, and mining in New Spain was indeed secured. But, as various Mexican delegates repeatedly pointed out, those reforms would not be truly efficacious without a revision of the monopolistic trade policy that funneled virtually all imports and exports—against all the canons of economic common sense—through the hands of a few merchants at Cádiz, Veracruz, and Mexico City. The Mexican delegates failed to secure any reform of trade policy in the Cortes of 1810–1813. The trade reform of 1820 came too late, for Mexico declared its independence before the reforms could be made effective. This significant failure of the Mexican deputies had important consequences. To the extent that economic grievances were the cause for the insurrection in New Spain—and, if we may believe the assertions of the Mexican deputies, economic injustices were an important source of disaffection—the failure of the Mexican delegates to the "liberal" Cortes of 1810–1813 to convince enough of their fellow deputies of the urgent need for a reform of trade policy contributed to the encouragement of those who were fighting for independence. Their failure made a mockery of the vaunted equality of Overseas Spaniards with Peninsular Spaniards as proclaimed by the Cortes.

The determination of the reasons for that failure would be a study in itself beyond the scope of this paper. Nevertheless, because of its significance, the point demands some attention in this appraisal of the Mexican deputies' role in promoting economic reform. Until October of 1811, the Cortes had seemed to be quite favorably disposed to a liberalization of trade policy, short of allowing foreign ships free access to Spanish American ports. After this time, some factor or factors led the Cortes to abandon the idea of a change in trade policy. The most plausible cause for the change was the violent propaganda campaign waged by the merchant guilds of Cádiz and Mexico City against any liberalization of trade policy. The reform-minded Mexican deputies urged the adoption of liberal trade reforms as a necessity, if Spain wished to hold the allegiance of her overseas provinces. The spokesman for the mercantile interests, on the other hand, alleged that the liberalization of trade policy was the shortest route to the dissolution of the Empire. The merchants charged that only the creoles supported that change in policy. And spurning the use of euphemisms, they frankly urged that the overseas provinces should continue to be treated economically as colonies, alleging that Spain's monopoly of their commerce was a small price to pay for the benefits and protection they received from the mother country, and that the Cortes' grant of equality did not extend to trade. In this context there is a great deal of meaning in Mendiola's charge that the mercantile elements were in fundamental opposition to the national interest.

One can only surmise why the liberal Mexican deputies themselves were not united on the question of the extent of trade reform that was desirable. In general they seemed to favor economic reforms that would make Mexicans masters of their own destiny. Their reluctance to support the complete free trade article may be thus explained, for it would not only expose Mexico's infant industry to possibly destructive competition but would also militate against the development of a Mexican merchant marine. There is possibly some significance in the fact that after the Cortes had approved the trade reform bill in 1820, Ramos Arispe resurrected an 1811 proposal for stimulating Mexico's merchant marine. And one may well ask whether he and those who thought as he did, were not looking toward the needs of an independent Mexico in their interest in seeing New Spain develop a merchant marine.

The spirit of all the economic reforms the Mexican deputies advocated is well summed up in a reminder addressed by Ramos Arispe to the Cortes of 1820:

Above all I take issue with a use of terms that I have noticed here and on other occasions, that is, the habit of calling the overseas provinces "our possessions." They are possessions no longer. The overseas provinces are as much a part of the Spanish Monarchy as are the provinces of the Peninsula. Finally I would that the European Spaniards not lose sight of the fact that they cannot enjoy complete prosperity, if they do not make it transmissible to their brothers of America.[46]

[46] Spain, Cortes, 1820, *Legislatura de 1820*, III, 2153.

Appendix A

Economic Proposals Presented to Cortes of 1810–1813

The six economic proposals presented to the Cortes of 1810–1813 by the American alternate deputies on December 16, 1810:

1) The natives and inhabitants of America may sow and cultivate whatever crops, nature and their skills make possible in those climates; and in a similar fashion, they may develop industries, manufactures, and arts without restrictions.

2) The Americas shall enjoy the widest freedom to export their products to the Peninsula and to allied and neutral nations, whether such products are raw materials or manufactures, and the Americas shall be permitted to import whatever they need, either in national or foreign bottoms, and to this end, all ports of the Americas shall be opened.

3) There shall be a free reciprocal trade between the Americas and the Spanish Asiatic possessions, with any privileges whatsoever opposed to this free trade hereby abolished.

4) There shall be established equal freedom of commerce between all the ports of America and those of the Philippine Islands, and with the ports of the rest of Asia, with a similar abolition of any privilege whatsoever to the contrary.

5) Every monopoly in the Americas shall be lifted and suppressed; but the Treasury shall be indemnified, to the amount of the net profits it realized from the monopolized articles, by equivalent taxes levied on each of these articles.

6) The exploitation of mercury mines shall be free and open to any individual; but the administration of their production shall remain the duty and responsibility of the Mining Tribunals, to the exclusion of the viceroys, intendants, governors, and the Tribunals of Royal Finance.[a]

[a] Spain, Cortes, 1810–1813, *Proposiciones que hacen al Congreso nacional los diputados de América y Asia*, p. 1.

Appendix B

Suggested Responsibilities of Provincial Deputations

Pertinent sections of Article 335 of the Spanish Constitution as they were presented to the Cortes, and the substitute for Section 18 which was submitted by Miguel Ramos Arispe:

Article 335, It shall fall to these deputations [i.e. provincial]:

5) To promote the education of youth and to foment agriculture, industry, and commerce, protecting the inventors of discoveries in any one of these branches of activity.

16) To foment agriculture, the arts, and trade, the provincial deputation shall present to the government the plans and projects it judges to be the most opportune.

18) In addition to what is provided in paragraph 10 of Article 335 of the Constitution, the overseas deputations shall see to it that the inhabitants scattered over the mountains and valleys are forced to live in villages in conformity with the requirements of the laws, proposing to the Government the measures they consider most suited to providing these people with land and the means to cultivate it, in conformity with what was determined by the Cortes in the decree of January 4th of this year.

19) The provincial deputation must consult with the Government and await its authorization for all the decisions in which the law demands this, and, in general, for all things and measures of more significant importance they shall direct all recourse and communications through the political chief, the president of the provincial deputation.

Ramos Arispe's article:

It shall also be the responsibility of the overseas deputations to establish missions among the infidels, to establish new villages of Spaniards, and to effect the movement of established villages to better areas, assigning and distributing the lands according to the Laws of the Indies, and giving an account to the Government of what has been done, for its information and approbation.[a]

[a] Spain, Cortes, 1810–1813, *Diario de sesiones de las Córtes generales e extraordinarias, 1810–1813*, VIII–IX, 5165, 5393, 5427–5428, 5400.

Appendix C

Recommendations for Reform of Trade Regulations

The Trade Committee's recommendations for reform of the trade regulations and for the guidance of the trade treaty negotiations with Great Britain, submitted to the Cortes on March 29, 1811:

1) All Spanish ships, whether from the Peninsula, the nearby islands, or the overseas provinces, may from now on go directly to any neutral or allied port of either hemisphere.

2) The products of any province of the Monarchy and all goods introduced into a Spanish port of either hemisphere may be carried to any other province of the kingdom.

3) The same Spanish ships may carry on trade directly and mutually with the Philippine Islands.

4) In order to foster our merchant marine, which is the training ground for our royal navy, all material and equipment for shipbuilding which it should be necessary to import into Spain or the Indies under any flag shall be declared free of duty.

5) With the same end, the first cargoes of Spanish ships in either hemisphere

newly built after the publication of this decree shall be free of royal duties on their maiden trips out and back.

6) The goods of licit commerce, whether foreign or Spanish, may be carried directly to any Spanish port that has been opened in either hemisphere, as well by English or neutral ships as by Spanish ships; however in the assessment of customs duties a proportion shall be maintained so that Spanish vessels pay less than foreign vessels, and so that among the foreign vessels, the English ships shall pay less than neutral ships.

7) English cotton goods and other foreign goods, the importation of which was forbidden, may be carried directly to the said ports not only by nationals but also by allies and neutrals, with the exclusion solely of coarse cotton goods and printed cotton goods; the introduction of these into the Peninsula shall cease as well.

8) The imports from neutrals must be paid for solely in products of the country, but the British may take one-third of the value of their imports in money and the other two-thirds in goods.

9) What is established here in favor of the British and concerning the admission of neutrals to the ports of America shall be valid for three years and no more, but what is here set forth for the benefit of national trade shall be permanent and perpetual.

10) Foreigners, both allied and neutral, may go only to certain designated ports which shall be ones that are sufficiently populated and garrisoned, and this shall be effected under all the safeguards the State deems necessary; the results of the negotiations conducted by the Regency on the basis of these proposals shall be presented to the Cortes for its sovereign approval.[a]

The free trade proposals approved by the Cortes in the first round of discussion:

1) The same as the Trade Committee's first proposal. (Approved on May 26, 1811)

2) The products of any province of the Monarchy and all goods licitly introduced into any Spanish port of either hemisphere may pass to any of the other provinces of the kingdom, as long as they are carried in Spanish ships, and there is no infringement of the government monopolies while these remain in force. (Approved on May 26, 1811)

3) The same as the Committee's third proposal. (Approved on August 11, 1811)

4) In order to foster our merchant marine, which is the training ground for our royal navy, material and equipment necessary for the construction of ships may enter ports of Spain and the Indies duty free. (Approved on August 11, 1811)[b]

---

[a] Joaquín Maniau, "Puntos de vista," *La libertad del comercio en la Nueva España en la segunda década del siglo XIX* (Vol. I of *Archivo histórico de Hacienda*), pp. 39–41.

[b] Spain, Cortes, 1810–1813, *Actas de las sesiones secretas*, pp. 294, 376.

A proposal made by the Spanish deputy, Oliveros, seemingly designed to prevent or at least delay implementation of the above trade reforms:

In order to establish the freedom of trade, conceded in the first and second proposals above, and which may be granted in succeeding proposals, [i.e., proposals 1 through 4], the customs duties for America and Spain shall first be set in such a way that they shall be the same on the goods and products introduced for their consumption. (Approved on May 27, 1811)ᶜ

The Trade Committee's fifth proposal was rejected in the first round of discussions on August 11, 1811. The following proposal was introduced as a substitute for it and submitted to the committee for its consideration:

The Regency shall assign to citizens who build new ships a premium proportionate to the size of the ships, which reward shall be deductible from the duties on the first cargo.

The committee's sixth proposal was rejected on August 13, 1811, and proposals seven through ten were not taken up.ᵈ

The following proposals are the final drafts of the approved trade reform articles as they were passed by the Cortes for the second time, before being returned to committee at the request of Joaquín Maniau. The italicized portions represent the changes that were introduced in the proposals between their first and second approval.

1) All Spanish ships, whether from the Peninsula and adjacent islands or from the overseas provinces, *manned according to the law,* may from now on, *as well on direct trips, as when making stops,* go to any allied or neutral port in either hemisphere, *and in a similar fashion, return directly from the port of departure, or else return from any other port of the Monarchy with goods* of lawful trade. (Approved on September 29, 1811)

2) The products of any province of the Monarchy, and all goods, *national or foreign,* lawfully introduced into any Spanish port of either hemisphere, *in conformity with the preceding article,* may pass to any other port of the rest of the provinces of the kingdom, as long as they are carried in Spanish ships and no infringement of the governmental monopolies occurs, while they subsist. (Approved on September 30, 1811)

3) The same national ships may conduct direct and mutual trade with the Philippine Islands, *with the Manila Galleon hereby abolished, and also the exclusive privileges enjoyed by the Philippine Islands Company.* (Approved on October 8, 1811)ᵉ

ᶜ *Ibid.,* p. 295.
ᵈ *Ibid.,* pp. 376–377; Maniau, "Puntos de vista," *La libertad del comercio,* p. 41.
ᵉ *Ibid.,* pp. 424–425, 433.

In this round of discussions Oliveros' proposal appeared as Article 5, and the former Article 4 reappeared in identical form as Proposal 6. The article now introduced as number 4 was an entirely new one, on which no action was taken. Article 5 of the first round of discussions was now approved in the following form as Proposal 7:

> 7) With the same end in view, the Regency is authorized to grant to the owners of Spanish ships, newly constructed in any port of the Monarchy, from the time of the publication of this decree, a premium proportionate to the tonnage of the ship, which premium shall be deducted from the duties owed on the cargo of the maiden voyage.[f]

[f] *Ibid.*, pp. 434–435.

Appendix D

Articles Pertaining to Freedom of Trade

The articles of the new customs regulation of 1820 which pertained directly to the granting of freedom of trade:

> 1) There shall be one general customs duty for all the Spanish monarchy, which regulation shall become effective from January 1, 1821 in Europe, and in the overseas provinces thirty days after the decree and the new customs rates arrive.
>
> 4) Only one tax shall be collected by the Treasury on the import and export of goods in foreign trade.
>
> 5) In the cases in which it is permitted to import or export goods in foreign bottoms, the cargoes shall bear the designated duty and one third more.
>
> 8) National and foreign goods of all types, except those which are prohibited, shall move freely within the lines of the interior check points which shall be established, without need of customshouse permits, and such goods shall also move freely in the intermediate territory between this line and the customshouse or in the intermediate area of the sea between two towns of one and the same province; however, for movement of goods beyond these lines the following rules shall be observed.
>
> 9) The carrying of goods of all sorts, outside the customs lines, from one port or anchoring ground to another . . . shall be done exclusively in Spanish bottoms.
>
> 11) Foreign goods on which the import duties have been paid in some port of the Peninsula can move freely and be shipped outside the customs line to another port of the Peninsula, or be exported to a foreign land, paying only the two-per-cent tax for administration costs in the port of embarcation and nothing in their new port of destiny; but such goods may not be re-exported to a port of Overseas Spain without paying for a second time the import duty on foreign goods; the same procedure shall be observed for foreign goods imported in a Spanish port in America or Asia; they shall not be

carried to other regions of America and Asia or to the Peninsula without paying the customs duties a second time.

12) A Spanish ship, carrying already imported foreign goods, or domestic produce which bears a consumer's tax, between Spanish ports, which shall anchor in or touch at a foreign port and justifies itself in a lawful way . . . shall pay at its port of destiny or wherever it unloads, the import duties and consumer's tax on all the indicated goods of its cargo even though it may show receipts to prove that it has already paid those duties and taxes.

17) All Spanish ships may travel from any open port of the monarchy to any foreign port, importing and exporting goods of licit commerce, provided customs and other regulations are observed.

19) Foreign ships shall be admitted in all the ports of the Spanish monarchy to the extent that each respective foreign nation admits Spanish ships in its home ports and those of its possessions.

26) Depots for maritime trade shall be established in the ports designated by the government and which the Cortes approves of; they shall be of two classes: first-class depots, in which both foreign goods and domestic produce subject to the consumer's tax may be stored, and second-class depots, in which only domestic goods subject to the consumer's tax may be stored; ports of both classes must be secure and well defended, possess a shelter for the ships in permanent moorings, a customshouse and necessary warehouses near the port, and a maritime guild; and among the ports which present these qualifications, those shall be chosen which export the greatest amount of domestic produce and manufactures.

29) Goods forbidden to be imported or exported shall be treated of in a separate article . . . with the list to be ratified or rectified by each legislature.[a]

[a] Spain, Cortes, 1820, *Legislatura de 1820,* I, 746–748.

Appendix E

Propositions for Mining Reform

Propositions for mining reform introduced by Sres. Cortazar, Ramos Arispe, Michelena, Alamán, Fagoaga, Pablo La-Llave, Couto, and Medina:

Since the mining industry of New Spain requires a change in the system of contributions which it pays and in the method by which it is governed, in order to avoid the absolute ruin which threatens it immediately, and in order to re-establish its ancient splendor, on which the very splendor of those provinces depends, this change shall be verified in the following terms:

1) The tax called the fifth is abolished, as is also the one per cent of seigniorage.
2) These shall be substituted for by a direct tax of eighteen per cent of the net profit of the mine.
3) To prove that they have paid this tax the owners or administrators of mines shall send a notarized copy of the weekly reports to the territorial mining deputation which shall in turn certify it and forward it to the national

cashier's office of the province, in which shall be deposited the sum realized, whether the amount be in money or in bullion.

4) This tax shall cease when in fulfillment of the proposal to the Cortes of November 3, 1820, made by Sres. Ramos Arispe, Michelena, Couto, Cortazar, and Fagoaga, there is established in New Spain the direct tax.

5) No more shall be charged for minting than the process actually costs.

9) Miners shall receive the gold which their silver ores contain.

11) There shall be carried out that which was commanded in the Royal decrees of January 13, 1783, November 12, 1791, December 6, 1796, freeing tools and supplies needed for mining and the extraction of the metals from all taxes of transit to or introduction into the mining villages, which, in violation of the above-mentioned Royal decrees, have been imposed during the late war.

12) There shall be similarly extinguished the new taxes, namely, the taxes of convoy, of war, and other denominations, also imposed on those goods during the late war.

13) The commerce in mercury shall continue free and the first sale not be verified in Seville, but rather in the qualified overseas ports to which it shall be conducted at the expense of the public Treasury, which shall not raise the price beyond the cost of the transport, and which shall see to it that it maintains a substantial stockpile of mercury in these parts, so that it shall never be in short supply.

14) The Mining Tribunal shall stop collecting the usual one *real* per *marco*.

15) Since the adoption of the Constitution has made useless the administrative and directive functions of this tribunal, the same shall be reorganized to reduce its members to a president and two deputies.

21) Since the Mining Tribunal henceforward shall be merely a judicial body not needing an agent at court, this post and salary shall be extinguished.

22) Since there is no longer any administration of funds, the post of factor or cashier shall be extinguished.

25) For the payment of the salaries of the employees of the tribunal, the profit from the sale of substandard coins of the mint shall be used, the which, until now, has not had a set destiny.

26) The same funds shall also pay the cost of maintaining the School of Mines, and whatever is left over shall go to endowments for establishing schools of mines in Guanajuato and Zacatecas.

27) In fulfillment of the Royal decree of December 22, 1814, the posts that are not of high rank which become vacant in the mints, shall be distributed to the students of the Schools of Mines.[a]

[a] Spain, Cortes, 1821, *Legislatura de 1821*, II, 1408–1409.

8. Reform as a Means To Quell Revolution

W. Woodrow Anderson

Reform was not a new theme when the American delegates made their appeals in the Spanish Cortes from 1810 to 1822. Suggestions for changes in Spain's colonial policy had been offered many times before the Americans were invited to participate in the formation of a government that would rule the empire while their king was in captivity and Spain was dominated by Napoleon. Some have speculated that had the reforms of Charles III in the latter eighteenth century been continued there would have been no American movements for independence from Spain. Without being overcritical of Spain's attitude toward her American possessions, Alexander von Humboldt, after his trip to the New World shortly before the rebellions broke out, noted in his subsequent account many of the ills which beset the Americas—ills that were to be reiterated by the American delegates to the Cortes.

However, a few weeks after the Cortes had convened, and before any regularly elected Mexican delegate had taken his seat, the business of the Cortes was complicated by rebellion in the overseas province of New Spain. On September 16 Father Miguel Hidalgo raised his standard against the Spaniards. Could further agitations be quelled by promising reforms to the colonies, as their delegates maintained? Or could the revolution be subdued by superior strength once Spain was freed from Napoleon's yoke? The Americans urged reforms in the face of revolution. The Spaniards wanted to leave things as they were, at least until the French had been driven from Spanish soil. But once begun, the fires of revolt could not be extinguished. Spain, a prisoner herself, had begun to lose an empire.

In explaining the causes of the revolution in the Cortes and making proposals for its termination, the Americans expressed the whole gamut of complaints against the mother country. They centered in the inequities and corruption of the colonial social system, governmental policies, and commercial conduct with the provinces. Among the Americans there was much bitterness toward the privileges of the European-born Spaniards and the discrimination against the Indians, the mestizos, the Negroes, and the *castas* (those with some Negro blood). In the governmental system the Americans were denied access to the most important positions; they also complained that too often the *gachupín* officials were despotic, indifferent, and inefficient. Spain's restrictive policies toward manufacturing and agriculture were thorns in the sides of the Americans. Throughout the sessions of the Cortes, the American delegates maintained that these were the principal areas of complaint in the overseas provinces and that they were the basis for the revolutionary movements. Until 1821 they energetically advocated that with the removal of these inequalities between the mother country and the colonies, peace would be restored and the desire for independence forgotten.

Four months before the rebellion tore the Mexicans into factions, the "bishop elect" of the province of Michoacán, Manuel Abad y Queipo, a Spaniard who had resided some thirty years in the New World, sent suggestions to the Regency in Spain for preventing an insurrection in America, and particularly in New Spain. Peace was precarious, he stated. Revolution was imminent if not prevented by wise actions of the government. He reported that the French Revolution had put into motion an ardent desire for independence. The Americans, thinking that Spain was lost when they had heard that she had been occupied, naturally began to think of independence and the means of realizing it in case Spain did not recover her freedom. According to this astute observer the situation in Mexico was rather confused by the ambiguous attitude of Viceroy José de Iturrigaray, which made those who favored independence believe that he also wanted it and would support it. A national junta was proposed, and as the word of it spread throughout the country, unrest rose to the boiling-point. The European merchants in the capital, believing that New Spain sought to abandon the mother country in its hour of need—and to do it with the aid of the viceroy—imprisoned Iturrigaray. Abad y Queipo reported that this act aggravated the rivalry between the European and creole elements of society. The succeeding viceroy, Pedro de Garibay, with the best intentions, far from having calmed the passions, had only incited them. And now there was a desire for independence on all sides. Nevertheless, in spite of all this, the people pledged their allegiance to Ferdinand VII because they considered him the unifying factor in their plans in case the metropolis succumbed, and as the cause of a more just and liberal government in case it survived.

This loyal Spaniard, Abad y Queipo, proceeded to report that peace depended almost entirely on what happened in the metropolis and the confidence the people had in the government. The first signs of unrest in Mexico, as well as all America, were the result of the prevailing opinion that the monarchy was in a deplorable state as a consequence of the reign of Carlos IV. He warned that if public order were disturbed, a dreadful anarchy would necessarily follow. Class would be pitted against class. Ruin and devastation, such as had occurred in Santo Domingo, could be expected. The situation would be that the American Spaniards, the Indians, and the *castas* would oppose the European-Spaniards—the Americans because of their desire to govern alone and to be the sole businessmen; the lower classes, deprived of property and living in a miserable state, because they hated and envied the foreigners.

In order to prevent rebellion in Mexico this churchman thought that concessions should be made quickly to placate the people, and he proposed the following measures: that the personal tribute be removed, that a tax on the general stores be eliminated, that there be some assurance that the recent loan of forty million asked by the Junta Suprema Central would be voluntary and not forced, that some twenty or thirty thousand soldiers be stationed in Mexico to keep peace and to prevent the loss of the provinces by revolution, that a military viceroy be sent quickly, that the government monopolies be removed and all the ports of the Spanish Peninsula and of America be granted the right of navigation and commerce with all parts of the world.[1]

This statement represented the valuable wisdom and studied judgment of a man aware of the situation through thirty-one years experience in America. His observations were to be borne out by subsequent events and also by the explanations of the Mexican delegates as to the reasons their people had rebelled. If his recommendations had received prompt attention, the confidence of this oppressed

[1] Manuel Abad y Quiepo, *Colección de los escritos más importantes que en diferentes épocas dirigió al gobierno D. Manuel Abad Queipo*, pp. 149–159.

people would most probably have been restored, if only partially in the beginning. The fate of his proposal, however, was to be that of other such proposals. On March 12, 1811, these suggestions were presented to the Cortes by the Council of the Indies; thereafter, they were lost in a committee.[2] The sad truth was that after September 16, any suggestion of reform probably came too late.

The Mexican delegates to the Cortes made mention of Father Hidalgo's rebellion for the first time in reference to eleven proposals presented as the means of terminating the disturbances in America. Seven of the Americans who sponsored the suggestions were Mexicans. According to Father José Servando Teresa de Mier, who was present in the Cortes, the Americans, tired of the government's discriminatory attitudes, resolutely demanded that a day be designated for the treatment of American matters. The Cortes finally resolved that the American delegation should meet to summarize the principal petitions of the people they represented. They should then propose to the Cortes what they considered expedient.[3]

Accordingly, on December 16, 1810, the American delegates presented eleven proposals which contained the main grievances of the colonists. As was to be the case with various subsequent recommendations, there is no record of their presentation in the *Diario* of the Cortes.[4] They are summarized as follows: 1) as a consequence of the decree of October 15, 1810, which declared equality of rights among all peoples of the empire, in the Cortes there should be equality of representation with Spain for the American provinces, in proportion to population; 2) the people of America should have agricultural, manufacturing, and mechanical trades free from restrictions; 3) Americans should enjoy the freedom to import and export whatever they desired, in national or foreign ships, and all American ports should be open to such trade; 4) there should be free and reciprocal trade between the Americas and the Asiatic possessions, and whatever exclusive privileges opposed such freedom should be abolished; 5) there should be freedom of commerce for all ports of America and the Philippines with other ports of Asia, and all

---

[2] Hubert Howe Bancroft, *The Works of Hubert Howe Bancroft*, XII, 443.

[3] José Guerra [José Servando Teresa de Mier Noriega y Guerra], *Historia de la revolución en Nueva España*, II, 646–647. Because of the lack of stenographers at that time, the records in the *Diario* pertaining to the business which preceded the proposals are inadequate.

[4] The accuracy of the date is verified by other references to it in the *Diario*.

privileges restricting such freedom should be removed at once; 6) all government monopolies should be suppressed, and compensation for the consequent loss of revenue should be made by a special duty on each article thus freed; 7) the exploitation of quicksilver mines should be free and open to all; 8) American Spaniards and Indians should have equal opportunity for all positions in the Cortes as well as any place in the monarchy, be it political, ecclesiastical, or military; 9) at least one-half of the positions in each kingdom should be given to natives of that territory; 10) for the surest success of the above proposal, a nominating board should be created; 11) the Jesuits should be restored because they were necessary for the spread of knowledge and for the progress of the missions.[5]

Several American delegates on January 2, 1811, pressed for the admission and discussion of the proposals. It was agreed to devote two days a week, Wednesday and Friday, to their consideration.[6] The debates began on the ninth of that month. On the first day the Mexican priest from Tlaxcala, José Guridi y Alcocer, in his argument for their acceptance, shed some light on the nature of the rebellion in Mexico, which he called "that fire which is spreading like a flood and burning up entire provinces." Tranquillity had disappeared from the provinces because of the laments of the people, laments embodied in the proposed remedies. He assured the Cortes that the Americans loved the mother country and would never want to separate themselves from her. However, they detested the despotism of the Spanish colonial policy and the scorn with which they were treated. The Americans maintained that their separation from Spain by the great oceanic expanse contributed to their being misunderstood in the metropolis. Moreover, the blaze which had been touched off could not be put out in any other way than by accepting and promulgating the eleven proposals as decrees. Otherwise, the Americas would be lost.[7] A few days later the delegate from Chiapas, Manuel de Llano, reenforced Guridi's statement by saying that the insurrectional movements were not a desire on the part of the Americans to separate themselves, but were born of anxiety to recover their rights as Spaniards.[8]

---

[5] Spain, Cortes, 1810–1813, *Proposiciones que hacen al Congreso Nacional los diputados de América y Asia.*

[6] Spain, Cortes, 1810–1813, *Diario de las discusiones y actas de las Cortes* (hereinafter referred to as *Diario de las Cortes*), II, 234.

[7] *Ibid.*, pp. 318–319.

[8] *Ibid.*, III, 3–4.

Shortly after arriving in Spain, Mariano Mendiola, the delegate from Querétaro, spoke on January 18, 1811, of the proposal of equal representation. His report was some of the earliest first-hand news to reach the Cortes concerning the revolution in New Spain. He stated that the delegates were not aware that the rebellion had spread like lightning throughout all of the provinces. The citizens of *his* city had remained loyal in the face of the insurgents, however, because they had been promised by the viceroy and the delegates to the Cortes that they would have equal representation with their European brothers in the Cortes.[9] In arguing for this same recommendation Guridi y Alcocer said that the Cortes had in its hands a most admirable means of calming those agitations, a means which would prevent a thousand disasters, something that would be more efficient and more powerful than cannons and bullets—equal representation for the Americans.[10] José María Gutiérrez de Terán declared that America would be happy joined to Spain but only if governed by the same law and accorded equality in every way, including representation in the Cortes.[11] Thus the Americans warned of the dangers of revolution if their suggestions for radical changes went unheeded.

In spite of heated debate, the first proposal was rejected, and all that the Americans could get was the promise of equal representation in a future Cortes. The three recommendations pertaining to trade were also the cause of much discussion; however, their further consideration was delayed until such time as the Cortes could obtain the opinion of various people in New Spain. Two years later, in March of 1813, Antonio Larrazábal said that the general decadence of the monarchy and the sad situation of the overseas provinces would ultimately bury them in misery if the commercial system, which was up to then sustained by private interest, was not changed.[12] The sixth proposal was postponed. The ninth and tenth were reserved for action after the constitution should be completed. The eleventh, the proposal for the restoration of the Jesuits, was rejected almost unanimously.[13]

---

[9] *Ibid.*, pp. 29–30. His reference was perhaps to the fact that the Cortes on October 15, 1810, decreed that the overseas provinces were equal in rights with the Spanish provinces.
[10] *Ibid.*, p. 98.
[11] *Ibid.*
[12] *Ibid.*, XVIII, 76.
[13] Bancroft, *Works*, XII, 446–448.

This was only the beginning of a long series of rejections of American proposals for restoring peace to the Americas.

Soon after Ignacio Beye de Cisneros arrived in Spain in April, 1811, he weakened the foregoing arguments of the Americans when he announced that the American delegates had referred to many things as the origin of the revolution, none of which was the actual cause.[14] The primary reason for the first revolutionary movements in New Spain this delegate from Mexico City attributed to the imprisonment of Viceroy Iturrigaray. The people of New Spain saw their chief insulted and an old military man substituted who had neither the ability to govern nor to instill confidence in people. Besides the Viceroy, many other distinguished people had been arrested, but young hoodlums escaped punishment for acts of vandalism they committed in the city.[15] Without awaiting the arrival of the new viceroy, the archbishop had removed the former ruler. And in June the order had come to place the power in the hands of the Audiencia. According to Beye, this order was a serious mistake because the public had little confidence in the Audiencia, as a result of the attitudes of some of its members in previous uprisings. This lack of confidence grew with the first acts of that tribunal, and all trust in that body was soon gone, as it undertook to retire the troops which the archbishop had begun to arm, and thereby confirmed the idea that was now widespread, that New Spain was to be given over to France. Beye therefore offered as the cause of the revolution the one which he said that the Americans gave—the fear that the Europeans would try to subject Mexico to the yoke of Napoleon if he succeeded in dominating Spain.[16]

In order to pacify the area and to prevent the loss of such rich dominions, Beye de Cisneros proposed that a system of provincial juntas be adopted, with a supreme representative governing junta of Spain to which the viceroy and the Audiencia would be subject. In case the whole of Spain was subjugated, the juntas would have the power to declare the eventual independence of the Americas. (The provincial juntas proposed by Beye de Cisneros are not to be confused with the provincial deputations that were established under the constitution. He was talking here of the various central govern-

[14] Lucas Alamán, *Historia de Méjico.* Beye's *Memoria* was not published in the *Diario*, but Mier has quoted from it in his *Historia de la revolución.*

[15] Mier, *Historia de la revolución*, I, 247–249.

[16] *Ibid.,* pp. 268–269.

ing juntas like the one attempted by Iturrigaray and those function-
ing at this date in Caracas, Buenos Aires, and elsewhere.) Mier states
that although this plan was approved by the overseas committee, the
Europeans opposed its reading on the grounds that it was revolutionary.[17] He quotes Beye's reaction: "A revolutionary plan! They are
fools because their system is good for nothing but to drive the Americans to independence."[18] When something was said in the Cortes that
offended the Americans, this popular delegate was fond of comforting
his countrymen with these words: "This, my friends, has no other
remedy than Father Hidalgo."[19]

After Beye's revealing statement as to the immediate reason for the
revolution, the Americans continued to warn of the threatening danger of spreading rebellion if specific measures were not taken. Freedom of the press had been declared by the Cortes as early as
November, 1810, but it had not been decreed in Mexico. In February
of 1812, Miguel Ramos Arizpe, from Coahuila, pleaded that prompt
action be taken. He argued that in Mexico the people had been made
to believe that the cause of Spain was lost and that they were destined
to suffer the same fate. Because they would never submit to such a
destiny, they were now involved in a disgraceful war. The Mexicans
needed to know about Spain's noble efforts against the French in-
vaders, and the only way this could be achieved would be for them to
have complete freedom of the press.[20] Gutiérrez de Terán also alleged that one of the main causes of the revolution was the lack of
general enlightenment in America and that the only remedy for this
was to allow the press free play. Only then would all of the disturbances cease.[21]

In the discussion of Article 22 of the Constitution, which refused
citizenship to the *castas*, Miguel Gordoa y Barrios stated that to approve that article would make the disastrous civil war a perpetual one
because, knowing the character and mentality of the *castas*, he felt
that they would not accept anything less than equality.[22]

The delegate from Michoacán, José Cayetano de Foncerrada, asked

[17] *Ibid.*, II, 655.
[18] *Ibid.*, p. 656.
[19] Alamán, *Historia de Méjico*, III, p. 63.
[20] Spain, Cortes, 1810–1813, *Diario*, XI, 441–442.
[21] *Ibid.*, p. 440.
[22] Spain, Cortes, 1810–1813, *Diario de sesiones de las Córtes generales y extraordinarias*, (hereinafter referred to as *Diario de sesiones de las Cortes*), pp. 1766–1767.

for a new audiencia in his province and said that the "recent sad events" would probably not have happened if there had been another audiencia for that vast stretch of territory, a tribunal to which the people could have taken their grievances. He stated that such a tribunal would still be useful for re-establishing order.[23]

According to Lucas Alamán, as the American representation increased, the Americans began to speak more boldly and threateningly in the Cortes. They were aided by the press, especially the well-known *El Español* of London, as well as by the progress of the revolution.[24]. Be that as it may, on August 1, 1811, thirty-three Americans made a report in a secret session of the Cortes.[25] It did not appear in the *Diario* of the Cortes, but José Blanco White included it in his March, 1812, edition of *El Español*. In the report the Americans discussed several causes of the disturbances in the provinces and offered various suggestions to remedy the situation. They first wanted, however, to dismiss from the minds of the Europeans the notion that a desire for independence from Spain had excited the Americans to rebellion at the time they had become aware that Spain was unable to suppress a revolt. There was more to it than that, they said. The original cause of the revolution was the oppression of bad government. The malevolence, growing day by day, had taken from the hearts of the Americans all hope of reform and had engendered the desire for independence as the only remedy. In Mexico the imprisonment of Iturrigaray by a part of the Europeans had aroused the rivalry existing between the Europeans and the creoles. This rivalry increased throughout the kingdom and resulted in the death and imprisonment of many Americans. Furthermore, it caused an "alarm," which, beginning in the town of Dolores on September 14 [sic], 1810, spread through the land. The report said, in addition, that the Americans, having heard what had happened in Spain, seriously feared being handed over to the French. Even if all of Spain were dominated by France, the Americans would never break all ties with relatives and friends in Spain, but they were not willing to be subjected to

[23] Spain, Cortes, 1810–1813, *Diario de las Cortes*, XIV, 248–249.

[24] Alamán, *Historia de Méjico*, III, 69–70.

[25] Mier (*Historia de la revolución*, II, 657) says that Guridi y Alcocer had drawn up the report. The Mexicans were José María Couto, Miguel Guridi y Alcocer, Máximo Maldonado, Miguel Gómez, Miguel González Lastiri, Antonio Joaquín Pérez, José María Gutiérrez de Terán, Manuel de Llano, Ignacio Beye de Cisneros, Miguel Gordoa y Barrios, Octaviano Obregón, Andrés Savariego, Eduardo de Cárdenas, and Miguel Ramos Arizpe.

the yoke of Napoleon. According to this report, the Europeans began insulting and ill-treating the Americans upon receiving the bad news of Spain's war with the French, but in no place was a disturbance started because an American had insulted a European. Consequently, one infers from all of this that although the Americans could be blamed for the desire for independence, they could not be blamed for the occasion of the actual break.

Furthermore, the desire for independence could be distinguished as either independence from the European Spaniards or independence from the government of the Peninsula. The Americans had not desired the former. What they wanted and explained in their proclamations and publications was to govern themselves, during the captivity of the king, by *juntas* which they themselves would form, for the reason that they had no confidence in those established in the Peninsula. They had therefore constituted themselves a government while Spain was unable to govern. Moreover, the Americans had sworn allegiance to the king because they did not consider that the Regency had had the right to transmit the sovereign power to the Junta Central. Therefore, since the sovereignty reverted to the people after the capture of the king, the people of Spain could not constitute a government that would be extended to the Americas without the consent of the Americans. The delegates believed that there was not a general desire for perpetual independence but only a desire for independence from a government they saw as illegitimate. They reasoned that the revolution was neither a rebellion, nor sedition, nor a schism, nor independence in the accepted sense of the term. It was, however, action stemming from a belief on the part of the Americans that they did not have to obey the government of the Cortes but could form their own government.

What was the antidote embodied in this treatise? As *men*, the Mexicans complained of being viewed with scorn as colonists, or as a second species of man. Therefore, it was necessary to remove the suspicion that Americans would not have equal representation in the Cortes. The American deputies suggested that the Cortes could liberate the Americas from this fear by permitting them to form provincial juntas to govern their districts, as those in the Peninsula were governed. As *living beings*, Mexicans were dependent for their food and comfort upon the fruits of the land and the products of industry; hence, the restrictions which prohibited them from benefiting fully from agriculture and manufacturing had to be eliminated. As *social beings,* they resented the despotism of their governors and waited longingly for the day when merit would be the basis for the distribution of positions and commerce would be open with every nation with whom they were at peace. They terminated the report by warning that as long as the motives for discontent were perpetuated, the disturbances would not cease.[26]

According to Alamán, this statement caused quite a stir in the Cortes; however, no action was taken beyond referring it to a committee.[27]

Miguel Ramos Arizpe of Coahuila made a report to the Cortes on November 7, 1811, in which, although he did not mention the Mexican revolution as such, he pointed out some injustices which, if eliminated or remedied, would relieve some of the "unhappiness" in Mexico. Expressing his faith in the prompt adoption of adequate measures which the Mexicans were asking through him, he began by pointing out maladies in the colonial policy, such as the sale of public offices to the highest bidder and the practice of appointing close friends, relatives, or military men to civil posts. And the lack of an orderly system of popular education—was it due to the location of the Interior Provinces or the indifferent attitude of the government? Or, he asked, was it a deliberate attempt to keep people in ignorance in order that they might more easily be enslaved? He noted that agriculture should have been flourishing in that fertile region but that because of restrictive government policies and a lack of population the land was going to waste. The area abounded in raw materials, he said, but because of restrictive commercial policies the people had to export raw materials and import manufactured goods which cost four times their original price. This economic slavery was worsened by the European monopolies of Veracruz and Mexico City.

Ramos Arizpe scathingly attacked the government of the provinces also. "It is a fact . . . that the government of the Spanish monarchy through error, through ignorance, and many times through family interest or other private designs, in the long space of three centuries, has directed all its efforts only to the luxury, aggrandizement, and extraordinary splendor of its rulers." He continued that the powerful provincial governors ruled despotically and ignorantly. There was a shortage of cabildos because they were naturally opposed to a mili-

[26] "Representación de la diputación americana a las Cortes de España. En 1 de Agosto de 1811," *El Español,* IV, 370–389.
[27] Alamán, *Historia de Méjico,* III, 70.

196 Mexico and the Spanish Cortes

tary government and would hinder the governor's movements. The governor did not have anyone to advise him on judicial matters, and the courts to which one could appeal were located at such distances outside the provinces that it made "recourse to them by citizens of moderate wealth impossible." He proposed that if these evils were to be redressed it would be absolutely necessary "to establish within these provinces an internal, centralized government for the purely administrative functions, as well as the judicial." It would also be essential to establish an executive council or a provincial deputation.[28] His report was circulated widely in America and strongly influenced thinking there.[29]

Pedro Bautista Pino, the newly arrived Mexican delegate from New Mexico, on November 19, 1812, several months after the promulgation of the Constitution, offered one of the most interesting observations as to the cause of the rebellion in Mexico. The problem, as he saw it, was that the millions of hungry, naked, despondent *castas* were without land of their own or the hope of ever possessing any. Moreover, the *castas* were not the only ones who had no land. In a country that needed forty million inhabitants, Pino said that it was a disgrace that there were six million landless people. Until decisive measures were taken to ameliorate the unhappy state in which selfishness and prejudice had kept them, the revolution would not be calmed. As the most efficient way of assuring peace he proposed that all the people in New Spain be compelled to live in towns, placed where they could benefit from the greatest possible comfort. Each family would be assigned enough land to sustain it in the allotment of four leagues of *ejidos* (common lands) that each town would receive. Pino assured the Cortes that as soon as this decree was published the rebel leaders would be left alone, because every man would rejoin the loyalists, to take advantage of the land that he so intensely wanted.[30]

Ferdinand VII was restored to his throne in the early part of 1814, and on May 4 he revoked the Constitution of 1812. In Mexico the open activities of the insurgents were slowly brought to an end. The leaders were dead or in hiding. For a while it appeared that order had been

[28] Miguel Ramos de Arizpe, *Report that Dr. Miguel Ramos de Arizpe . . . Presents to the August Congress.*
[29] *Ibid.,* p. xi (introductory remarks).
[30] Spain, Cortes, 1810–1813, *Diario las Cortes,* XVI, 161–162.

restored. Then Agustín Iturbide, sent to do battle with a revolutionary band in 1820, made an agreement with the foe and in February, 1821, declared Mexican independence from Spain.

Meanwhile, a year earlier, on March 7, 1820, a military revolt had forced the king to restore the Constitution. The Cortes having been dissolved with the revocation of the Constitution in 1814, new elections were held for the ordinary session of 1820–1821. At least fifty-nine deputies were elected to represent Mexico in the Cortes, forty-four of whom had taken their seats before the first session closed on June 30, 1821, so that by that date, with the seven alternates, Mexico had a representation of fifty-one members.[31] Shortly after the elections, the attorney of the Audiencia of Mexico, José Hipólito Odoardo, reported to the Minister of Ecclesiastical Affairs and Justice that the general attitude of the Mexicans had changed entirely since February, 1820. Among all classes of society one noticed fear, suspicion, and hope regarding possible reforms. As the means of conserving peace, he suggested the suspension of the Constitution until tranquillity had been assured.[32]

The American delegates to the Cortes, however, came up with a far different plan. Two Mexicans, Mariano Michelena and Miguel Ramos Arizpe, who were serving in the reinstated Cortes as alternate delegates, actively petitioned that more time be spent in resolving the problems of the overseas provinces. It was well known that the Americans wanted to present new proposals for the pacification of their land. Finally, on May 3, 1821, the Spanish Conde de Toreno proposed that a committee, composed of Spaniards and Americans, present to the Cortes a proposal containing adequate measures for bringing peace to America. In his opinion, if the Cortes acted upon a matter of such importance before the sessions were scheduled to end on June 30, it would have achieved its greatest work up to then.[33] This proposal met with the approval of the Cortes and on the following day a committee of four Spaniards and five Americans was named. The Americans included one delegate from Venezuela, Felipe Fermín

[31] See Chapter I, *supra*. Nettie Lee Benson, "Iturbide y los planes de independencia," *Historia Mexicana*, II (Enero–Marzo, 1953), 440, included the deputies from Guatemala and Chiapas in her figures because Guatemala joined Mexico under Iturbide.

[32] Alamán, *Historia de Méjico*, V, 55.

[33] Spain, Cortes, 1821, *Diario de sesiones de las Cortes*, II, 1389.

Paúl, and four Mexicans—Lucas Alamán, Francisco Fagoago, Bernardino Amati, and Lorenzo Zavala.[34] Alamán notes that their meetings were frequent but fruitless—as was evident in their report to the Cortes.

Six days before the session was to end, Toreno read the report of the pacification committee. It was apparent that the Americans on the committee had not participated in the preparation of the report. In fact, the Americans presented their own ideas the following day. The report had only praise for Spain's greatness in America, as evidenced for example, by her desire to spread the benefits of her culture to the aborigines and her zealous attempts, as expressed in the Laws of the Indies, to see that the Americans were treated with the same consideration and equality as the Spaniards. Any disorder or injustice was attributable neither to the laws nor the interests or ambitions of the metropolis but to the irresponsible acts of governors who took advantage of the ills that grieved Spain or of the distance between Spain and the overseas provinces. Furthermore, it could be said in praise of America that the beginning of the dissidence had a noble origin which resembled that which caused Spain to defend herself against the enemy invasion. The Americans distrusted their governors and preferred to separate themselves from the Peninsula rather than suffer foreign domination. Moreover, if any of the insurgent leaders had any less pure motives, he saw it necessary to misrepresent them and conceal them under the pretext of a just and worthy cause. The report stated that the committee had met several times with the king's ministers. However, because the ministers were not prepared to take a definite stand on the matter, the committee felt that it could do nothing else except recommend that the government be encouraged to present for the consideration of the Cortes the means it thought convenient for bringing a lasting peace to America.[35]

The king's ministers were by no means the only ones who were uncompromising and uncooperative in the matter before the pacification committee. Its report made no mention of the activities of the Americans on the committee. As the closing date for the Cortes drew near, the Americans decided to offer the committee their own proposals for pacification.[36] Mariano Michelena had conceived a plan of

[34] *Ibid.*, p. 1406.
[35] *Ibid.*, III, 2447–2448. See also "Documento numero 18," in Alamán, *Historia de Méjico*, V, 932–933.
[36] Alamán, *Historia de Méjico*, V, 510–511.

government for the Americas before the elected delegates from Mexico had arrived. When some of the newly elected Mexican delegates arrived in April they considered his ideas, which Ramos Arizpe put in writing, and submitted them for the consideration of the pacification committee.[37] These ideas were widely discussed but were rejected by the committee as not being the solution to the problem of America. And because the report of the committee to the Cortes did not mention them, the Americans presented their own report the following day, June 25.

The Americans pointed out that the situation in America was critical and that in spite of the expensive measures taken to maintain those areas under Spanish dominion, a new revolution had arisen in Mexico. Furthermore, they emphasized that absolute pacification would not be achieved until the motives for unrest were removed. According to the report, oppressive governors had failed to obey the Constitution, as they had failed to obey the Laws of the Indies. The people had known despotism before, but with a difference. They had at one time seen themselves as sheep belonging to one or several owners, or as slaves who ought blindly to obey their masters; but now it had been announced that they were free and that they should make known their thoughts and ideas. However, as soon as they had tried it, "the ax had fallen on them." Moreover, the system of elections established by the Constitution was inconvenient. The fact that delegates were to be sent biennially to Spain meant that they would be separated from their countries, families, and businesses for at least three years, in addition to being burdened with the expense of the trip. Furthermore, it was impractical that Americans should meet with Europeans to make laws for people some "four or five thousand leagues away" [*sic*]. The laws made for the Peninsula would not always be good for each one of the American provinces, nor could the American delegates be expected to legislate very well, isolated from the people they represented and that they should consider in making laws. These remarks served as a prelude to what the Americans offered as the way to bring an end to the revolution led by Iturbide.

They recommended that 1) there should be three divisions of the Cortes in America, the first to be comprised of the delegates of all New Spain, including the interior provinces and Guatemala, another to be composed of those of the kingdom of New Granada and the

---

[37] *Historia Mexicana*, II, 441.

provinces of Tierra Firme, and the third of those of Peru, Buenos Aires, and Chile; 2) these Cortes should meet at the times designated in the Constitution for the meeting of the regular general Cortes and govern themselves in every way prescribed by the Constitution; 3) the capitals should be Mexico City, Santa Fé de Bogotá, and Lima; 4) there should be in each division an appointee to exercise executive power in the name of the king; 5) these executive offices should be intrusted to a subject named by the king, without excluding a member of the royal family, and subject only to the king and the general Cortes in matters relating to conduct, and removable at the discretion of the king, but the ministers of the king's appointee should be responsible to the Cortes of the region over which he presided; 6) there should be four ministers in each region—government, finance, ecclesiastical affairs and justice, and army and navy; 7) each region should have a supreme tribunal of justice, composed of a president, eight ministers, and an attorney; 8) likewise, each should have a council of state, composed of seven individuals; 9) the commerce between the Peninsula and the Americas should be considered as that between one province and another in a monarchy; 10) everyone should have the same civil rights and the same opportunity to jobs and public offices; 11) New Spain and the other provinces that comprised its legislative division would assume the obligation of sending to Spain the sum of 200 million *reales* in the space of six years as a contribution to the payment of the foreign debt; 12) New Spain would also promise to contribute to the expenses of the navy the sum of forty million *reales* annually, with payment to begin the first year the Cortes for that region began to meet, and the amount to be increased when the situation in New Spain so allowed; 13) the other countries of America would contribute to the Peninsula in a way to be settled at a later date; 14) New Spain would agree to pay all of the public debt contracted in its territory by the government or its agents; 15) the deputies of the various Cortes, upon taking the oath of office, would swear to uphold the Constitution of the monarchy and to fulfill and execute this law.[38] Thus, the Americans reiterated certain proposals, such as free trade and equal opportunity for all, but introduced the idea of a commonwealth-type relationship between Spain and her

[38] Spain, Cortes, 1821, *Diario de las sesiones de Cortes: Legislatura de 1821,* pp. 2471–2477. The recommendations were also published in *Exposición presentada a las Cortes por los diputados de ultramar en la sesión de 25 de junio de 1821.*

colonies. The offers to reimburse the mother country were, of course, contingent upon the acceptance of the other proposals. Furthermore, the Americans gave no proof that the proposals would be accepted in their countries. The plan, however, would never get that far.

The government answered the committee in writing, stating that, although the intentions of the king and his ministers could not be more decidedly in favor of giving America all the benefits in its power, four obstacles were found to the American plan: the proposals were contrary to the Constitution, and therefore the government could not and would not take any action on them; moreover, it would be a horrible example for the Cortes to allow someone to take the lead in doing something for which the delegates had no power; public opinion in the Peninsula and America was not prepared for a novelty of such dimensions. Furthermore, the deputies who signed the proposals had not said how they would be received in America.[39]

By now it was apparent that the regular session of the Cortes would come to a close without any action being taken on the pacification of America. Sr. Calatrava on June 26 read the report of the committee charged with informing the Cortes of the political state of the nation. According to the report, the most powerful measure to assure public order would be the continued operation of the Cortes, and the committee proposed that the king be petitioned to grant extra sessions to take care of pending legislation. Among the most "interesting and urgent" business pending in the Cortes was the division of Spanish territory and the codification of laws for the army and the navy. There was no mention of the American problem.[40] Americans immediately began to argue that the most important business—the state of the American provinces—definitely had to be included in the proposed extra session.[41]

Calatrava answered that in the opinion of the committee the matter of the pacification of America could not be considered because, by the action of the Cortes on the twenty-fourth, the matter had been left up to the executive branch of the government, not to the Cortes. If the matter was pending, it was pending the action of the government, not of the Cortes.[42] It was then proposed by four Americans that in the

---

[39] Alamán, *Historia de Méjico*, V, 512–513.
[40] Spain, Cortes, 1821, *Diario de las sesiones de Cortes. Legislatura de 1821*, III, 2512–2513.
[41] *Ibid.*, pp. 2514–2516.
[42] *Ibid.*, p. 2514.

petition to the king the business of America be included.[43] After some further discussion, the point was declared sufficiently discussed and the addition was approved.[44]

The extraordinary session was granted; it opened in Madrid on September 22, 1821. Although the American problem had been included for discussion, the delegates spent relatively little time treating that subject. In fact they involved themselves more with the consideration of such topics as a penal code, freedom of the press, national militias, commerce, and the division of Spanish territory. The Americans finally insisted that it was time to hear what the government would propose in place of their ideas which it had rejected.

One month after the session had opened, Sr. Paúl of Venezuela proposed that the government, as depository of all the information concerning the subject, should present its suggestions for re-establishing order in America. The ideas would be passed to a committee for examination and opinion, and then they would be discussed by all the delegates.[45]

Lucas Alamán expressed doubt that this appeal would be effective, since the Cortes had tried twice to get the government to act. He stated that because of the rapid progress of the revolution in New Spain, any proposed action would probably be too late.[46]

The suggestions of the government were delivered to the Cortes on January 17, 1822, less than a month before the session was to close. They do not appear in the *Diario*; however, they were later summarized in a speech by Alamán as requesting: 1) that an armistice be signed with the overseas provinces; 2) that the purpose of the armistice be to open discussions of the disagreements between the provincial deputations of the overseas provinces and the Cortes; 3) that the delegates to the Cortes be given the right to suspend those articles of the Constitution which they thought harmful to the provinces; 4) that the decrees relative to the outrages against the clergy, the suppression of the monastics, and so forth, be abrogated; 5) that free trade be declared between the Peninsula and the American provinces; 6) that free trade be conceded to foreign powers for a limited time of six years; 7) that public lands in America be distributed to those with-

[43] *Ibid.*, p. 2515.
[44] *Ibid.*, p. 2517.
[45] Spain, Cortes, 1821–1822, *Diario de las sesiones de Cortes. Legislatura Extraordinaria*, I, 391–392.
[46] *Ibid.*, p. 392.

out land; 8) that the arbitration of foreign powers be sought in bringing about peace in America.[47] It appeared that Spain was at last
ready to concede that changes had to be made in her colonial policies
in order to save her empire. But she had tarried much too long before
she began to speak of "armistice," "discussions," and "concessions."

The opinion of the overseas committee concerning these ideas was
read on the twenty-fourth. The members did not feel it necessary to
occupy the time of the Cortes with the government proposals, for
several reasons. Some suggestions, they said, pertained to matters
over which the legislature had no authority. Others had already been
agreed upon in the Cortes, and still others were not suitable for discussion; nor would they have favorable results if they had been. In
place of the ideas of the executive branch of the government, the
committee suggested that selected individuals be sent as soon as
possible to the places in America where there were established governments, where they would hear and receive in writing any proposals
that the Americans might make. They were to send them immediately
with their own observations to the government of the metropolis so
that the Cortes might consider them and bring an end to the hostili-
ties. The Cortes would remain in session until such action had been
taken.[48]

In the discussion of the opinion offered by the overseas committee,
which began on January 17, the Spanish deputy Francisco Golfín
offered suggestions which would have led to the establishment of a
confederation and perhaps could have preserved the Spanish Empire.
They were not his own ideas but those of a private citizen, Miguel
Cabrera de Nevares. According to him, the report of the overseas
committee was unsatisfactory. There was no need to find out what
the Americans wanted; for years they had been asking for independence. Furthermore, the Americans would not make an agreement that
did not include a recognition of their independence. They had sworn
not to enter into any transaction or receive any emissary from Spain
who was not authorized to recognize their independence. The creoles
were suspicious and would probably think that it was Spain's intention to gain time to recover the American provinces. Moreover, the
proposals were harmful because it would require at least a year to
carry them out; other nations would take advantage of this and make

[47] *Ibid.*, III, 2029.
[48] *Ibid.*, pp. 1975–1976.

trade treaties with the Americans. Spain would be the last and the least favored. The American governments were growing stronger every day and it was becoming increasingly difficult to make advantageous agreements with them. Spanish commerce was being paralyzed. Wealth belonging to Spaniards was in danger of falling into rebel hands, and it was doubtful that it would be returned if independence were not recognized. Pointing out the political and economic disadvantages of the committee's report, this sagacious Spaniard proposed that representatives be sent to recognize the independence of the Americas and to sign a treaty based on that recognition. He proposed a trade agreement based on the principle of free trade. He further suggested a confederation of the different states of America and Spain, with King Ferdinand as its ruler, and a federal congress, composed of representatives of each government.[49] There was no motion to discuss these ideas.

In the same day's session a Mexican at last acknowledged the fait accompli of American independence. Lucas Alamán said that the question that was now before the Cortes was the position that the Peninsula should take in relation to America. In his opinion a treaty should be made whose purpose would be the formal recognition of American independence. However, first of all, some form of communication and understanding had to be established and in his opinion, the committee report offered the easiest, surest, and quickest way.[50] Although there were obvious allusions to the recognition of American independence in the report under consideration, this was the first outright suggestion to that effect by an American delegate to the Cortes.

On the following day, José María Puchet, the delegate from Puebla, proclaimed that any measure presented to the Cortes by the government would not attack the root of American problems. The causes of insurrection and independence in New Spain were not what the majority believed, he said. Old and now humanly impossible to reform, the roots lay in legislative defects, abuses of power, bad economics, and even worse politics in the distribution of jobs, and the conduct of the Spanish government in fanning the fire of discord in the hearts of Americans and Spaniards. He favored the views of the committee in their entirety.[51]

[49] *Ibid.*, pp. 2022–2024.
[50] *Ibid.*, pp. 2028–2030.
[51] *Ibid.*, p. 2038.

A secretary in the Overseas Ministry rose to say that the feeling was being expressed that the report was a move toward recognition of independence, or that it at least alluded to independence, and that it would certainly be acclaimed as such in America. He doubted government approval unless the following clause were added: ". . . without it being understood that this move is any other thing than a pure means of conciliation." The president suspended discussion of the matter until the Cortes had heard the opinion of the government concerning the committee report.[52] On the thirteenth, the secretary from the Overseas Ministry announced that the king and his ministers thought the report was quite good, but because it used the word "independence" several times it would be highly advantageous, if not absolutely necessary, to add the clause proposed by the government official a few days before.[53] Juan Goméz de Navarrete of Michoacán accused the government of trying to destroy the report and impede the Cortes in carrying out the only means to end the war.[54] The additional clause was passed to the overseas committee.

Two days before the session was to close, the delegates began debate of the added clause. According to Gómez de Navarrete and Tomás Murfi, time would be wasted if it were considered in the Cortes, and the opportunity for substituting past relations of dependence for friendly relations in the future might be lost to foreigners. If Spain did not help the overseas provinces to organize their governments on a solid base, someone else would do so.[55] Alamán voiced his opinion that so much had been said that perhaps it would not be possible to achieve the good ends that the committee had originally proposed and which the Cortes had been about to accept. He thought that with the addition of the clause in question, the simplest and most reasonable part had been substantially removed.[56] By then it was obvious to everyone that the American deputies favored Spanish recognition of American independence. Soon thereafter, all consideration of the American question was to be quickly and completely terminated by the action of two Spaniards.

The Spanish delegates Toreno and Moscoso proposed four additions to "the opinion of the majority of the committee." The first

---

[52] *Ibid.*, p. 2044.
[53] *Ibid.*, p. 2062.
[54] *Ibid.*, pp. 2062–2064.
[55] *Ibid.*, p. 2276.
[56] *Ibid.*, pp. 2280–2281.

was that the Cortes declare that the Treaty of Córdoba, celebrated between General O'Donojú and General Iturbide, and any act or stipulation relative to the acknowledgment of Mexican independence in general, were illegitimate and void in their effect on the Spanish government and its subjects. Moreover, the Spanish government would consider as a treaty violation the recognition of the independence of her overseas possessions by any friendly nation as long as the problems between Spain and America were unresolved. The third suggestion was that the government try by all possible means to conserve and strengthen the ties with the metropolis and propose to the Cortes appropriate measures for doing so. The fourth suggestion had the sting of a scorpion for the American delegates. It was recommended that those provinces which had declared independence from Spain, or those which did not recognize the supremacy of the Spanish government, while in such a state should not have representatives in the Cortes.[57] After a brief debate, the first, second, and third points were approved. The fourth had been withdrawn by "the committee."[58]

The consideration by the Cortes of the problem of American revolution and independence ended in a familiar way. On February 13 Toreno remarked that the committee felt it would be all right if the American business was left for the next Cortes. The president so moved and the Cortes approved his motion. With this action the session was closed.[59] It is likely that on that day no American remained in the Cortes.

For six years the Mexican delegates had argued that Spain could preserve her extensive empire if reforms were made in her colonial policies. It can be said in their favor that they were keenly aware of those circumstances that aggravated the colonial peoples. And, if accepted by the Spaniards, some of their proposals were potentially capable of reducing the tensions which existed between America and Spain and of reestablishing some of their former bonds to their mutual benefit. As far as can be ascertained, there is no evidence to prove that the representatives of Mexico to the Spanish Cortes had any other attitude toward the revolution than that which they expressed before that body. They were convinced that although it was set off by the results of Napoleon's conquest of Spain, it had much deeper, underlying causes which kept it in motion, even after Ferdi-

[57] *Ibid.*, p. 2298.
[58] *Ibid.*, p. 2308.
[59] *Ibid.*, p. 2309.

nand was restored to his throne. They proposed certain measures such as free trade and equal opportunity for all. Beginning with the proposals of Beye de Cisneros in early 1811, they fostered the idea of some form of self-government for America, knowing that the Americans would never again settle for their former status. Beye suggested provincial juntas and a representative governing junta to whom the viceroy and Audiencia would be subject. The combined statement of the Americans in August, 1811, repeated the recommendation of provincial juntas like those in Spain and requested that the Americas be allowed regional governments. The idea of self-government grew, and in 1821 the Americans offered a plan for governments whose only official link to Spain was an executive named by the king. All other governmental functions were to be the responsibility of American officials. By this time the Americans had begun to think of the eventuality and inevitability of complete independence from Spain. In a letter to his brother Rafaelito, dated June 6, 1821, Ramos Arizpe, after explaining the new proposals to be offered to the Cortes, expressed a fear that it was too late for them and that independence for all of Latin America would come as it had already to Colombia.[60] With the rejection of their proposals, many of the Americans sailed for home at the conclusion of the regular session of the Cortes of 1821. Those who stayed for the extra session asked that the Cortes recognize the independence of America and seek some form of reconciliation that would be mutually advantageous. With the repudiation of these suggestions, the Americans ended their efforts in the Spanish Cortes and returned home, some of them to take an enthusiastic part in shaping the future destinies of independent republics.

Whether Spanish concessions would have at any time preserved her empire is history's secret. Perhaps once the revolution had begun, the unavoidable conclusion of it was complete independence from Spain.

[60] Miguel Ramos Arizpe, *Carta escrita a un americano.*

Conclusion   *Nettie Lee Benson*

The new generation of creoles followed two routes to independence in the period beginning in 1810: "that of insurrection and that of parliamentary debate" as Luis González states in his "Estudio Preliminar" to *El Congreso de Anáhuac 1813*. A great deal of study and writing has been devoted to the insurrectionists and their ephemeral Constitution of Apatzingán, whereas little attention has been given to those Mexicans who followed the route of parliamentary or congressional debate in the Spanish Cortes during the period 1810–1822, although they were the ones who laid the real foundations for constitutional government in Mexico. Through their participation in the Cortes of Spain, they not only gained valuable experience which was to be well employed in the constituent congresses of 1822–1824 and the later regular congresses but helped prepare the people of Mexico for participation in constitutional government—educating them through municipal and provincial elections, obtaining for them some little experience in local and provincial government and in freedom of expression, and pointing to the need and possibility of economic, military, and religious reforms. The guidelines for future developments in all these areas, as well as many others not treated here, were sketched by those who traveled the path of parliamentary debate. Their work was less dramatic but more enduring, and is worthy of much more study and recognition than it has received.

As stated in the Introduction these eight chapters do not cover all that the Mexicans to the Cortes attempted to realize for their country through legislation. Other topics yet to be developed to complete the story relate to local, provincial, and national government; educational, land, and judicial reform, etc.; and should include as well a complete analysis of the Mexican delegation as a whole, its common interests, objectives, and supports. These chapters here presented do, however, demonstrate rather clearly the common interests, objectives, and support of the Mexican deputies in relation to the topics covered and show that in nearly every instance when a roll-call vote was recorded on a subject, the Mexicans acted as a unit. While these papers do not answer all questions, they do cause one to question such allegations as that the Mexican people were not prepared to participate in governing themselves, their elections were tumultuous and unruly, freedom of the press was grossly abused by them, and that the government set up in Mexico in 1824 resulted from a poor translation of the United States Constitution and an arbitrary breaking-up of a highly centralized viceroyalty.

Too long historians and political scientists, in writing of this and the immediately subsequent period, have relied almost entirely on Bancroft, who used as his primary source the extremely partisan history of Lucas Alamán, a conservative who longed for a return to the colonial or monarchical form of government and who wrote history as Father Mariano Cuevas admitted doing when he said, "I write history not as it occurred, but as I want people to believe it did."

Alamán's thesis that Mexico was arbitrarily dismembered by ignorant and ill-prepared Mexican political figures has led to a black legend of Mexican political ignorance, much as Las Casas' denunciations of the treatment of the Indians created that legend of Spanish cruelty. Alamán's portrait of his progressive contemporaries as politically ignorant has served to obscure the fact that his account is neither a complete nor true history of Mexico between 1810 and 1850. It has successfully closed the door on any studies of the effect of the inherent regionalism which was recognized in the Spanish Constitution of 1812 through the creation of provincial deputations and the elimination of the viceroy and his replacement by various regional political chiefs. When historians awake to the fact that much is yet to be learned about what actually occurred during the period of 1810–1857, perhaps someone will investigate the overwhelming desire of Mexico City and its immediate area to control all of Mexico and will see this desire as a significant factor in the chaos of the period, much as the determination of Buenos Aires to control the provinces resulted in chaos for the whole Río de La Plata area. An important question also yet to be investigated is: if centralized government was the proper form of government for Mexico in 1821 to 1850, why did it fail so miserably and quickly each time it was attempted during that period? Many other subjects for interesting studies might emanate from minds uninfluenced by what has been the continued and almost exclusive reliance on biased historical writings, both contemporary and secondary.

Bibliography

Primary Sources

Abad Queipo, Manuel. *Colección de los escritos más importantes que en diferentes épocas dirigió al gobierno D. Manuel Abad Queipo.* México: Imprenta de M. Ontiveros, 1813.

———. Representación a S. M. el 20 de junio de 1815 por el obispo electo de Michoacán el Excmo. Dn. Manuel Abad y Queipo, sobre la situación política de nuestras Américas. Photostatic copy of original in the Cuevas Collection in the Latin American Collection of The University of Texas Library.

Alba, Rafael de (ed.). *La constitución de 1812 en la Nueva España.* 2 vols. (Vols. IV and V in *Publicaciones del Archivo General de la Nación*). México: Tip. Guerrero Hnos., 1912–1913.

Albuerne, Manuel de. *Origen y estado de la causa formada sobre la real orden de 17 de mayo de 1810, que trata del comercio de América.* Cádiz: Imprenta de Vicente Lema, 1811.

Álvarez, Francisco. *Anales históricos de Campeche, 1812 a 1910.* 2 vols. Mérida: Imp. del "Colegio S. José" de artes y oficios, 1912.

Argüelles, Agustín de. *Exámen histórico de la reforma constitucional que hicieron las Córtes generales y extraordinarias.* 2 vols. London: Imprenta de Carlos Wood e Hijo, 1835.

Austin. The University of Texas Library. Latin American Collection, Alejandro Prieto Papers.

———. Genaro García Papers.

———. Hernández y Dávalos Papers.

———. Printed Decrees, 1792–1822.

Austin. The University of Texas Library. Archives of Eugene C. Barker History Center. Bexar Archives.

———. Nacogdoches Archives.

Bárcena, Manuel de la. *Manifiesto al mundo de la justicia y la necesidad de la independencia de la Nueva España.* Impreso en Puebla y en México: Oficina de D. Mariano Ontiveros, 1821.

Bernardo Bonavía to Secretaría de Estado y del Despacho de la Gobernación de Ultramar, Durango, March 16, 1814. Archivo General de Indias, Seville, Legajo 297, No. 4. Typescript copy in the possession of Nettie Lee Benson, Austin, Texas.

Bustamante, Carlos María. *Campañas del general D. Félix María Calleja, comandante en gefe del ejército real de operaciones, llamado del centro.* México: Impr. del Aguila, 1828.

——. Copia de la memoria de Iturbide con comentarios. Manuscript in Hernández y Dávalos Collection, Expediente 17, No. 8.4255, in Latin American Collection of The University of Texas Library.

Cádiz, Merchant Guild of. *El Comercio de Cádiz representado legítimamente recurre la segunda vez a S.M. en 12 de octubre exponiendo el resultado ruinoso que causaría al Estado el proyecto de comercio libre.* Cádiz: Imprenta real, 1811.

——. *Informe dirigido a S.M. por el Consulado y Comercio de esta plaza en 24 de julio sobre los perjuicios que se originarían de la concesión del comercio libre de los extrangeros con nuestras Américas.* Cádiz: Imprenta real, 1811.

——. *Tercera exposición del Comercio de Cádiz a las Cortes generales y estraordinarias por medio de una diputación especial, ampliando sus ideas y observaciones sobre el proyecto de comercio libre de las Américas con las naciones extrangeras.* Cádiz: Imprenta real, 1812.

Calleja, Félix María. "Informe del exmo. sr. virrey d. Félix Calleja sobre el estado de la N.E. dirigido al Ministerio de Gracia y Justicia en 18 de agosto de 1814." Manuscript in the Latin American Collection of The University of Texas Library.

Cañedo, Juan de Dios. *Manifiesto á la nación española sobre la representación de las provincias de ultramar en las próximas Córtes.* Madrid: Imprenta de Vega y Companía, 1830; reprinted in México in 1820 by Alejandro Valdés.

Canel Acevedo, Pedro. *Reflexiones sobre la Constitución española, Cortes nacionales y estado de la presente guerra.* Oviedo: D. Francisco Candid Pérez Prieto, 1812.

Cárdenas, José Eduardo. *Memoria a favor de la provincia de Tabasco, en la Nueva España, presentada a S.M. las Cortes generales y extraordinarias por el dr. Joséf Eduardo de Cárdenas.* Cádiz: Imprenta del Estado Mayor General, 1811.

Censor, El. Cádiz. 1811.

Coahuila. Archivo municipal de Saltillo. Expediente 60 (1811–1813). Typescript copy.

Correo americano del sur. 1813.

Delgado Román, Ricardo (comp.). *Valentín Gómez Farías, ideario reformista.* Guadalajara: Gobierno del Estado, 1958.

Despertador americano, El. December 20, 1810–January 17, 1811.

Diario de México. 26 vols. México, 1805–1817.

Documentos históricos mexicanos. Edited by Genaro García, 7 vols. México, 1910.

El hispano-americano constitucional. Mérida, 1820.

Español, El. 8 vols. London, 1812–1814.

Exposición presentada a las Cortes por los diputados de ultramar en la sesión de 25 de junio de 1821, sobre el estado actual de las provincias de que son representantes. Madrid: Imprenta de Don Diego García y Campay, 1821.

Fernández de Lizardi, José Joaquín. *Cincuenta preguntas del Pensador a quién quiera responderlas.* México: Imprenta Imperial de D. Alejandro Valdés, November 21, 1821.

———. *El Pensador mejicano.* México: Imp. de Doña María Fernández de Jáuregui, 1812.

[Foncerrada, José Cayentano de]. *Comercio libre vindicado de la nota de ruinoso a la España y a las Américas.* Cádiz: Imprenta del estado-mayor general, 1811.

Gaceta del gobierno de Guadalajara. Guadalajara, 1820–1822.

Gaceta del gobierno de México. 12 vols. México, 1810–1821.

Gaceta del gobierno imperial de México. 2 vols. México: Impr. imperial de Alejandro Valdés, 1821–1822.

Gaceta de México. 1805–1817.

Gaceta extraordinaria del gobierno provisional mexicano. August, 1817.

Gaceta imperial de México. México, 1821–1822.

García, Genario (ed.). *Documentos históricos mexicanos.* 7 vols. México, 1910.

Gómez Pedraza, Manuel. *Manifiesto que Manuel Gómez Pedraza, ciudadano de la república de Méjico, dedica a sus compatriotas; o sea una reseña de su vida pública.* Guadalajara: Brambila, 1831.

González, José Eleuterio. *Colección de noticias y documentos para la historia del estado de Nuevo-León, recogidos y ordenados de manera que formen una relación seguida.* 2d ed. 2 vols. Monterrey: Imprenta del Gobierno, 1885.

Guadalupes to Morelos, The, December 7, 1812. In Correspondencia de los guadalupanos. Contemporary copies of originals in the Archives of the Indies in the Latin American Collection of The University of Texas Library.

Guatemala. Ayuntamiento. *Instrucciones para la Constitución fundamental de la monarquía española y su gobierno . . . dadas por el M. I. Ayuntamiento de la Ciudad de Guatemala a su diputado el Sr. Dr. D. Antonio de Larrazábal.* Guatemala: Editorial del Ministerio de Educación Pública, 1953.

Guerra, José [José Servando Teresa de Mier Noriega y Guerra]. *Historia de la revolución en Nueva España antiguamente Anáhuac ó verdadero origen y causas de ella con la relación de sus progresos hasta el presente año de 1813.* 2 vols. London: La Imprenta de Guillermo Glindon, 1813.

Guridi y Alcocer, José Miguel. "Contestación de Don José Miguel Guridi y Alcocer a lo que contra él y los decretos de las Cortes se ha vertido en los números 13, y 14 del *Telégrafo americano*," *Censor extraordinaro*. Cádiz: Imprenta de Agapito Fernández, 1812.

Hernández y Dávalos, J. E. (comp.) *Colección de documentos para la historia de la guerra de independencia de México de 1808 a 1821*. 6 vols. México: J. M. Sandoval, 1877–1882.

Illustrado americano. May, 1812–April, 1813.

Illustrador nacional. April–May, 1812.

Iturbide, Agustín de. *Carrera militar y política de don Agustín de Iturbide*. México: M. Ximeno, 1827.

Juguetes contra el Juguetillo. 1812.

Juguetillo, El. 1812.

Juguetón, El. 1812.

Lagranda, Francisco. *Consejo prudente sobre una de las garantías*. México, 1821.

Lily, Cristóbal; Ausel y Domínguez, Juan Manuel; Ayesterán, José Joaquín; and Michelena, José Mariano. *Representación presentada á la Junta Superior de Galicia por los Americanos residentes en esta Provincia*. Reprinted in Puebla: Oficina del Gobierno, 1820.

López Cancelada, Juan. *Ruina de la Nueva España si se declara el comercio libre con los estrangeros*. Cádiz: Imprenta de Manuel Santiago de Quintana, 1811.

M. M. *Acta celebrada en Iguala. El primero de marzo juramento al día siguiente presto el sr. Iturbide con la oficialidad y tropa a su mano*. México, 1821.

Maniau, Joaquín. "Puntos de vista de D. Joaquín Maniau diputado de la Nueva España en las Cortes de Cádiz, sobre el tratado de comercio que se negociaba en 1811, entre Inglaterra y España," *La libertad del comercio en la Nueva España en la segunda decada del siglo XIX* (Vol. I of *Archivo histórico de hacienda*). México: Secretaría de Hacienda y Crédito Público, Dirección de Estudios Financieros, 1943.

Mateos, Juan A. *Historia parlamentaria de los congresos mexicanos de 1821 a 1857*. 25 vols. México: Vicente S. Reyes, Impresor, 1877–1912.

México. Archivo General de la Nación. Ramo de Historia: Vols. 398, 401–404, 417, 442–448. Ramo de Guerra: Vols. 30–31. Provincias Internas: Vols. 185–187. Microfilm.

México. Constitution. *Acta constitutiva de la Federación mexicana*. México, 1824.

———. *Colección de constituciones de los Estados Unidos Mexicanos*. 3 vols. México: Imprenta de Galván, 1828.

———. *Constitución federal de los Estados Unidos Mexicanos sancionada por el Congreso general constituyente, el 4 de octubre de 1824.* México, 1824.

———. *Decreto constitucional para la libertad de la América mexicana, sancionada en Apatzingán a 22 de octubre de 1814.* Reimpreso en la oficina de D. Mariano de Zúñiga y Ontiveros, 1821.

Mexico. Laws, statutes, etc. *Colección de los decretos y órdenes del soberano congreso mexicano, desde su instalación en 24 de febrero de 1822 hasta 30 de octubre de 1823 en que cesó.* México: Imprenta del Supremo govierno de los Estados Unidos Mexicanos, 1825.

———. *Colección de los decretos y órdenes que ha expedido la soberana junta provisional gubernativa del Império Mexicano, desde su instalación en 28 de septiembre de 1821 hasta 24 de febrero de 1822.* México: D. Alejandro Valdés, 1822.

———. *Legislación mexicana o colección completa de las disposiciones legislativas expedidas desde la independencia de la república.* 34 vols. México: Imprenta del Comercio, á cargo de Dublán y Lozano, hijos, 1876–1904.

Mexico, Secretariat of Foreign Relations. *La constitución de 1812 en la Nueva España.* 2 vols. (Vol. V of Publicaciones del archivo general de la nación) México: Tip. Guerrero Hnos., 1913.

Noticioso general, El. México, 1815–1823.

Nuevo León. Archivo general del Gobierno del estado de Nuevo León. Año 1820, Carpeta Núm. 5. Typescript copy.

Oficios y Contestaciones de la Diputación Provincial desde el día 1º de Mayo de 1814. Archivo General del Estado de Nuevo León, Monterrey, México. Typescript copy in the possession of Nettie Lee Benson, Austin, Texas.

Parral, Mexico. Archivo de Hidalgo del Parral, El, 1631–1821. Microfilm.

Pensador mejicano, El. México, 1812–1813.

Pérez Antonio Joaquín, to Calleja, Félix María, April 14, 1816. In "Controversía entre el obispo de Puebla y el virrey Calleja," *Boletín del Archivo general de la nación.* IV, No. 5 (September, 1933), 657–664.

Pérez-Maldonado, Carlos. *Documentos históricos de Nuevo-Leon anotados y comentados.* 2 vols. Monterrey: Ciudad de Nuestra Señora de Monterrey, 1947–1948.

Pérez y Comoto, Florencio. *Representación que a favor del libre comercio dirigieron al excelentísimo señor Don Juan Ruíz de Apodaca, Virrey, Gobernador y Capitán General de Nueva-España, doscientos veinte y nueve vecinos de la ciudad de Veracruz.* Habana: Oficina de Arazoza y Soler, 1818.

Pino, Pedro Bautista. *Noticias históricas y estadísticas de la antigua provincia del Nuevo Méjico.* México: Imprenta de Lara, 1849.

Proyecto de ley constitutiva del ejército, presentado a las Cortes por las comisiones unidas de organización de fuerza armada y de milicias. México, 1821.

Quirós, José María. *Ideas políticas económicas de gobierno, Memoria de instituto, formada por D. José María Quirós, secretario de la junta gubernativa del Consulado de Veracruz.* Veracruz: Imprenta del gobierno imperial mejicano de Priani y socios, 1821.

——. *Memoria de estatuto, Idea de la riqueza que daban a la masacirculante de Nueva España sus naturales producciones en los años de tranquilidad, y su abastimiento en las presentes conmociones.* Veracruz, 1817.

——. *Memoria de Instituto en que se manifiesta que el comercio marítimo ha llamado siempre la atención de todas las naciones; y cada una ha hecho los mayores esfuerzos para su posesión exclusiva.* Habana: Oficina de la Cena, 1814.

Ramos Arizpe, Miguel. *Carta escrita a un americano sobre la forma de gobierno que para hacer practicable la constitución y las leyes, conviene establecer en Nueva España atendida su actual situación.* Madrid: Ibarra, Impresor de Cámara de S.M., 1821.

——. *Ideal general sobre la conducta política de d. Miguel Ramos de Arizpe, natural de la provincia de Coahuila.* México: Oficina de Doña Herculana del Villar y Socios, 1822.

——. *Memoria que el Doctor D. Miguel Ramos de Arizpe, presenta a el augusto Congreso.* Cádiz: Imprenta del Estado Mayor General, 1812; Guadalajara, 1813.

——. *Papel que la diputación mexicana dirige al excmo. señor secretario de estado y del despacho de guerra.* Madrid: Ibarra, Impresor de Cámara de S.M., 1821.

——. *Report That Dr. Miguel Ramos de Arizpe, Priest of Borbon and Deputy in the Present General and Special Cortes of Spain for the Province of Coahuila, One of the Four Eastern Interior Provinces of the Kingdom of Mexico, Presents to the August Congress on the Natural, Political, and Civil Conditions of the Provinces of Coahuila, Nuevo Leon, Nuevo Santander, and Texas of the Four Eastern Interior Provinces of the Kingdom of Mexico.* Translation, annotations, and introduction by Nettie Lee Benson. The University of Texas Institute of Latin American Studies, Latin American Studies, No. 11. Austin: University of Texas Press, 1950.

Redactor mexicano, El. Mexico, 1814.

Representación que los Americanos Españoles, residentes en Madrid, han entregado á S.M. por medio de los Sres. Marqués de Cárdenas de Montehermoso, D. Manuel Inca Inpanqui, y D. Gabriel Señero, el día 4 del presente mes de abril [dated March 31, 1820, and signed by 146 individuals]. Reprinted in México: Alejandro Valdés, 1820.

Revillagigedo, Juan Vicente de. "El Virrey de Nueva España, conde de Revillagigedo, informa en el expediente sobre averiguar si hay decadencia en el comercio de aquellos reinos. Reproduced in *Colección de documentos para la historia del comercio exterior de México*, IV, 5–59. México: Publicaciones del Banco Nacional de Comercio Exterior, S.A., 1960.

Semanario patriótico americano. México, July, 1812–January, 1813.

Semanario político y literario. México, 1810–1821.

Spain, Constitution. *Constitución política de la monarquía española, promulgada en Cádiz á 19 de marzo de 1812.* Cádiz: n. p., 1812; México: A. Valdés, 1820.

Spain. Cortes, 1810–1813. *Diario de las discusiones y actas de las Cortes.* 24 vols. Cádiz: Imprenta Real, 1811–1813.

———. *Diario de sesiones de las Cortes generales y extraordinarias.* 9 vols. Madrid: Imprenta de J. A. García, 1870–1874.

———. *Instrucción para los ayuntamientos constitucionales juntas provinciales, y gefes políticos superiores decretada por las Cortes generales y extraordinarias en 23 de junio de 1813.* México: Imprenta de J. Bautista Arispe, 1820.

———. *Lista de los señores diputados de las Cortes generales y extraordinarias de la nación española.* Cádiz: La imprenta real, 1811.

———. *México en las Cortes de Cádiz: Documentos.* México: Empresas Editoriales, S.A., 1949.

———. *Proposiciones que hacen al Congreso Nacional los diputados de América y Asia.* Madrid: Imprenta de Francisco de Paula Periu, 1811.

———. *Reglamento para el gobierno interior de las Cortes* [dated November 24, 1810]. Cádiz: La imprenta real, 1810.

———. *Representación de la diputación americana a las Cortes de España en 1° de agosto de 1811.* (Con notas del editor inglés). London: Imprenta de Schulze y Dean; México: Reimpreso en la Oficina de Alexandro Valdés, 1820.

Spain. Cortes, 1813–1814. *Actas de las sesiones de la legislatura ordinaria de 1813.* 2d ed. Madrid: Imprenta de la Viuda e Hijos de J. Antonio García, 1876.

Spain. Cortes, 1814. *Actas de las sesiones de la legislatura ordinaria de 1814.* Madrid: Imprenta de la Viuda e Hijos de J. Antonio García, 1876.

Spain. Cortes, 1820. *Diario de las sesiones de Cortes: Legislatura de 1820.* 3 vols. Madrid: Imprenta de J. A. García, 1871–1873.

Spain. Cortes, 1820–1821. *Diario de las actas y discusiones de las Cortes:*

Legislatura de los años de 1820–1821. 23 vols. Madrid: Imprenta especial de las Cortes, 1820–1821.

Spain. Cortes, 1821. Diario de las sesiones de Cortes: Legislatura de 1821. 3 vols. 2d ed. Madrid: Imprenta de J. A. García, 1871–1873.

Spain. Cortes, 1821–1822. Diario de las sesiones de Cortes: Legislatura extraordinaria. 3 vols. Madrid: Imprenta de J. A. García, 1871.

Spain, Cortes, 1822. Diario de las sesiones de Cortes. Legislatura de 1822. 3 vols. 2d ed. Madrid: Imprenta de J. A. García, 1872–1873.

Spain. Council of Regency. Decreto de 14 de febrero de 1810.

Spain. Junta Suprema Central Gubernativa de España e Indias. Decreto de 29 de enero de 1810: El rey y a su nombre la suprema Junta Central Gubernativa de España é Indias. N.p., n.d.

Spain. Laws and Statutes, 1810–1822. Colección de los decretos y órdenes que han expedido las Cortes generales y extraordinarias. 9 vols. Madrid: Imprenta nacional, 1820–1822.

Spain. Laws, Statutes, 1813–1833 (Ferdinand VII). Instrucción conforme a la cual deberán celebrarse en las Provincias de Ultramar las elecciones de Diputados de Cortes para las ordinarias de 1820 y 1821 [signed by Ferdinand VII at Madrid, March 24, 1820].

———. Recopilación de leyes de los reinos de las índias. Madrid: Consejo de la Hispanidad, 1943.

Tena Ramírez, Felipe (comp.). Leyes fundamentales de México, 1808– 1957. México: Editorial Porrúa, S.A.

Twitchell, Ralph E. The Spanish Archives of New Mexico: Compiled and Arranged with Historical, Genealogical, Geographical and Other Annotations, by Authority of the State of New Mexico. 2 vols. Rapid City: Torch Press, 1914.

Valdés, Alejandro. Guía de forasteros de esta imperio mexicano y calendario para el año de 1822. México: Alejandro Valdés [1822 ?].

Ventura Beleña, Eusebio. "Informe reservado del oidor de la Audiencia de México sobre el atual estado del comercio del mesmo reino." Reproduced in Colección de documentos para la historia del comercio exterior de México, IV, 60–122. México: Publicaciones del Banco Nacional de Comercio Exterior, S.A., 1960.

Vera, Fortino Hipólito. Colección de documentos eclesiásticos de México, o sea antigua y moderna legislación de la iglesia mexicana. 3 vols. Amecameca: Imprenta del Colegio Católico, 1887.

V[idaurre y Encalada?], M. [L. de]. Manifiesto sobre los representantes que corresponden a los americanos en las inmediatas Córtes. Madrid: Imprenta de Vega y Compañía, 1820; reprinted in México by Alejandro Valdés, N.D.

Villanueva, Joaquín Lorenzo. Mi viaje á las Córtes. Madrid: Imprenta nacional, 1860.

Voto de la nación española, El. Seville, 1809. Pamphlet, republished in México, 1810.

Secondary Sources

Alamán, Lucas. *Historia de Méjico desde los primeros movimientos que prepararon su independencia en el año de 1808, hasta la época presente.* 5 vols. México: Imprenta de J. M. Lara, 1849–1852; Editorial Jus., 1942.

Alessio Robles, Vito. *Coahuila y Texas en la época colonial.* México: Editorial Cultura, 1938.

Almada, Francisco R. *Apuntes históricos de la región de Chínipas.* Chihuahua: Talleres Linotipográficas del Estado del Chihuahua, 1937.

———. *Diccionario de historia, geografía y biografía Sonorenses.* Chihuahua: Talleres Arrendatarios de Impresora Ruiz Sandoval, 1952.

Amador, Elías. *Bosquejo histórico de Zacatecas.* 2 vols. Zacatecas: Talleres Tipográfico "Pedroza," AGS, 1943.

———. *History of California.* 2 vols. San Francisco: History Company, 1885.

———. *History of the North Mexican States and Texas.* 2 vols. San Francisco: History Company, 1889.

Ancona, Eligio. *Historia de Yucatán desde la época más remota hasta nuestros días.* 5 vols. Barcelona: Imprenta de Jaime Jesús Roviralta, 1889–1905.

Bancroft, Hubert Howe. *History of Mexico.* 6 vols. San Francisco: A. L. Bancroft, 1883–1887.

———. *The Works of Hubert Howe Bancroft.* 39 vols. San Francisco: A. L. Bancroft & Company, 1883–1890.

Barker, Eugene C., "The Government of Austin's Colony, 1821–1831," *Southwestern Historical Quarterly,* XXI (January, 1918), 223–252.

Bayle, Constantino. *Los cabildos seculares en la América Española.* Madrid: Sapienta, 1952.

Benson, Nettie Lee. "Iturbide y los planes de independencia," *Historia mexicana,* II, No. 3 (January–March, 1953), 439–446.

———. *La diputación provincial y el federalismo mexicano.* México: El Colegio de México, 1955.

———. "Texas' Failure To Send a Deputy to the Spanish Cortes, 1810–1812," *Southwestern Historical Quarterly,* LXIV (July, 1960), 1–22.

———. "The Contested Mexican Election of 1812," *Hispanic American Historical Review,* XXVI (August, 1946), 336–350.

———. "The Provincial Deputation in Mexico, Precursor of the Mexican Federal State." Unpublished Ph.D. dissertation, The University of Texas, 1949.

———. "Washington, Symbol of the United States in Mexico, 1800–1823," *The Library Chronicle of The University of Texas* (Spring, 1847) II, No. 4.

Berlanga, Tomás. *Monografía histórica de la ciudad de Saltillo.* Monterrey: Imprenta Americana, 1922.

Bolton, Herbert E. *Guide to Materials for the History of the United States in the Principle Archives of Mexico.* Washington, D.C.: Carnegie Institute, 1913.

Bustamante, Carlos María de. *Cuadro histórico de la revolución mexicana iniciada el 15 de septiembre de 1810 por el C. Miguel Hidalgo y Costilla cura del pueblo de Dólores en el obispado de Michoacán.* 5 vols. México, 1961.

Castro y Rossi, Adolfo. *Cortes de Cádiz.* Madrid: Imprenta de P. Pérez de Velasco, 1913.

Cavazos Garza, Israel. *El muy ilustre ayuntamiento de Monterrey desde 1596.* Monterrey, 1956.

Cossío, David Alberto. *Historia de Nuevo León.* 6 vols. Monterrey: Talleres Linotipográficos de J. Cantu Leal, 1925.

Dealey, James Q. "The Spanish Sources of the Mexican Constitution of 1824," *The Quarterly of the Texas State Historical Association,* III, No. 3 (January, 1900), 161–169.

Delgado, Jaime. *La independencia de América en la prensa española.* Madrid: 1949.

Enciclopedia Universal Illustrada Europeo-Americana. Bilboa: Espasa Calpe, S. A.

Esquivel Obregón, Toribio. *Apuntes para la historia del derecho en México.* 5 vols. México: Editorial Polis, 1938.

Fisher, Lillian Estelle. *The Background of the Revolution for Mexican Independence.* Boston: Christopher Publishing House, 1934.

———. *Champion of Reform, Manuel Abad y Queipo.* New York: Library Publishers, 1955.

———. *The Intendant System in Spanish America.* Berkeley: University of California Press, 1929.

Gamboa, José M. *Leyes constitucionales de México durante el siglo XIX.* México: Oficina Tip. de la Secretaría de Fomento, 1901.

García, Genaro. "Secretarios de Estado del Gobierno Mexicano." Unpublished manuscript in Latin American Collection, The University of Texas Library, Austin.

García Gutiérrez, Jesús. *Acción anticatólica en Méjico.* 2d ed. México: Editorial Campeador, 1956.

Garza, David Trippe. "Spanish Origins of Mexican Constitutionalism: An Analysis of Constitutional Development in New Spain, 1808 to Independence." Unpublished Master's Thesis. The University of Texas, 1965.

González Palencia, Angel. *Estudo histórico sobre la censura gubernativa en España, 1800–1833.* 3 vols. Madrid, 1934.

Haggard, J. Villasana. "Spanish Archives Calendar Oct. 30, 1807, to May

13, 1809. Copied from Card Calendar prepared by Archivists and Staff, Revised by J. Villasana Haggard, Translator of The Spanish Archives." Archives of The University of Texas, 1941.

Haring, Clarence H. *The Spanish Empire in America.* New York: Oxford University Press, 1947.

Humboldt, Alexander von. *Ensayo político sobre Nueva España.* 6th Spanish edition. 5 vols. México: Robredo, 1941.

Index to El Archivo del Hidalgo del Parral, 1631–1821. Cleveland: Microphoto, Inc.

Jiménez Gregorio, Fernando. "La convocatoria de Cortes Constituyentes en 1810. Estado de la opinión española en punto a reforma constitucional," in *Estudios de Historia Moderna,* Núm. V, (Barcelona, 1955), 223–347.

King, James F. "The Colored Castes and the American Representation in the Cortes of Cádiz," *Hispanic American Historical Review,* XXXIII (February, 1953), 33–64.

Labra y Cadrana, Rafael María de. *América y la constitución española de 1812.* Madrid: Tip. "Sindicato de publicidad," 1914.

Labra y Martínez, Rafael M. de. *Los presidentes americanos de las Cortes de Cádiz: Estudio biográfico.* Cádiz: Imprenta de Manuel Alvarez Rodríguez, 1912.

Lafuente y Zamolloa, Modesto. *Historia general de España desde los tiempos primitivos hasta la muerte de Fernando VII.* 6 vols. Barcelona: Montaner y Simón, Editores, 1877–1882.

Lanz, Manuel A. *Compendio de historia de Campeche.* Campeche: Tip. "El Fénix" de Pablo Llovera Marcín, 1905.

Lea, Charles Henry. *Chapters from the Religious History of Spain Connected with the Inquisition.* Philadelphia, 1890.

Lerdo de Tejada, Miguel. *Comercio esterior de México desde la conquista hasta hoy.* México: Impreso por Rafael Rafael, 1853.

Llave Hill, Joaquín de la. *El municipio en la historia y en nuestra constitución.* México: Universidad Nacional Autónoma de México, 1960.

McAlister, Lyle N. *The "Fuero Militar" in New Spain, 1764–1800.* Gainsville: University of Florida Press, 1957.

Martínez Marina, Francisco. *Teoría de las Cortes ó grandes juntas nacionales.* 3 vols. Madrid: Imprenta de D. Fermín Villalpando, 1813.

México. Congreso. Cámara de Senadores. *El Congreso de Anáhuac 1813.* México: Cámara de Senadores, 1963.

México en las Córtes de Cádiz: Documentos. México, 1949.

Molina Solís, Juan Francisco. *Historia de Yucatán durante la dominación española.* 3 vols. Merida: Imprenta de la Lotería del Estado, 1904–1913.

Mora, José María Luis. *Obras Sueltas.* 2 vols. Paris: Librarie de Rosa, 1837.

Moreno Carvajal, Gustavo. *El municipio mexicano*. México: Universidad Nacional Autónoma, 1963.

Muro, Manuel. *Historia de San Luis Potosí*. 3 vols. San Luis Potosí: Imp. de F. L. González, 1910.

O'Gorman, Edmundo. *Breve historia de las divisiones territoriales: Aportación a la historia de la geografía de México*. México: Editorial Polis, 1937.

Parkes, Henry Bamford. *A History of Mexico*. Boston: Houghton Mifflin Company, 1938.

Parry, J. H. *The Sale of Public Office in the Spanish Indies under the Hapsburgs*. Berkeley: University of California Press, 1953.

Pérez-Maldonado, Carlos. *Narraciones históricas regiomontañas*, 2 vols. Monterrey: Ciudad de Nuestra Señora de Monterrey, 1947–1948.

Pimentel, Francisco. *Historia crítica de la poesía en México*. 5 vols. Vol. V: *Obras completas de don Francisco Pimental*. México: Tipografía economía, 1903–1904.

Priestley, Herbert I. *José de Gálvez, Visitor-General of New Spain (1765–1771)*. Berkeley: University of California Press, 1916.

Priestley, Herbert Ingram. *The Mexican Nation: A History*. New York: Macmillan Company, 1923.

Ramos, Demetrio, "Las Cortes de Cádiz y America," *Revista de Estudios Políticos*, Num. 126 (Madrid, November–December, 1962), 433–639.

Richman, Irving S. *California under Spain and Mexico, 1535–1847*. Boston: Houghton Mifflin, 1911.

Rivera Cambas, Manuel. *Los gobernantes de México: Galería de biografías y retratos de los vireyes, emperadores, presidentes y otros gobernantes que ha tenido México desde don Hernando Cortés hasta el C. Benito Juárez*. México: Imp. de J. M. Aguilar Ortíz, 1873.

Robertson, William Spence. *Iturbide of Mexico*. Durham: Duke University Press, 1952.

Rolland, M. C. *El desastre municipal en la república mexicana*. México: Molina, 1939.

Sánchez Agesta, Luis. *Historia del constitucionalismo español*. Madrid: Instituto de Estudios Políticos, 1955.

Schmitt, Karl M. "The Clergy and the Independence of New Spain," *Hispanic American Historical Review*, XXXIV, No. 3 (August, 1954), 289–312.

Smith, Robert Sidney. "Shipping in the Port of Vera Cruz, 1790–1821," *Hispanic American Historical Review*, XXIII (February, 1943), 5–20.

Sosa, Francisco. *Biografías de mexicanos distinguidos*. México: Oficina Tipográfica de la Secretaría de Fomento, 1884.

Spell, Jefferson Rea. "Fernández de Lizardi: A Bibliography," *Hispanic American Historical Review*, VII (November, 1927), 490–491.

———. *The Life and Works of José Joaquín Fernández de Lizardi.* Philadelphia: University of Pennsylvania, 1931.

Sprague, William Forrest. *Vicente Guerrero, Mexican Liberator: A Study in Patriotism.* Chicago: R. R. Doubleday & Sons, 1939.

Suárez, Federico. *La crisis política del antiguo régimen en España.* 2d ed. Madrid: Ediciones Rialp, 1958.

Tandron, Humberto. "The Commerce of New Spain and the Free Trade Controversy, 1796–1821." Unpublished Master's thesis, The University of Texas, 1961.

Timmons, Wilbert H. "Los Guadalupes: A Secret Society in the Mexican Revolution for Independence," *Hispanic American Historical Review,* XXX, No. 4 (November, 1950), 453–479.

———. *Morelos: Priest, Soldier, Statesman of Mexico.* El Paso: Texas Western College Press, 1963.

Toreno, Conde de. *Historia del levantamiento, guerra y revolución de España.* 5 vols. Madrid: M. Rivadeneyra, 1872.

Torre Revello, José. *El libro, la imprenta y el periodismo en América durante la dominación española.* Buenos Aires, 1940.

Torres Lanzas, Pedro. *Independencia de América. Fuentes para su estudio. Catálogo de documentos conservados en el archivo general de Indias de Sevilla.* Madrid: Establecimiento Tipográfico de la Sociedad de Publicaciones Históricas, 1912.

Trens, Manuel B. *Historia de Veracruz.* 6 vols. Jalapa: Talleres Linotipográficos del Gobierno del Estado de Veracruz, 1948–1950.

Valle Iberlucea, Enrique del. *Los diputados de Buenos Aires en las Cortes de Cádiz y el nuevo sistema de gobierno económico de América.* Buenos Aires: Martín García, 1912.

Velásquez, María del Carmen. *El estado de guerra de Nueva España, 1760–1808.* México: Colegio de México, 1950.

Villaseñor y Villaseñor, Alejandro. *Biografías de los héroes y caudillos de la independencia.* Vol. III: *Obras del Lic. Alejandro Villaseñor y Villaseñor.* México: Imp. de "El Tiempo," 1910.

Walker, Thomas Fonso. "Pre-Revolutionary Pamphleteering in Mexico, 1808–1810." Unpublished Ph.D. dissertation, The University of Texas, 1951.

Ward, Henry George. *Mexico.* 2d ed. London: H. Colburn, 1829.

Zamacois, Niceto de. *Historia de Méjico, desde sus tiempos más remotos hasta nuestros días.* 22 vols. Barcelona and México: J. F. Párres y Comp., 1876–1903.

Zarate, Julio. *La guerra de independencia.* 5 vols. Vol. III: *México a través de los siglos.* Edited by Vicente Riva Palacio. Barcelona: 1886–1889.

Zerecero, Anastasio. *Memorias para la historia de las revoluciones en México.* México: Imp. del gobierno a cargo de J. M. Sandoval, 1869.

Index

Abad y Queipo, Manuel: in defense of colonies, 138; and decoration of Venegas, 140; criticizes Callejo, 146; on prevention of rebellion in Mexico, 186–187

absolutism: and king's veto, 54; desire of Mexican Cortes delegates to limit, 55

Acevedo, Juan: replaced on Supreme Censorship Board, 104

Acevedo, Pedro: named to Mexico City censorship board, 107

Acta celebrada en Iguala: censored, 108

Acta constitutiva: and Mexican Constitution of 1824, 58

Actas de la sesiones secretas: and Cortes' opposition to trade reform, 163–164

agriculture: proposed reforms of, 154, 155, 162, 175, 178, 188, 194; and public domain lands, 160; fostered by tariffs, 171; and classification of ports, 172; restrictions on, and Mexican revolution, 186, 195; mentioned, 179. SEE ALSO land, distribution of; schools, agricultural

Aguirre, Guillermo: serves on censorship board, 88; replacement nominated for, 91

Alamán, Lucas: describes elections of 1820, 32; elected to 1821 Cortes, 34, 124; in Mexican government, 39, 131; as author of *Historia de Méjico*, 40; on lack of town councils, 61; on Jesuits, 117; on acceptance of Constitution of 1812, 123; on *El Español*, 139; on Calleja and Mexican revolution, 145, 146; on Novella, 151; and economic reform, 154; and land distribution, 161; and mining legislation, 173, 174, 183; reports on American demands in Cortes, 193,

195; as member of Cortes pacification committee, 198; on causes of Mexican revolution, 202; reports on suggestions to pacify rebels, 202; on Spanish recognition of Mexican independence, 204, 205; influence of, on interpretation of history, 209

Alcalá, José María: serves on Mexican censorship board, 101, 107; denied transportation to Cortes, 144

Alcaraz, Conde de: elected to 1821 Cortes, 34; and mining school legislation, 174

Aldama, José María de: chosen deputy for 1813–1814 Cortes, 24

Alfaro, Miguel: elected to 1813–1814 Cortez, 24

Alméida, Pedro: serves on Yucatán censorship board, 102

Alonso y Pantiga, Angel: chosen for 1813–1814 Cortes, 24; attends 1813–1814 Cortes, 26; signs monarchist manifesto, 102

Alvarado, Ignacio: chosen for 1813–1814 Cortes, 25

Álvarez, Melchor: and municipal elections, 78

Álvarez, Ramón: chosen for 1813–1814 Cortes, 25

Amati, Bernardino: elected to 1821 Cortes, 34; serves on Cortes pacification committee, 198

Amigo de la Patria: precensored, 95

Anaya, Rafael: elected alternate to 1822–1823 Cortes, 38

Apartado, Marqués del: elected alternate for 1813–1814 Cortes, 24; elected to 1821 Cortes, 34; named alternate to Mexico City censorship board, 107

Apezechea, Fermín Antonio de: chosen for 1813–1814 Cortes, 25

Apodaca, Juan Ruíz de: position of, as

dress of, to Cortes, 145; and economic reform, 154, 167, 168; and
mining legislation, 173; mentioned,
44
Governing Board of Mexico: composition of, 151
governors, provincial: injustice of, and
Mexican revolution, 195, 196, 198,
199
Guadalupe ring: and elections for Cortes, 143, 144; smashed, 145
Gual, Manuel: elected for 1822–1823
Cortes, 38
Guardiola, Marqués de: serves on censorship board of Mexico, 101; asks
to be excused, 107
Güereña, Juan José: elected deputy for
1810–1813 Cortes, 16; offices held in
Cortes, 16; on Church reform, 114,
115, 121, 131; and economic reform, 158, 160; and trade legislation, 168; mentioned, 73
Guerra, Francisco: elected to 1821
Cortes, 34
Guerra, José Basilio: elected to 1821
Cortes, 34
Guerrero, Vicente: and Mexican Revolution, 83–84, 134
guilds
—, maritime: objected to, 170
—, merchant: oppose free trade, 163,
166, 176
Guillén, José María: elected alternate
to 1822–1823 Cortes, 39
Guridi y Alcocer, José Miguel: elected
deputy for 1810–1813 Cortes, 16;
career of, 40, 131, 135; on equal
representation, 44, 45, 47, 48–49;
50, 51, 52, 53, 190; opposes second
veto for king, 54; on ministries, 56;
elected to provincial deputation, 56,
144; and freedom of the press, 92,
100, 111; and censorship, 104, 107;
on trade legislation, 116, 155–156,
165, 168; and Church reform, 131;
and military, 134–135, 141; and decoration of Venegas, 140; and economic reform, 154, 155, 156, 174,
175; and distribution of public lands,
160; favors English mediation, 169;
and mining legislation, 173; and
causes of Mexican revolution, 189;
mentioned, 44, 154

Gutiérrez, Antonio: and freedom of
the press, 106, 111
Gutiérrez de Lara, Bernardo: in San
Antonio de Béjar in 1813, 77
Gutiérrez de Teran, José María: offices
held in Cortes, 15; selected substitute deputy to 1810–1813 Cortes, 15;
attends 1813–1814 Cortes, 26; punished for liberal views, 28, 102, 123;
elected to 1821 Cortes, 34; and freedom of the press, 90; and trade reform, 167, 168; and equal representation, 190; and Mexican Revolution,
192

Hernández Chico, José María: elected
to 1821 Cortes, 34; career of, 40, 131
Hidalgo, Miguel, Father: and Mexican
rebellion, 124, 134, 185, 188, 192;
and Cry of Dolores, 138; defeated,
139; and need for military reform,
141; and need for land reform, 160;
mentioned, 99
Historia de México, describes 1820
elections, 32; cited by Ramírez, 174
Huerta, José de Jesús: elected alternate
to 1822–1823 Cortes, 39
Humboldt, Alexander von: on Spanish
militia, 136; and ills besetting
America, 185

Ibáñez de Corvera, Juan María: elected
for 1810–1813 Cortes, 16
Ilizaliturri, José María: appointed to
Guadalajara provincial censorship
board, 108
independence, Mexican: and Spanish
constitutional monarchy, 4–5, 135,
208; recognition of, 151–152, 204,
205, 206, 207. SEE ALSO Revolution,
Mexican
Indians: exempted from personal tax,
160; and distribution of public lands,
160; discrimination against, and
Mexican Revolution, 186, 187; Mexican deputies' proposal concerning,
189
industry: Mexican deputies' proposals
on, 154, 155, 174, 175, 178–179,
188, 194; fostered by tariffs, 171;
and classification of ports, 172
Inquisition: and freedom of the press,
93, 124